T0389412

Corpus Use in Cross-linguistic Research

Studies in Corpus Linguistics (SCL)

ISSN 1388-0373

SCL focuses on the use of corpora throughout language study, the development of a quantitative approach to linguistics, the design and use of new tools for processing language texts, and the theoretical implications of a data-rich discipline.

For an overview of all books published in this series, please see *benjamins.com/catalog/scl*

Volume 113

Corpus Use in Cross-linguistic Research
Paving the way for teaching, translation and professional communication
Edited by Marlén Izquierdo and Zuriñe Sanz-Villar

Corpus Use in Cross-linguistic Research

Paving the way for teaching, translation and professional communication

Edited by

Marlén Izquierdo
Zuriñe Sanz-Villar
University of the Basque Country, UPV/EHU

John Benjamins Publishing Company
Amsterdam / Philadelphia

The paper used in this publication meets the minimum requirements of the American National Standard for Information Sciences – Permanence of Paper for Printed Library Materials, ANSI Z39.48-1984.

Cover design: Françoise Berserik
Cover illustration from original painting *Random Order*
by Lorenzo Pezzatini, Florence, 1996.

DOI 10.1075/scl.113

Cataloging-in-Publication Data available from Library of Congress:
LCCN 2023036196 (PRINT) / 2023036197 (E-BOOK)

ISBN 978 90 272 1430 0 (HB)
ISBN 978 90 272 4931 9 (E-BOOK)

John Benjamins Publishing Company · https://benjamins.com

Table of contents

Cross-linguistic research and corpora

Paving the way for application(s)

Marlén Izquierdo & Zuriñe Sanz-Villar
University of the Basque Country / Euskal Herriko Unibertsitatea

Over the past two decades, a number of linguistics conferences have been devoted to research conducted from a corpus approach, in the framework of a great variety of disciplines, displaying a number of ever-refining methods and in pursuit of various real-life applications. One such conference is the *International Symposium on Parallel Corpora: Creations and Applications*, informally known as PaCor. Originally conceived of as a biennial series, its very first edition was promoted by the research group SpatiALEs from the University of Santiago de Compostela (Spain), and held in December 2016 (Doval and Sánchez Nieto 2019). The second edition took place in November 2018 at the Universidad Complutense de Madrid (Spain), under the aegis of the research group FUNCAP (Lavid-López, Maíz-Arévalo & Zamorano-Mansilla 2021). It was then decided that the third edition would be organised by the research group TRALIMA-ITZULIK, from the University of the Basque Country (Spain), intent on homing a face-to-face conference in Vitoria-Gasteiz in November 2020. The outbreak of the COVID-19 pandemic a few months earlier forced us not only to postpone the conference until 2021, but also to conduct it virtually.

While rather an unconventional way to disseminate research, it still meant an opportunity to do so, and we are immensely grateful to all the scholars who seized it and made PaCor 2021 possible. The third edition focused special attention on the ways in which the insights derived from cross-linguistic research may be a solid foundation for applications for real-life language users. Another highlight of the conference was making room for under-researched languages and/or domains, as this has been a niche long called to fill in corpus linguistics in general and in parallel corpus research in particular. A good number of researchers from different academic background and research profiles participated in the conference sharing their expertise, knowledge and curiosity not only regarding the themes indicated above, but also with regard to the creation and annotation of corpora featuring language combinations hitherto rare to find and/or challenging to process. In addition to interesting and inspiring talks, one positive outcome

https://doi.org/10.1075/scl.113.intro

of PaCor 2021 is the present volume, which features a selection of papers that shed light on the way corpora have been both origin and consequence of cross-linguistic research consolidation. Indeed, the alliance between cross-linguistic research and corpus linguistics paves the way to applications of language that meet real needs of communication.

As the corpus linguistic community grows, so does the interest and need for the creation, annotation, processing and application of corpora, opening up new themes of discussion and creating new spaces for contact and collaboration among researchers and practitioners. Subsequently, the ACTRES research group at the University of León (Spain) will be hosting the fourth edition of PaCor in November 2023.

1. (Parallel) corpora in cross-linguistic research

Cross-linguistic research unfolds at the crossroads between contrastive linguistics and translation studies, their common ground being an approach to language through understanding how languages might relate to one another. In other words, cross-linguistic research examines languages both in contrast and in contact. Being an empirical approach, present-day cross-linguistic research is by definition corpus-based. In fact, if Granger anticipated back in 2003 the potential of corpus linguistics in the field, only five years later the impact of parallel corpora on cross-linguistic research had already been felt as dramatic (Aijmer 2008).

PaCor is mainly concerned with parallel corpora, as illustrated by all the contributions in the present volume, yet corpus linguistics as a whole should be credited with the revival and ensuing reinforcement of cross-linguistic research, for it has benefited enormously not only from parallel corpora but also comparable ones (Granger 2010). Whatever type of corpus, cross-linguistic research is provided with a reliable source of empirical data that enables observation of language-related aspects that would be hard to see by the human eye, or formidable to track without browsing or statistical techniques, even likely to go unnoticed if not overtly juxtaposed or compared to other kind of data.

The combination of comparable and parallel corpora has not only fine-tuned research in contrastive linguistics and translation studies, independently as well as jointly, but has also opened up new research avenues that have in turn shaped or diversified the description of language as well as the application(s) of language. The former instantiates, amongst others, in the growing interest in domains, text types or language varieties never before researched, and the need for further examination of minority or under-represented languages. Accordingly, the latter would refer to the use of description-based findings in applied fields like language pedagogy, which is widely aware of the benefits of corpus-informed materials and theories (Römer 2011; Meunier 2011); in translator training, where the exposition to authentic translation practices would enhance the actual practitioner's self-confidence and autonomy, through decision-making, as well as analytical skills, through awareness-raising exercises (Bowker 2003; Pearson 2003); in accessibility, a prospering field within translation studies in need of theorisation and description as much as application(s), given that translation occurs in a variety of forms to overcome barriers and enable communication among people in and with the world around (Neves 2022); and in natural language processing (NLP), which reverts positively to corpus building, processing, annotation and browsing, to name a few (Hovy & Lavid 2010). In short, corpus-based cross-linguistic research can rely on various types of corpora to fine-tune theories with descriptive adequacy, and to develop applications with descriptively accurate robustness. All this is possible thanks to the fact that cross-linguistic research is inherently computer-mediated. Both facets are intertwined, as shown by all the chapters in this volume, irrespective of their being primarily linguistic or computational. Indeed, they complement each other, for all descriptions are application-oriented, as much as application is description-informed. In other words, applications could be hardly developed without the knowledge gained from description.

Over the course of time, language corpora have been improved not only technically but also qualitatively. Computational efforts joint with linguists' or researchers' needs for discovery have upgraded browsing functionalities to a remarkable extent, making corpus-based searches more and more precise and accurate, fast and reliable, even 'tidy' to ease interpretation (Anthony 2019). Likewise, many corpora that are purposefully built for cross-linguistic research have been (re)designed bidirectionally, in order to triangulate contrastive and translated data, or enable further applications. The case-studies exploiting P-ACTRES 2.0[1] and COVALT[2] in this volume would be a working example of this. Other collections include original texts and translations from several languages, following suit to the pioneering Oslo Multilingual Corpus (Johansson, 2005), which features six different languages. This corpus was arguably the result of reusing existing parallel corpora, all featuring Norwegian, a practice recently encouraged within the corpus community for the sake of sustainability, standardization and protocol replicability (Rabadán 2019). The work by Marco and Bracho Lapiedra is

1. P-ACTRES 2.0. is the second version of the ACTRES Parallel Corpus; ACTRES, in turn, stands for *Análisis Contrastivo y Traducción Especializada/English-Spanish* (in English Specialized/English-Spanish Contrastive Analysis and Translation.

2. COVALT stands for *Çorpus Valencià de Literatura Traduïda* (Valencian Corpus of Translated Literature).

based on COVALT, a multilingual corpus featuring French, Spanish, English and Catalan, the latter arguably considered a minority language. Similarly, Li's study draws data from an *ad hoc* trilingual corpus of newspaper articles written in English, Spanish and Chinese. While the number of Chinese speakers is huge, this is still a language far less represented in corpus linguistics, let alone compared to languages so far typologically different, which makes the contribution rather unique in the field.

Ad hoc corpora have been felt more and more necessary to bring to the research agenda under-represented languages or under-researched domains, interest in which has mostly grown out of the need for real applications. This is clearly illustrated by the LEXB[3] corpus, compiled by De Camillis and Contarino to contrast Italian and South-Tyrol German, a combination rare in the parallel corpus literature, especially so considering the German variety within. Most importantly, the corpus features specialised texts daily produced in the local administration realm, which would be considered a narrow domain (Skadiņa et al. 2010). The same is observed in the writing application GEFEM 2.0.©[4] developed by Ortego for professionals of the cold-meat industry in need of producing texts in English. While the language combination, namely English-Spanish, is a dominant one in cross-linguistic research, the text type would have unlikely attracted scholarly attention would it not be for a real academic-industry alliance resulting from an application-oriented research project. This brings to light the paramount importance that the collaboration between experts in complementary fields has. Remarkably, such a collaboration is not based on a service-customer relation, but on a researcher-to-researcher relation that would guarantee expertise, accountability and co-responsibility, as reflected in the co-authority of some of the contributions in the volume (Chapters 10 and 11). It is thanks to such tight collaborations that applications like GEFEM 2.0.©, or robust corpus techniques and well-thought resources like the various corpora referred to in this volume have made description possible, a *sine qua non* for ultimate applications that are not only necessary and justified, but must be correct, acceptable and reliable.

3. LEXB Corpus refers to the parallel corpus of South-Tyrolean legislation.

4. GEFEM 2.0. stands for *Generador de Fichas descriptivas de Embutidos* (Generator of dried meat product cards).

2. Structure and contributions of this volume

This volume consists of twelve chapters that can be grouped in two main parts. The first one focuses on linguistic description while the second one focuses on corpus building and concrete applications.

The first nine chapters report corpus-based research in a variety of linguistic disciplines ranging from contrastive linguistics to audiovisual translation, accessibility, and critical discourse analysis. Furthermore, a comprehensive overview of corpus-based descriptive analysis is provided given that the case studies are conducted at different levels of language delicacy: from lexis and word formation, to lexicogrammar, discourse analysis, and pragmatics. Regarding the corpora for the various analyses, data is taken not only from written corpora well-known for contrastive and translation studies like COVALT, PaGeS[5] or P-ACTRES 2.0., but also audiovisual corpora, in turn featuring different genres. The backbone of this first part of the book is the use of corpora for language description as a necessary stage that will enable future applications of different nature, to which all contributions refer, even instantiate. Such applications include translation practice and training, as stated by most contributions; language teaching, this being the reason and purpose behind the analysis conducted by Labrador; and media accessibility, in particular opera audio description, as justified by Hermosa. The remaining three chapters have a more computational profile; they relate to corpus building, corpus alignment, and the development of a corpus-informed tool for professional translation and writing. Particularly interesting are the language combinations involved as well as the domains or text types dealt with, which would contribute to filling an existing niche in the field.

The first two chapters of the volume represent, each, a case-study of light verb constructions (LVCs), rarely analysed from the perspective of translation studies. Both case studies rely on contrastive and translated data, yet Marco and Bracho Lapiedra approach it from a semantic point of view, while Rabadán adopts a lexical perspective. Either way, these two chapters foreground another asset of corpus linguistics, namely, inductive theorising.

The study by J. Marco and L. Bracho Lapiedra in the first chapter aims to test Halverson's Gravitational Pull Hypothesis (GPH). Data is drawn from four parallel and bilingual corpora (English-into-Catalan, English-into-Spanish, French-into-Catalan, and French-into-Spanish) and two monolingual corpora (in Catalan and Spanish), all of which belong to the COVALT corpus (*Corpus Valencià de Literatura Traduïda*). As a result, there are two comparable corpora for translated language (one with Catalan and the other with Spanish as translated language)

5. PaGeS is the German/Spanish parallel Corpus.

and another two comparable corpora for (the same) non-translated language(s). LVCs made up of Catalan *fer* (do/make) and Spanish *dar* (give) in collocation with nouns denoting dynamic events and emotional states were carefully chosen as object of study. The study confirms the hypothesis that LVCs with *fer* and *dar* conveying emotional events are under-represented in most sub-corpora (3 out of 4). As for the hypothesis concerning dynamic events, this was confirmed in two corpora (both parallel sub-corpora with Catalan as the target language). In light of the insights gained, the role of corpora in the translation classroom and the benefits of making translation trainees aware of translated language characteristics are highlighted, on the assumption that knowing which items of the target language are over- or underrepresented in translations, and why, can help students 're-think' their translation choices.

In Chapter 2, R. Rabadán analyses the English-into-Spanish translations of LVCs in two text genres (fiction and nonfiction) within P-ACTRES 2.0., to examine whether the semantic features of LVCs (the light verb-noun combinatorial capabilities) influence the translation choices. Five English light verbs are queried in the PoS tagged, bidirectional and parallel corpus first, and then, concordances are analysed examining translation patterns, "semantic features-translation choice association", and register variation. The author identifies five recurrent translation patterns, with single-verb constructions being the preferred translation option. In addition, the results corroborate the initial hypothesis that the semantic features of LVCs are expected to influence on translation choices. In addition, register-related variations are also observed. According to the author, computer-aided tools can only benefit from the findings of such studies; by including information regarding LVCs (and other constructions) in machine translation systems, post-editing aids (such as PETRA©) or authoring support apps (such as Gedire©) the quality of the products involved can be enhanced.

In Chapter 3 T. Molés-Cases analyses the translation of manner-of-speaking in Spanish-into-German narrative texts by focusing on reporting verbs introducing direct speech. While the author acknowledges the existence of similar studies featuring other language combinations, this is the first and only translation study of narrative texts from original Spanish into translated German. Data was taken from ten contemporary novels selected from the PaGeS (Parallel Corpus German Spanish) corpus. Molés-Cases concludes that the translation technique that seems to prevail in the translation of manner-of-speaking verbs is transference. In other words, manner-of-speaking is mostly maintained in translation and, thus, rarely affected by translation. Secondly, it has also been observed that there are differences between motion and speech events when translating manner. While manner-of-motion is often added in Spanish-into-German translations, typological differences seem not to be that important with speech events, as additions are rare when translating manner-of-speaking verbs in the same language combination and directionality. The author points out the benefits of her results for the development of contrastive competence in German-Spanish specialised translation, especially addressed to translation trainees.

Within the framework of German-Spanish translation applied contrastive studies, Chapter 4 by M.T. Sánchez Nieto also showcases a study at the lexicogrammatical level, the object of study being the dative passive. This is a pervasive construction in day-to-day German language use, with no parallel construction in the target language, i.e, Spanish. Despite its frequency, Sánchez Nieto denounces a dearth of studies about it from a contrastive perspective, reason why she embarks on a joint contrastive and descriptive analysis of translations in both directions, German into Spanish and Spanish into German. At the stage of data selection from PaGeS 2.0, the author resorts to the CQL functionality built in SketchEngine, as it allows her to make very specific queries. Subsequently, the author uses ATLAS.ti to label and examine the results obtained from SketchEngine. The results show that the so-called *bekommen* passive is much more frequent than the *kriegen,* and particularly the *erhalten* passives of which no occurrences were found in the corpus. Regarding the German-to-Spanish direction of analysis, Sánchez Nieto concludes that it is not always easy for the translators to maintain the semantic function of the passives under analysis. The contribution ends with pertinent suggestions for the general German-into-Spanish translation classroom, as well as thought-provoking observations into what needs to be considered when using parallel corpora in translation practice courses or in foreign language learning settings.

N. Ramón carries out a corpus-based cross-linguistic analysis of two near-synonym English verbs, 'begin' and 'start'. Both verbs indicate ingressive aspect and occur in similar syntactic constructions. In order to identify possible semantic differences between the mentioned near-synonyms, their corresponding translation options are analysed browsing P-ACTRES 2.0., and the two datasets are juxtaposed to determine if semantic similarities or dissimilarities can be observed. The results reveal syntactic differences between 'begin' and 'start', as the former is more often followed by a to-infinitive clause, while 'start' occurs near clausal complements as much as it does near transitive and intransitive patterns. The cross-linguistic analysis shows differences to previous research studies with the same object of study (Egan 2012) but different language combination. In English-into-Spanish translations statistically significant differences were found between 'begin' and 'start' when followed by a to-infinitive, since 'start' was more often translated with other ingressive verbs. When occurring in intransitive patterns, there are also remarkable differences between both verbs. Modulation and the use of other ingressive verbs is again more often found in the translations of 'start'. The author concludes that sense relations other than initiation of an action are triggered by 'start' to a greater extent than by 'begin'; in other words, apart from indicating the initiation of an action, the Spanish translations of 'start' may include more detailed or precise sense relations.

B. Labrador's analysis of Spanish translations of English 'run' in Chapter 6 is done with a foreign language teaching application in mind. The ultimate purpose is to gain insight into the use of core vocabulary, and more specifically the use of the word 'run', apparently a simple, one-dimensional verb that in context, nevertheless, takes on complex connotations of meaning. The occurrences extracted from the fiction and non-fiction sub-corpora from P-ACTRES 2.0 are manually analysed, both intra- and inter-linguistically. The former analysis shows the real use of 'run' in terms of meanings, grammar, or collocational or syntactic patterns in English. In the latter, by contrast, English-into-Spanish translation solutions of motion verbs were analysed. Density change, i.e. the use of a single verb in the Spanish translations, is the solution that stands out, but perspective change is also frequent. The pedagogical implications of this corpus-based study such as different approaches (such as Data-Driven Learning, DDL, or Computer-Assisted Language Learning, CALL) to make students aware of cross-linguistic differences of English and Spanish, and the acquisition of patterns expressing motion in English, are included in the paper. While the main 'recipients' of Labrador's research are L2 learners and teachers of English, translation students could also benefit from such a corpus-based study.

C. Gutiérrez Lanza analyses the use of discourse markers (DMs) in cinema scripts, aiming to compare the translation strategies used from English into Spanish and the use of DMs originally written in Spanish. The rationale behind is that if there are certain features in film dialogue whose use is statistically different in translated language compared to non-translated language (i.e. dubbese), then as long as using them can be avoided, the quality, acceptability, and tenor of the audiovisual texts can be enhanced. For that purpose, the author compiled TRACEci, an innovative parallel corpus that includes English source texts, the translated action films in Spanish (TT1), and the corresponding adapted versions (TT2), which are often not easy to source. The tool used for the compilation of the corpus was TAligner 3.0, an open access tool that enables simultaneous alignment of more than two texts. A relevant reference corpus in Spanish, CORPES XXI, and more specifically the *guiones* subcorpus (composed of scripts), is used for the analysis of non-translated cinema scripts. The comparison between TT1 and TT2 revealed that the use of conversational markers (CMs) dropped by 39.74% during the synchronisation process. On the other hand, the overuse of CMs, mostly in TT1 but also in the synchronised translations, may be an indicator of the existence of statistical dubbese. However, the author argues that the quality of the translated product is enhanced after the synchronisation process, since there is a considerable reduction of some CMs. Undoubtedly, both translation trainees and professionals can benefit from the results of such pilot study, as indicated by Gutiérrez-Lanza. Being aware of general trends in translated texts, such as the overuse of CMs in draft translations, can help them be more aware of the specificities of translated language compared to non-translated texts.

In Chapter 8 I. Hermosa focuses on a different audiovisual product, namely opera scripts, and more specifically audio descriptions (AD) and audio introductions (AI). Not only are opera AD and AI compared, but also AD scripts in Catalan and in Spanish, from the two main opera houses in Spain: the Liceu Opera House and the *Teatro Real*. The goal is to determine where in the spoken-written continuum opera AD falls, which makes Hermosa's a pioneering study in the field. To this end, a corpus divided into four sub-corpora, two devoted to ADs (AD_ES and AD_CAT) and another two to AIs (AI_ES and AI_CAT), had to be purpose-built. Five parameters were chosen to describe the four sub-corpora in terms of their spoken and written characteristics, namely, lexical density, lexical variation, mean word length, mean sentence length and the Flesch-Szigriszt readability index. A variety of tools such as Sketch Engine, Wordsmith Tools and the free software INFLESZ were combined, which not only echoes Rabadán's call for recycling and reprocessing available resources (2019), but also suggests that this may be the course of action with under-researched domains, languages or text-types. The results of some of the parameters indicate (mean sentence and word length, and the Flesch-Szigriszt readability results) that AI texts tend to be closer to the written pole than AD texts, but AD and AI share characteristics proper not only of written language, but also of spoken discourse.

B. Li in Chapter 9 reports on a parallel- and multilingual corpus-based analysis of journalistic texts translated from English into Chinese and Spanish. The innovation of the study is manyfold: it combines imageology and translation studies to look into image construction in news translation, paying special attention to news labels and the translation of headlines. The contribution is not only interesting because of its interdisciplinary character but also for its methodology, since journalistic texts – "tritexts" in this case – are not easily available for the compilation of parallel, let alone multilingual corpora. The analysis of the parallel texts shows that the image of China differs in the Spanish and Chinese versions of the *New York Times*, which might respond to the writers' intended effect on the writers' way of thinking or opinion about China.

The second part of the book groups together three chapters dedicated to cross-linguistic corpus resources and tools.

In Chapter 10 we learn about the LEXB Corpus, compiled by F. De Camillis and A. Contarino to examine parallel legal-administrative texts written in Italian and German from South Tyrol. The bilingual resource was then used to adapt an Italian-German machine-translation system (ModernMT) with domain-specific texts and its quality evaluated. Additionally, De Camillis and Contarino developed a terminology evaluation framework to report on legal terminology accuracy of machine-translated texts. The results of the automatic metrics show that the quality of texts translated with the domain-adapted MMT model improved. Although terminology improvement is more limited, the terminology evaluation framework itself is of great interest. It is also noteworthy that publicly available textual resources were used to compile the parallel corpus from scratch, as described in detail, and both the LEXB corpus as well as the automatic terminology evaluation tool are publicly available. Thus, the impact this kind of research may have on real users of the language, civil servants working in South Tyrol in this case, is of great value. It can also serve as inspiration for researchers working in machine translation adaptation, especially for low resource languages or language varieties.

The collaboration between linguists and data scientists has been essential for conducting the research presented in Chapter 11. *Politova et alter* present a manually annotated gold dataset for the language pair Russian-Chinese, distant languages for which no gold standard was available. Such a dataset was then used to train a word-alignment model, stage that resorted to the Russian-Chinese parallel corpus (RuZhCorp) consisting of 3.5 million words. The alignment rules for this language combination are thoroughly described by the authors, which can be helpful for researchers interested in improving word-alignment models, irrespective of the language combination. Tests showed that the inclusion of a set of manually aligned sentences improves the alignment quality considerably.

Last but not least, in Chapter 12 T. Ortego describes the development of GEFEM 2.0.©, a corpus-informed tool for real use by Spanish professionals, either technical writers or translators, interested in the transfer of dried meat product cards from Spanish into English. In addition to the actual tool, the author explains the corpus-based analyses previously conducted to describe, in terms of both form and content, the text types needed by the abovementioned professionals. This study shows how multilevel corpus-based analysis, based on both parallel and comparable corpora, are essential for developing tools like the one presented in this last chapter, a reliable and acceptable writing aid that can help small and medium-sized agri-food companies overcome language barriers. As shown by the author, the cross-linguistic comparison of the results of both corpora, comparable (C-GEFEM) and parallel (P-GEFEM), accounts for the correctness, acceptability and reliability of such a tool.

As shown by the contributions in this volume, parallel corpora have come a long way, which continues ahead. We hope the volume contributes to knowledge building and transfer in the corpus community in general, and particularly among corpus-based cross-linguistic researchers. It will surely spark curiosity, paving the way of a discipline that evolves systematically, catering for theories, descriptions and applications within.

References

Aijmer, Karin. 2008. Parallel and comparable corpora. In *Corpus Linguistics. An International Handbook*, Anke Lüdeling & Merja Kytö (eds), 275–292. Berlin: Walter de Gruyter.

Anthony, Laurence. 2019. *New directions in corpus design and corpus tools development.* Lecture given at Hong Kong Metropolitan University (HKMU). Retrieved from HKMU channel: <https://www.youtube.com/@HKMUChannel/search?query =Laurence%20Anthony> (26 May 2023).

Bowker, Lynn. 2003. *Computer-aided Translation Technology. A Practical Introduction.* Ottawa: University of Ottawa.

Doval, Irene & Sánchez Nieto, M. Teresa. 2019. *Parallel Copora for Contrastive and Translation Studies. New Resources and Applications* [Studies in Corpus Linguistics 90]. Amsterdam: John Benjamins.

Granger, Sylviane. 2010. Comparable and translation corpora in cross-linguistic research. Design, analysis and applications. *Journal of Shanghai Jiaotong University* 2: 14–21.

Granger, Sylviane, 2003. The corpus approach; A common way forward for contrastive linguistics and translation studies? In *Corpus-based Approaches to Contrastive Linguistics and Translation Studies* [Approaches to Translation Studies 20], Sylviane Granger, Jacques Lerot & Stephanie Petch-Tyson (eds), 17–29. Amsterdam: Rodopi.

Hovy, Eduard & Lavid, Julia. 2010. Towards a 'science' of corpus annotation: A new methodological challenge for corpus linguistics. *International Journal of Translation* 22(1): 13–36.

Lavid-López, Julia, Maíz-Arévalo, Carmen & Zamorano-Mansilla, Juna Rafael. 2021. *Corpora in Translation and Contrastive Research in the Digital Age* [Benjamins Translation Library 158]. Amsterdam: John Benjamins.

Meunier, Fanny. 2011. Corpus linguistics and second/foreign language learning: Exploring multiple paths. *RBLA* 11(2): 459–477.

Neves, Josélia. 2022. Translation and accessibility. The translation of everyday things. In *The Routledge Handbook of Translation and Methodology*, Federico Zanettin & Christopher Rundle (eds), 441–456. London: Routledge.

Pearson, Jennifer. 2003. Using parallel texts in the translator training environment. In *Corpora in Translator Education*, Federico Zanettin, Silvia Bernardini & Dominic Stewart (eds), 15–24. London: Routledge.

Rabadán, Rosa. 2019. Working with parallel corpora. Usefulness and usability. In *Parallel Corpora for Contrastive and Translation Studies*, Irene Doval, Maite Sánchez Nieto (eds), 57–78. Amsterdam/Philadelphia: John Benjamins.

Römer, Ute. 2011. Corpus research applications in second language teaching. *Annual Review of Applied Linguistics* 31: 205–225.

Skadiņa, Inguna, Vasiļjevs, Andrejs, Skadiņš, Raivis, Gaizauskas, Robert, Tufiş, Dan & Gornostay, Tatiana. 2010. Analysis and evaluation of comparable corpora for under resourced areas of machine translation. In *Proceedings of 3rd Workshop on Building and Using Comparable Corpora. LREC 2010*, Valletta: ELRA.

CHAPTER 1

Light Verb Constructions as a testing ground for the Gravitational Pull Hypothesis

An analysis based on the COVALT corpus

Josep Marco & Llum Bracho Lapiedra
Universitat Jaume I | Universitat Politècnica de València

This study aims to test out the Gravitational Pull Hypothesis (GPH) on Light Verb Constructions (LVCs) conveying emotional states and dynamic events in a number of language combinations, with English and French as source and Catalan and Spanish as target languages. It draws on the corresponding sub-corpora of the COVALT translation corpus. The GPH posits three cognitive causes of translational effects: source or target language salience and connectivity. Different configurations of these causes are expected to result in over- or under-representation of target language features. This study attempts to push the theory forward by formulating hypotheses at the more abstract level of LVC types rather than individual LVCs. The effects predicted (under-representation of LVCs conveying emotional states and no significant differences for those conveying dynamic events) are confirmed in five out of the eight situations at the intersections of LVC types and language pairs.

Keywords: Gravitational Pull Hypothesis, Light Verb Constructions, emotional states, dynamic events, COVALT

1. Introduction

The aim of this chapter is to test out the Gravitational Pull Hypothesis (GPH) on certain types of Light Verb Constructions (LVCs). The study draws on the English-Catalan (EN-CA), English-Spanish (EN-ES), French-Catalan (FR-CA), and French-Spanish (FR-ES) sub-corpora, and the non-translation components (CA and ES), in COVALT. COVALT stands for *Corpus Valencià de Literatura Traduïda* (Valencian Corpus of Translated Literature).

https://doi.org/10.1075/scl.113.01mar

The outline of the chapter is as follows. Section 2 briefly sketches the main features of the GPH. Section 3 introduces the concept of Light Verb Construction and deals briefly with its definition and typology. Section 4 presents the methodology, and Section 5 provides the results of the analysis and discusses them. Finally, Section 6 offers some concluding remarks.

2. The Gravitational Pull Hypothesis

Halverson's Gravitational Pull Hypothesis (GPH, Halverson 2003, 2017) is first and foremost an attempt to show that "the various lexical/semantic patterns that have been subsumed under the heading 'translation universals' may be explained with reference to general characteristics of human cognition" (2003: 197–198). It both pertains to a higher level of generalisation than the various hypotheses subsumed under the heading of translation universals (or, less ambitiously, features of translation) and purports to provide a cognitive explanation for them. On a more concrete level, it is also an attempt to bridge the gap between two of those alleged features of translation, over- and under-representation of target language typical features. Even if empirical evidence has been found for both of them, they cannot be true at one and the same time.

The GPH posits three potential causes of translational effects: patterns of salience in the target language (factor 1 – magnetism); patterns of salience in the source language (factor 2 – gravitational pull); and patterns of connectivity, which reflect relationships between the source and the target languages (factor 3 – connectivity). One effect is predicted for each potential cause, or factor – and there is also the possibility of interactions between them. The effect of factor 1 will be over-representation; the effect of factor 2 will be over-representation too; and the effect of factor 3 may be over- or under-representation. Different configurations of these three factors for particular linguistic items in particular language pairs will result in over- or under-representation. The hypothesis draws on various theoretical sources, the most significant being Langacker's (e.g. 2008) Cognitive Grammar and bilingual theory (e.g. de Groot 2011). In spite of its highly promising explanatory potential, it is under-researched so far. Empirical studies drawing on the GPH include Halverson (2017), Hareide (2017a, 2017b), Vandevoorde (2020), Lefer & De Sutter (2022), Marco (2021), and other studies by members of the COVALT group, in press or in preparation.

3. Light Verb Constructions

Light Verb Constructions (LVCs) are made up of a light (or support) verb and a predicative noun. A light verb is a verb with a very general meaning that is partly de-semanticised (or bleached) when co-occurring with a predicative noun. It serves as a syntactic prop for a nominalised event. The predicative noun embodies such an event. The main condition for a noun to qualify as predicative is that it should have internal argument structure, i.e. it should be able to assign semantic roles. In 'give a kiss', for example, 'kiss' has two roles – the kisser and the person/object kissed. The number of roles assigned by the predicative noun must be compatible with the light verb's internal structure, as the former must be accommodated by the latter. When used as a full verb (as in 'I gave my son a toy'), 'give' has three arguments: the giver, the thing given and the recipient of the gift. When used as a light verb (as in 'I gave my son a kiss'), the thing given becomes an event with its own argument structure, so that 'my son' fulfils a double role as recipient of the gift and person kissed. A light verb assigning fewer than three semantic roles would not have been able to accommodate the event structure typical of 'kiss.' As a result, the co-occurrence of light verbs and predicative nouns operates under selection restrictions – not all predicative nouns can co-occur with a given light verb. This is nicely summarised by Wittenberg-Kuypers (2014: 8) as follows:

> According to Jackendoff's Parallel Architecture [...], the combination of a light verb and a particular noun leads to the creation of a complex predicate, composed out of the meaning and arguments of the noun, and at least the argument structure and probably some semantic features of the light verb.

LVCs have been studied in a variety of theoretical frameworks and national traditions, which makes even a brief summary unthinkable here. Let it suffice, then, to mention a few contributions in order to give a general idea of the multiplicity of approaches. Some studies are strictly monolingual, with the odd reference to other languages for the sake of comparison – e.g. Helbig (1979) or López-Campos Bodineau (1997) and many others for German, or Ronan and Schneider (2015) for English. The latter study is important in that it draws on previous studies such as Algeo (1995) and Allerton (2002) with a view to determining the most often used light verbs and LVCs in British and Irish English. It is corpus-based and uses automatic parsing and machine learning in order to reach acceptable rates of precision and recall in LVC detection. Other studies are more clearly contrastive in nature. Thus, Bustos Plaza (2005) deals with similarities and differences between German and Spanish LVCs. Ginebra (2008) makes the theoretical point that a 'phraseological' approach to LVCs is more fruitful than one that regards them as the sum of independent lexical items, and illustrates it with LVCs based on the Catalan verb *tenir* and their English equivalents in dictionaries. Castell (2011) focuses on how LVCs are dealt with in German and Catalan monolingual and bilingual dictionaries. And Ginebra and Navarro (2015) throw light on a number of contrasts as regards LVCs between two such closely related languages as Catalan and Spanish. A third group of studies might be referred to as language-independent because of their wide scope, even if examples are inevitably taken from a particular language or a number of them. Butt (2003), for instance, provides a schematic review of the concept of light verb in a number of languages and some conclusions on how these verbs behave as a class. Alonso Ramos' (2004) is an extremely well-documented and solidly argued book-length study of the lexical and semantic nature of LVCs, with Spanish as its pivotal language. Finally, Wittenberg-Kuypers (2014) gives an account of a number of experimental studies setting out to "examine questions of mental representation, cognitive processing, and event construal to provide insights into the architecture of the language system" (2014: 2). To that end, LVCs are seen against the backdrop of their non-light counterparts, and evidence suggests that the former are processed differently from the latter.

This wealth of studies on LVCs at large would seem to warrant a proportional wealth of translation-oriented studies on the same subject, but that is hardly the case. LVCs have received some attention from the field of Machine Translation (see e.g. Babych, Hartley & Sharoff 2009 or Marzouk 2021) but otherwise very few studies deal with the topic. One such study is Rabadán (2023, in this volume), which uses corpus-based methodology to find out how English LVCs fare in Spanish translation. Five English light verbs are chosen, corpus matches are manually scanned in order to discard false positives and a number of the resulting true LVCs are analysed in order to identify the translation solutions employed. Five solution types are distinguished: LVC in Spanish (e.g. 'give permission' → *dar permiso* 'give permission'); correlated single verb (e.g. 'give guidance' → *aconsejar* 'advise'); fuller, more specialized verb (e.g. 'give permission' → *conceder permiso* 'grant permission'); other full lexical verbs (e.g. 'make holes' → *perforar* 'drill'); other. The most often used translation solutions turn out to be, in descending order, other full lexical verbs, correlated single verb, LVC in Spanish.

Over and above the brief presentation just provided, a few aspects of LVCs need to be highlighted. Firstly, light verbs tend to be form-identical with full verbs (Butt 2003: 3), i.e. they also function as full verbs – e.g. 'make an analysis' vs 'make shoes'. Secondly, they may show varying degrees of emptiness, i.e. some are emptier than others. Compare 'have' with 'commit', which is much more specific. As claimed by Alonso Ramos (2004) and many others, an inverse proportion may be posited between specificity and productivity, so that the more specific a light verb, the less productive it will be. And thirdly, LVCs often have a full-verb counterpart (e.g. 'make an analysis/analyse'), but that does not imply that the two are semantically equivalent. LVCs perform different communicative functions from full verbs. At least two such functions need to be mentioned here. The first one is their potential for signalling *Aktionsart*, especially as regards the stage of development of an event as conveyed by the threefold distinction 'inchoative/continuative/terminative'. The first two stages may be illustrated by the German LVCs *in Bewegung setzen/halten* or its English equivalents 'set/keep in motion', whereas the terminative meaning is present in the English constructions 'be at an end' or 'bring something to an end'. The second function is that of individuation, as highlighted by Colominas Ventura (2001: 70). Whereas 'walk' (as in 'I walk with Ryan every day') is non-count, its LVC counterpart 'take a walk' turns the action of walking into an item and thus makes it countable.

In order to operationalise the concept of LVC and make it amenable to the kind of analysis to be performed in this study, two things need to be done: defining the notion as precisely as possible and adopting a suitable classification. As to definitions, many have been put forward, with varying degrees of narrowness. Here we will follow Colominas Ventura (2001), who claims that an LVC, besides constituting a complex predicate made up of a light verb and a predicative noun, as said above, must have a meaning that can be compositionally derived. That excludes all kinds of figurative meanings and places LVCs firmly in the realm of collocations, half-way between fixed expressions and free combinations.

As to classifications, it is assumed that predicative nouns, insofar as they designate events, can be semantically classified along the same lines as verbs (e.g. Colominas Ventura 2001: 68 and ff.; Alonso Ramos 2004: 157). Vendler (1967) classified events into states, activities, achievements and accomplishments on the basis of three criteria: dynamicity, telicity and duration. This classification lies at the basis of many subsequent attempts, which are variations on the same categories but may differ in their degree of granularity and the number of underlying criteria. Alonso Ramos (2004) claimed that the semantic classification of predicative nouns cannot be language-independent and posited a seven-fold typology for Spanish which identified the following categories: state, quality, action, activity, act, process, and event. They are based on the distinction static/dynamic and the criteria of volition (or agentivity) and duration. Volition is certainly not the same as telicity, but in most other respects Alonso Ramos' classification is similar to previous ones.

In this study we will draw on the static/dynamic distinction, so there is no need here to go into the details of further sub-divisions of these categories. In fact, our initial focus was on LVCs conveying emotional events, as we realised that Catalan *fer* and Spanish *dar* are rather productive in this sense and do not have formal counterparts in English (a literal translation of *fer por* or *dar envidia*, for instance, would be 'make fear' or 'give envy', respectively). We did not expect many differences to arise from the remaining types of events across languages, and that is why we decided to group acts, actions and activities together under the more general category of dynamic events.

4. Methodology

LVCs were chosen as a potentially fertile ground to test out the GPH because both the varying degree of isomorphism between types of LVCs across languages and the relative salience of different types of LVC in the target and source languages may crucially impact their frequencies in translated as opposed to non-translated texts. The hypotheses, then, focus on LVC types, not individual LVCs – a decision that involves a number of limitations for the operationalisation of each factor. Some of them are inherent to the decision whereas others derive from data manageability. These limitations can be summarised as follows:

a. Target language salience (or magnetism) was established across the emotional state/dynamic event divide. Therefore, we were in the domain of semasiological salience: we needed to determine whether LVCs based on *fer* in Catalan and *dar* in Spanish tended to fall under the category of emotional states or dynamic events. Onomasiological salience was left out of the picture, as will be explained below.
b. Source language salience (or gravitational pull) was established on the same basis. A large English reference corpus was queried for LVCs based on the two closest English equivalents of *fer* and *dar* ('make' and 'give', respectively), and the same operation was performed on the two closest French equivalents, *faire* and *donner*, with a view to determining whether LVCs based on those four SL verbs tended to fall under the category of emotional states or dynamic events.
c. Connectivity between LVCs conveying emotional states or dynamic events in the source and target languages was formulated on the basis of magnetism and gravitational pull, as established in a and b above. But the main limitation in this respect concerns not hypothesis formulation but hypothesis testing. ST triggers for TT LVCs conveying emotional states and dynamic events were identified as a necessary step in the method, but the complementary step of finding out the TT matches of those triggers was not carried out for reasons of data manageability. The number of TT LVCs under scrutiny in this study (36, as will be seen later) is rather high, and ST triggers typically span a number of options, often with no option playing a dominant role; therefore, for the picture of connectivity to be complete, a very high number of concordances would need to be manually scanned and categorised. One of the consequences

of this limitation is that onomasiological salience at the target pole has not been mapped. In other words, we do not know whether a given LVC or LVC type in the SL tends to be translated as a TL LVC or as any of the alternative options (e.g. as identified by Rabadán, 2023): a correlated full verb (e.g. 'give a kiss' → *besar* 'kiss'), a more specialized verb, etc. This was left for future research, as undertaking it in this study would have required an extremely time-consuming analysis based on individual LVCs in both directions (TL → SL and SL → TL) in the four language combinations.

Now that the limitations of the study have been highlighted, let us look at its achievements. The study draws on four sub-corpora of the COVALT corpus: English-Catalan, English-Spanish, French-Catalan and French-Spanish. COVALT was initially made up of the Catalan translations published in the region of Valencia between 1990 and 2000 of narrative works originally written in English, French and German. A Catalan non-translated component was later added so that the translated components in the three sub-corpora and the non-translated component would constitute a comparable corpus in all relevant respects (literary genre and place and period of publication). The next step was to compile three sub-corpora featuring Spanish translations (whenever available) of the same source texts already present in the corpus. So the two sets of parallel corpora (i.e. those having Catalan and those having Spanish as their target language) might be regarded as *comparable* (in the sense proposed by Hareide 2017b) in most relevant respects, although the criteria of place (Valencian region) and period (1990–2000) of publication could not be met in all cases. Finally, a Spanish non-translated component was also added so that a comparable corpus for Spanish would be available as well. Figure 1 and Table 1 show the general make-up of COVALT and the size of the components used for this study, respectively.

Corpus queries focused on two highly frequent light verbs: *fer* ('make/do') in Catalan and *dar* ('give') in Spanish. The choice of these two verbs was motivated by their frequency and productivity in their respective languages[1] and also by the patterns emerging from the analysis of CA and ES. *Fer* is often regarded as the most basic and productive light verb in Catalan; since analysis of its noun collocates in CA clearly yielded two patterns (emotional states on the one hand

1. Colominas Ventura (2001: 21) mentions *fer* ('do/make'), *tenir* ('have'), *donar* ('give') and *prendre* ('take') as the most productive light verbs in Catalan. Corpus-based studies focusing on English, such as Algeo (1995) and Ronan and Schneider (2015), have found out that 'have', 'make', 'give' and 'take' are the most common light verbs in English, although their ranking order may vary across regional varieties. The same would hold for Spanish: *tener* ('have'), *dar* ('give'), *hacer* ('do/make') and *tomar* ('take') are usually regarded as the most frequent light verbs in that language.

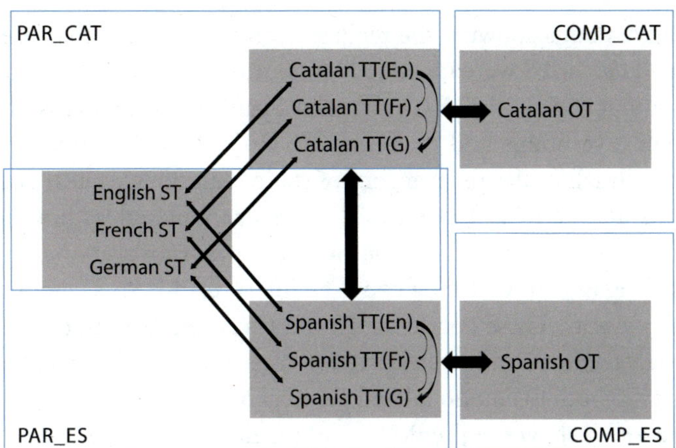

Figure 1. General make-up of the COVALT corpus

Table 1. Size of the corpus components used in this study

COVALT CORPUS	
Component	**Size**
CA	1,551,521
ES	4,170,178
EN-CA (ST)	1,201,757
EN-CA (TT)	1,343,631
EN-ES (ST)	1,131,061
EN-ES (TT)	1,122,299
FR-CA (ST)	551,869
FR-CA (TT)	566,998
FR-ES (ST)	540,741
FR-ES (TT)	565,481

and acts/actions/activities on the other), *dar* was chosen for Spanish because it both features prominently in LVCs conveying dynamic events and largely collocates with nouns expressing the same emotional states as *fer* + noun in Catalan (e.g. *fer por* = *dar miedo*).[2] The COVALT corpus was indexed with Corpus Workbench, which uses the Corpus Query Processor (CQP) as browser. First of all,

2. In fact, Ginebra and Navarro (2015: 222) claim that "Spanish often uses the support verb *dar* when Catalan uses *fer*" – although they hasten to add that this by no means happens in all cases.

the predicative nouns showing the highest degree of collocational strength with *fer* in CA and *dar* in ES were identified.[3] So our point of departure was the non-translated component both for Catalan and Spanish. On the basis of these two lists of predicative nouns and their ensuing LVCs, two basic meaning patterns emerged, which fall under the category of static (emotional states) and dynamic (acts, actions and activities) events. All LVCs encountered within the relevant portion of the list belonged to one of the two types. However, there were a few that were ambiguous in that they could be interpreted both as emotional states and dynamic events. These had to be left out because categorisation would have required analysis on an individual basis. A case in point is *fer mal* ('do harm'), which may refer both to emotional and physical harm.

Tables 2 and 3 show the predicative nouns most strongly associated with *fer* in CA and *dar* in ES. The analysis focuses on the LVCs made up of *fer* or *dar*, as the case may be, and the 10 predicative nouns denoting emotional states and dynamic events most strongly associated with those light verbs within the 100 top-ranking collocates. However, only 8 were found for emotional states, both in Catalan and Spanish, so the list for that type of predicative noun is shorter. The choice of 10 LVCs per LVC type and target language is admittedly arbitrary, as the figure could easily have been higher or lower. At any rate, we wished to keep corpus data within manageable limits, as we intended to perform not only a quantitative but also a qualitative analysis. A total of 36 LVCs were thus processed, first in non-translations and then in translations; and in the latter ST triggers had to be considered too.

Once a manageable list of individual LVCs has been selected for analysis, the relative salience of each type in each target language must be determined. Be it noted that salience is here operationalised as corpus frequency. This is admittedly a controversial decision, as there may be more to salience than just (corpus) frequency. In fact, Halverson (2017: 16) argues for the need to combine several sources of evidence in order to establish both salience and connectivity, and illustrates that possibility by adopting a mixed-methods approach in which corpus data are supplemented with data from elicitation and translation tests. We intend

3. The collocation utility in CQPweb ranks collocates according not to raw frequency of the collocation (i.e. node + collocate) but collocational strength, or strength of the association between the two, which can be quantitatively measured by means of different statistical tests. Most of them are based on the relationship between observed and expected frequency, i.e. the actual frequency of a given collocational chain in a corpus as compared to the frequency with which it would occur if association between node and collocate were random. Out of the several metrics used by CQPweb, log-likelihood was chosen, on the strength of Evert's (2005: 112) comparison among a number of statistical measures. The collocation window was 3L, 3R, with the minimum frequency of the collocate at 5.

Table 2. List of predicative nouns most strongly associated with light verb *fer* in Catalan non-translations

LVCs with Catalan *fer*	
Emotional states	**Dynamic events**
gràcia ('be funny, please')	gest ('make a gesture')
il·lusió ('give a thrill')	petó ('give a kiss')
por ('frighten')	esforç ('make an effort')
ràbia ('infuriate')	pregunta ('ask a question')
llàstima ('rouse pity')	broma ('make a joke')
mandra ('feel lazy')	ullada ('look, glance')
fàstic ('disgust')	volta ('turn (round)')
goig ('look good')	tomb ('take a stroll')
	pausa ('pause, stop')
	glop ('take a gulp')

Table 3. List of predicative nouns most strongly associated with light verb *dar* in Spanish non-translations

LVCs with Spanish *dar*	
States	**Dynamic events**
miedo ('frighten')	vuelta ('turn (round)')
pena ('rouse pity')	paso ('take a step')
vergüenza ('feel ashamed')	salto ('take a jump')
ganas ('feel like')	beso ('give a kiss')
asco ('disgust')	orden ('give an order')
lástima ('rouse pity')	paseo ('take a walk')
grima ('set teeth on edge')	explicación ('give an explanation')
escalofrío ('give the shivers')	gracias ('give thanks')
	muestra ('show signs of')
	codazo ('nudge')

to perform those kinds of tests on several indicators in the future. But in this particular study only corpus evidence is used, so that the most plausible way to operationalise salience (and connectivity, as will be seen later on) seems to be frequency. Table 4 shows the raw and normalised frequencies of the two types of

LVCs with *fer* in CA and *dar* in ES. LVCs conveying dynamic events are more frequent than those conveying emotional states in both CA (362 vs 218, with normalised frequencies at 233.5 and 140.6 per million words, respectively) and ES (938 vs 327, with normalised frequencies at 224.9 vs 78.4 per million words). So we conclude that the former are more salient than the latter in both languages.

Table 4. Raw and normalised frequencies (per million words) of LVC types with *fer* in CA and *dar* ES

	CA		ES	
	Raw f	Norm f	Raw f	Norm f
Emotional states	218	140.6	327	78.4
Dynamic events	362	233.5	938	224.9

As explained at the beginning of this section, in order to establish SL salience (i.e. gravitational pull) we decided to examine the predicative nouns collocating with the closest equivalents of *fer* and *dar* in English and French: 'make' and 'give', and *faire* and *donner*. The main thing to be determined was whether the distribution of LVCs across types favoured one type or the other. Here is a summary of the findings:

a. The top-ranking 100 collocates of the verb 'make' were scanned for predicative nouns in the ST component of EN-CA. None of the 49 LVCs thus identified conveyed an emotional state. All of them conveyed dynamic events of the types included in the study (acts, actions and activities), although the ascription of one ('make difference') is rather doubtful.
b. The same procedure was repeated for 'give' in EN-ES and only 3 of the LVCs found conveyed emotional states ('give courage/pleasure/strength'). As in the case of 'make', all the remaining ones fell under the general category of dynamic events.
c. In order to complement a and b, the English Web 2020 corpus in Sketch Engine (36,561,273,153 words) was queried for noun collocates of 'make' and 'give'. The top-ranking 400 collocates of each light verb were manually scanned for LVCs denoting emotional states or dynamic events. Out of the 88 LVCs found for 'make', 82 conveyed dynamic events and 6 were of doubtful ascription. No cases of LVCs denoting emotional states were found. As for 'give', 112 different LVCs were identified, out of which 94 referred to dynamic events, 8 to emotional states, 8 to other types of states and 2 were of doubtful ascription. These results confirm to a large extent those presented in a and b. 'Make' and 'give' mostly tend to co-occur with predicative nouns denoting dynamic events, even if 'give'

is more likely to enter into LVCs conveying states generally, including emotional ones, than 'make'.

d. As for French, since the ST components of FR-CA and FR-ES in COVALT do not allow for collocation search, the French Web 2017 corpus in Sketch Engine (5,752,261,039 words) was queried instead. As in the case of English, the top-ranking 400 collocates of *faire* were scanned for LVCs denoting emotional states or dynamic events, with just one case of the former (*faire plaisir*) and a vast majority of the latter.
e. The same procedure was repeated for *donner* with quite dissimilar results: *donner* co-occurs with such predicative nouns as *plaisir, goût, sentiment, joie, peine, confiance, illusion* and *espoir*, conveying emotional states. This shows that, even though in the vast majority of cases the construction *donner*+predicative noun still conveys dynamic events, not emotional states, it is much more productive in the latter sense than *faire*+predicative noun.

On the basis of this data, then, it is fair to expect a relatively high degree of overlap and, therefore, of connectivity between LVCs with *fer* in Catalan and *dar* in Spanish, on the one hand, and LVCs with 'make' and 'give' in English and *faire* and *donner* in French, on the other hand, when these LVCs convey dynamic acts. However, for LVCs conveying emotional states, a relatively low degree of connectivity is to be expected in all four slots.

Drawing on these salience and connectivity patterns, the following hypotheses are put forward:

1. LVCs denoting emotional states will be under-represented both in EN-CA and EN-ES as compared to CA and ES, respectively, on account of both low TL salience of those constructions and low connectivity with their ST triggers.
2. LVCs denoting emotional states will be under-represented in both FR-CA and FR-ES as compared to CA and ES, respectively, on account of low TL salience of those constructions and low connectivity.
3. LVCs denoting acts/actions/activities will show no significant frequency differences either in EN-CA and FR-CA as compared to CA or in EN-ES and FR-ES as compared to ES.

The next step is to determine the frequencies of the LVCs identified in CA and ES in the four parallel sub-corpora and to establish similarities and differences in order to test out the hypotheses. This is the most crucial step in the study. However, it will be supplemented with a brief analysis of a number of selected LVCs so that more light is thrown on the interaction between the three factors in the GPH. To that end, the main triggers of a given TL LVC will be identified, so that connectivity patterns can be established – even if they are incomplete, as argued above.

5. Results and discussion

5.1 Quantitative analysis: The category level

The queries already performed for CA and ES (i.e. the Catalan and Spanish non-translated components of the comparable corpora) were repeated for EN-CA, EN-ES, FR-CA and FR-ES. All query matches were then manually analysed so that false positives could be discarded. Raw frequencies were normalised per 1,000,000 words for ease of comparison, as the corpus components to be compared were unequal in size. Finally, log-likelihood was calculated for each type of LVC (emotional states and dynamic events) across the translation/non-translation divide, i.e. by comparing frequencies between CA/EN-CA and CA/FR-CA, on the one hand, and between ES/EN-ES and ES/FR-ES, on the other. Be it remembered in this respect that we are concerned here with the category level (i.e. LVC types), not with individual LVCs.

The combination of language pairs and types of LVCs yields a total of 8 different sets of results, which are shown in Tables 5–8. In each table, columns 1, 3 and 5 provide raw (after manual analysis) frequencies and columns 2, 4 and 6 provide normalised frequencies. Tables 9 and 10 provide the totals per category for ease of comparison.

Table 5. Results for LVCs with *fer* conveying emotional states in EN-CA and FR-CA

fer	CA		EN-CA		FR-CA	
	Raw f	Norm f	Raw f	Norm f	Raw f	Norm f
gràcia	75	48.3	20	14.9	3	5.3
il·lusió	26	16.8	1	0.7	4	7.1
por	60	38.7	69	51.4	22	38.8
ràbia	17	11	0	0.00	2	3.5
llàstima	11	7.1	6	4.5	4	7.1
mandra	9	5.8	0	0.00	0	0.00
fàstic	9	5.8	5	3.7	2	3.5
goig	11	7.1	3	2.2	1	1.8
TOTAL	218	140.6	104	77.4	38	67.1

Table 6. Results for LVCs with *dar* conveying emotional states in EN-ES and FR-ES

dar	ES		EN-ES		FR-ES	
	Raw f	Norm f	Raw f	Norm f	Raw f	Norm f
miedo	152	36.4	27	24.1	19	33.6
pena	63	15.1	7	6.2	6	10.6
vergüenza	51	12.2	7	6.2	6	10.6
gana	27	6.5	2	1.8	4	7.1
asco	13	3.1	2	1.8	3	5.3
lástima	10	2.4	1	0.9	2	3.5
grima	4	1	1	0.9	0	0.00
escalofrío	7	1.7	1	0.9	0	0.00
TOTAL	327	78.4	48	42.8	40	70.7

Table 7. Results for LVCs with *fer* conveying dynamic events in EN-CA and FR-CA

fer	CA		EN-CA		FR-CA	
	Raw f	Norm f	Raw f	Norm f	Raw f	Norm f
gest	78	50.3	38	28.3	24	42.3
petó	53	34.2	0	0.00	0	0.00
esforç	40	25.8	47	35	15	26.5
pregunta	47	30.3	47	35	38	67
broma	34	21.9	25	18.6	11	19.4
ullada	20	12.9	57	42.4	5	8.8
volta	35	22.6	50	37.2	29	51.1
tomb	13	8.4	6	4.5	2	3.5
pausa	20	12.9	37	27.5	0	0.00
glop	22	14.2	5	3.7	0	0.00
TOTAL	362	233.5	312	232.2	124	218.6

Table 8. Results for LVCs with *dar* conveying dynamic events in EN-ES and FR-ES

dar	ES		EN-ES		FR-ES	
	Raw f	Norm f	Raw f	Norm f	Raw f	Norm f
vuelta	288	69.1	155	138.1	49	86.7
paso	176	42.2	42	37.4	19	33.6
salto	67	16.1	46	41	21	37.1
beso	76	18.2	4	3.6	21	37.1
orden	89	21.3	48	42.8	15	26.5
paseo	57	13.7	24	21.4	11	19.5
explicación	51	12.2	5	4.5	3	5.3
gracia	79	18.9	35	31.2	19	33.6
muestra	33	7.9	17	15.1	12	21.2
codazo	22	5.3	2	1.8	4	7.1
TOTAL	938	224.9	478	336.9	174	307.7

Table 9. Totals per category for CA, EN-CA and FR-CA

	CA		EN-CA		FR-CA	
	Raw f	Norm f	Raw f	Norm f	Raw f	Norm f
fer (emotional states)	218	140.6	104	77.4	38	67.1
fer (dynamic events)	362	233.5	312	232.2	124	218.6

Table 10. Totals per category for ES, EN-ES and FR-ES

	ES		EN-ES		FR-ES	
	Raw f	Norm f	Raw f	Norm f	Raw f	Norm f
dar (emotional states)	327	78.4	48	42.8	40	70.7
dar (dynamic events)	938	224.9	478	336.9	174	307.7

And finally, Table 11 provides the results of the log-likelihood test performed on totals per category across the translation/non-translation divide in all four language pairs.

Table 11. Log-likelihood results[4]

	CA/EN-CA	CA/FR-CA	ES/EN-ES	ES/FR-ES
fer/dar (emotional states)	**LL = 26.51**	**LL = 20.95**	**LL = 17.83**	LL = 0.39
fer/dar (dynamic events)	**LL = 0**	**LL = 0.39**	LL = 118.96	LL = 13.40

In Table 11, log-likelihood values that are aligned with the hypotheses are marked in bold.

Hypothesis 1, concerning emotional states in translations from English, is confirmed both for EN-CA and EN-ES. In EN-CA (Table 5), all LVCs are under-represented except *fer por* ('frighten'). In EN-ES (Table 6), all individual LVCs are under-represented.

Hypothesis 2, concerning emotional states in translations from French, is confirmed for FR-CA but not for FR-ES. As in EN-CA, all LVCs are under-represented in FR-CA except *fer por* (see Table 5). This may be accounted for by both low magnetism and low connectivity, the French verb *faire* not being very productive as far as LVCs conveying emotional states are concerned. As to FR-ES (Table 6), the difference between the overall frequency of LVCs in Spanish translations and Spanish non-translations is not significant. This means that low TL salience may have been compensated for by connectivity, stemming from the fact that the verb *donner* is more productive than *faire* in LVCs denoting emotional states. Individual LVCs are under-represented in 5 and over-represented in 3 cases (out of 8).

Finally, hypothesis 3 concerning dynamic events is only confirmed for two language combinations, EN-CA and FR-CA (Table 7), not for the remaining two having Spanish as TL (Table 8). Both in EN-CA and FR-CA, overall frequency differences between translations and Catalan non-translations are not significant, even though there are remarkable differences at the level of individual LVCs. In EN-CA, over- and under-representation cancel each other, as 5 LVCs are over- and 5 under-represented (out of 10). The same applies to FR-CA, even if as many as 7 LVCs are under-represented, whereas only 3 are over-represented (again out of 10). In EN-ES and FR-ES, however, differences between translations and non-translations are significant, contrary to what was predicted by hypothesis 3. In both cases, too, they lean towards over-representation. In EN-ES, 6 LVCs are over- and 4 under-represented. In FR-ES, there are 7 cases of over- and 3 of under-representation. Since the overall normalised frequencies of LVCs convey-

4. The critical value of the log-likelihood test is 3.84 at a 95% level of confidence (i.e. for a p value of < 0.05). Therefore, any LL value lower than 3.84 indicates that differences do not reach the threshold of statistical significance.

ing dynamic events are very similar in CA and ES (233.5 vs 224.9, respectively), the significant difference between ES and translations in EN-ES and FR-ES as regards this type of construction ought to be explained, at least to some extent, by a relatively high degree of connectivity between Spanish *dar* and its ST triggers both in English and French. We will come back to this point in Section 5.2.

5.2 Qualitative analysis: The individual LVC level

As regards hypothesis 1, a typical example of an LVC denoting an emotional state which is under-represented in EN-CA, thus aligning itself with the hypothesis, is *fer gràcia* ('be funny/please'). The normalised frequency of this construction per million words is 48.3 in CA and 14.9 in EN-CA, and the most obvious explanation for this significant difference is low degree of connectivity between *fer gràcia* and its ST triggers: there are as many as 14 (out of 20 occurrences of the Catalan LVC) and the top-ranking one (the verb 'like') accounts for just 5 of them. The same is true of *dar miedo* ('frighten') in EN-ES, which is also under-represented as compared to ES, normalised frequencies being 36.4 in the latter and 24.1 in the former. This construction has 14 different triggers (out of 27 occurrences) in English, the top-ranking ones being 'be afraid' (9) and 'fear' (5). But the Catalan equivalent of *dar miedo* ('frighten'), *fer por*, is a counterexample to the negative impact of low degree of connectivity on frequency, as it is the only Catalan LVC conveying emotional states which is not under-represented in EN-CA even though it has as many as 27 different triggers, with only one of them ('be afraid') accounting for a moderately high number of occurrences (18 out of 60). This is probably to be explained on the grounds of magnetism: *fer por* is the most neutral way of expressing in Catalan that something is frightening, other options (e.g. *espantar, esglaiar, espaordir* and others) being more laden with connotation.

Hypothesis 2 was based on the assumption that the convergence of the three factors (low magnetism, low gravitational pull and low connectivity) would lead to under-representation of LVCs conveying emotional states in FR-CA. The data, as seen above, bear out the hypothesis only for FR-CA, not for FR-ES. Analysis reveals that the triggers for such TL constructions rarely feature an LVC. The main exception to that is *fer por* in FR-CA and *dar miedo* in FR-ES, which are precisely the only LVCs of any importance (most other LVCs showing a very low frequency in both language pairs) which are not under-represented. *Fer por* occurs 22 times in FR-CA, with a normalised frequency of 38.8 vs 38.7 in CA. It has 6 different triggers, and one of them (*faire peur*, a very close formal equivalent of Catalan *fer por*) accounts for 14 out of 22 occurrences (64%, a relatively high percentage). In FR-ES, *dar miedo* occurs 19 times, with a normalised frequency of 33.6 vs 36.4 in ES. It has 6 different triggers in the STs, one of which (again, *faire peur*) accounts for 10 out of 19 occurrences (53%). This shows that the degree of connectivity between TL LVCs and their ST triggers can vary widely across individual LVCs, over- or under-representation depending to a large extent on that kind of variation.

Finally, hypothesis 3 predicted no significant differences in the frequency of LVCs conveying dynamic events between translations and non-translations for the four language combinations. The hypothesis was borne out by the data only for the sub-corpora having Catalan as TL. In both EN-ES and FR-ES, in fact, such constructions are significantly over-represented. As remarked above, this might be due to a relatively high degree of connectivity between LVCs with *dar* denoting dynamic events and their ST triggers in English and French. However, the magnetism of some individual constructions might also be a factor at play. *Dar salto* ('make jump'), for instance, is over-represented in both EN-ES and FR-ES, even though no significant degree of connectivity is observed between this LVC and any ST trigger. *Dar salto* has 24 different triggers in EN-ES for 46 occurrences, and 14 different triggers in FR-ES for 21 occurrences. But magnetism may be closely allied with connectivity, as in *dar gracias*, which is again over-represented in both EN-ES and FR-ES. Source concentration on a single trigger is high in both language pairs: the English verb 'thank' acts as a trigger for *dar gracias* in 26 out of the 35 occurrences of the Spanish LVC (74.29%), and the French verb *remercier* does as much in 14 out of 20 occurrences in FR-ES (70%). A similar case is *dar orden*, also over-represented in both EN-ES and FR-ES. The triggers 'give order' (16) and 'order' (10), taken together, account for 26 out of 48 occurrences of this LVC in EN-ES (54.17%). In FR-ES, the very close formal counterpart *donner ordre* acts as a trigger for *dar orden* in 9 out of 16 occurrences (60%). Magnetism and connectivity may be said to go hand in hand in these and other cases.

Individual LVCs conveying dynamic events in EN-CA and FR-CA, even if hypothesis 3 is confirmed by the data on the category level, show huge variation, as can be seen in Table 7. This clearly demonstrates that a different configuration of factors is at play for each particular LVC in each particular language pair even when a general pattern is discernible on the category level. Thus, low degree of connectivity may be said to account for the under-representation of *fer gest* ('make gesture') in EN-CA, which features 23 different triggers for a total of 38 occurrences. However, this LVC is also under-represented in FR-CA, where a higher degree of connectivity is observed between *fer gest* and its closest French counterpart *faire geste* – 11 cases out of 23, 46%. This seems to suggest low magnetism of the Catalan LVC. In other cases, though, degree of connectivity plays a discriminating role between EN-CA and FR-CA. *Fer pausa* ('make pause') is over-represented in EN-CA, with only 4 different triggers for 37 occurrences, the English verb 'pause' acting as a trigger in as many as 34 cases (91.89%). Degree of connectivity is very high, then, between these two elements. On the other hand, *fer pausa* does not occur at all in FR-CA.

Finally, gravitational pull may be regarded as the only factor at play in the over-representation of *fer ullada* ('give look') in EN-CA. It is over-represented in this language pair but not in FR-CA even if degree of connectivity between the Catalan LVC and its English triggers is rather low, as witnessed by the fact that it features 24 different triggers for a total of 57 occurrences. English is rich in verbs denoting ways of looking (e.g. 'look', 'glance', 'glimpse', 'peer', 'peep', 'stare', etc., as well as the corresponding nouns entering into LVCs in English, such as 'catch a glimpse' or 'take a look'), so that the 'looking' network may be said to be salient in the source language, resulting in gravitational pull. A parallel phenomenon is not observable in FR-CA, where *fer ullada* is under-represented.

6. Concluding remarks

The present study is perhaps somehow unorthodox in that it sets out to test the GPH not on particular lexical items but on the more abstract level of (certain types of) LVCs – a type of construction which is not easy to grasp in the first place. If hypotheses had been formulated on the level of individual LVCs, it would have been possible to establish the relative onomasiological salience of TL LVCs vis-à-vis their alternatives in the semantic networks they belong to, and the same could have been done with their most frequent ST triggers. It was impossible to do that for all the LVCs under scrutiny in the space of a book chapter. Even so, we thought it worthwhile to take the risk of formulating hypotheses at the more abstract category level, hinging upon the distinction between LVCs conveying emotional states or dynamic events, since these two patterns were discernible for *fer*+predicative noun in Catalan and *dar*+predicative noun in Spanish. That involved some clear methodological limitations, as explained at the beginning of Section 4. However, formulating hypotheses on the level of abstract categories could also be seen as a way of pushing the theory forward beyond the lexical level. This line of work must be replicated in the future to see if it is worth pursuing or not.

As seen in the previous section, the hypotheses put forward were only partly borne out by the data, i.e. in five out of the eight slots in the grid where the two types of LVCs converge with the four language combinations. We would like to argue that this is probably due not to shortcomings in the theory (i.e. to lack of explanatory validity) but to the methodological limitations of the study. By placing our focus at a relatively high level of abstraction, we may have missed important facts about the magnetism and gravitational pull of individual LVCs. More particularly, we may have under-estimated the magnetism of LVCs based on *dar* in Spanish when they convey dynamic events, which must go a long way towards explaining their over-representation in both EN-ES and FR-ES. These LVCs, together with others belonging to other types and in different language combinations, provide an ideal testing ground for the GPH on a more concrete level. That would imply looking at onomasiological salience too by performing analyses both from the target and the source ends, which would in turn enable us to draw a full picture of connectivity. This is a line of research to be pursued in the near future.

At any rate, the individual cases singled out for brief analysis at the end of the results and discussion section provide hints, it is hoped, of what a more thorough analysis along the lines just sketched would yield. In spite of the methodological limitations, a shifting picture emerges in which different configurations of factors for each LVC in each language pair pull towards over- or under-representation, or towards lack of significant difference, as the case may be. All in all, it seems possible to explain most particular cases on the basis of the three factors, which may be taken to confirm the potential of the GPH to account for translation facts.

This study was driven by the descriptive and explanatory urge which clearly permeates the GPH. Translation facts were accounted for on the basis of gravitational pull, magnetism and connectivity. However, it is not difficult to envisage practical applications of the results of the study, especially in the field of translator education. Corpora have the potential to be used in the translation classroom on a regular basis to raise awareness of different aspects of language use, either at the source or the target pole, or of contrastive issues concerning specific language pairs. The results of this study show, among other things, that translations in three of the four language pairs involved (EN-CA, EN-ES and FR-CA) tend to underuse LVCs with *fer* and *dar* denoting emotional states. That means that such idiomatic constructions as *fer gràcia* ('be funny, please') or *fer il·lusió* ('give a thrill') in Catalan, and *dar pena* ('rouse pity') or *dar ganas* ('feel like') in Spanish tend to be (perhaps unconsciously) avoided in favour of more formal options. If translator trainees become aware of this kind of fact, they may feel prompted to redress the balance in their practice. And what is important here perhaps is not the particular case of (certain types of) LVCs, but the more general category of target language resources that are not fully exploited in translation because of the lack of a formal counterpart in the source language. 'Translationese' is admittedly a descriptive label with no pejorative meaning; but there is no reason why it should be turned into an alibi for conservative translation practices which do not seek to improve on earlier attempts. In that respect, corpora may be said to be valuable *heuristic* tools, as they facilitate the discovery of potential areas for improvement.

Funding

This work was supported by the Spanish Ministry for Science, Innovation and Universities (PID2019-103953GB-I00 / AEI / 10.13039/501100011033). We are hugely indebted to Sandra Halverson for her close reading of an earlier draft of this chapter and for her suggestions, which did much to improve it.

References

Algeo, John. 1995. Having a look at the expanded predicate. In *The Verb in Contemporary English: Theory and Description*, Bas Aarts & Charles F. Meyer (eds), 203–217. Cambridge: CUP.

Allerton, David J. 2002. *Stretched Verb Constructions in English*. London: Routledge.

Alonso Ramos, Margarita. 2004. *Las construcciones con verbo de apoyo*. Madrid: Visor.

Babych, Bogdan, Hartley, Anthony & Sharoff, Serge. 2009. Evaluation-guided pre-editing of source text: Improving MT-tractability of light verb constructions. In *Proceedings of the 13th Annual Conference of the EAMT*, 36–43, Barcelona, May 2009. <https://aclanthology.org/2009.eamt-1.6/> (26 May 2023).

Bustos Plaza, Alberto. 2005. Poner en movimiento / in Bewegung setzen: ¿verbos pseudocopulativos españoles frente a verbos funcionales alemanes? In *Fraseología contrastiva: Con ejemplos tomados del alemán, español, francés e italiano*, Ramón Almela, Estanislao Ramón Trives & Gerd Wotjak (eds), 185–196. Murcia: Universidad de Murcia.

Butt, Miriam. 2003. The light verb jungle. *Harvard Working Papers in Linguistics* 9: 1–49.

Castell, Andreu. 2011. El tractament de les construccions amb verb suport en els diccionaris monolingües i bilingües de l'alemany i el català. *Zeitschrift für Katalanistik* 24: 73–88.

Colominas Ventura, Carme. 2001. La representació semàntica de les construccions de suport des d'una perspectiva multilingual. PhD dissertation, Universitat Autònoma de Barcelona.

Evert, Stefan. 2005. The Statistics of Word Cooccurrences: Word Pairs and Collocations. PhD dissertation, University of Stuttgart.

Ginebra, Jordi & Navarro, Pere. 2015. Concurrències lèxiques en català i en espanyol: Uns quants contrastos. In *Actes del Setzè Col·loqui Internacional de Llengua i Literatura Catalanes. Universitat de Salamanca, 1–6 de juliol de 2012*, Àlex Martín Escribà, Adolf Piquer Vidal & Fernando Sánchez Miret (eds), 217–228. Barcelona: Publicacions de l'Abadia de Montserrat.

Ginebra, Jordi. 2008. Els verbs de suport en català i en anglès. Estudi contrastiu a partir d'un petit corpus paral·lel. *Els Marges* 85: 53–72.

doi de Groot, Annette M. B. 2011. *Language and Cognition in Bilinguals and Multilinguals. An Introduction*. New York NY: Psychology Press.

doi Halverson, Sandra. 2003. The cognitive basis of translation universals. *Target* 15(2): 197–241.

Halverson, Sandra. 2017. Developing a cognitive semantic model: Magnetism, gravitational pull, and questions of data and method. In *Empirical Translation Studies. New Methods and Theoretical Traditions*, Gert de Sutter, Marie-Aude Lefer & Isabelle Delaere (eds), 9–45. Berlin: Mouton de Gruyter.

Hareide, Lidun. 2017a. The translation of formal source-language lacunas. An empirical study of the *Over-representation of Target-Language Specific Features* and the *Unique Items Hypothesis*. In *Corpus Methodologies Explained. An Empirical Approach to Translation Studies*, Meng Ji, Michael Oakes, Li Defeng & Lidun Hareide (eds), 137–187. London: Routledge.

Hareide, Lidun. 2017b. Is there gravitational pull in translation? A corpus-based test of the Gravitational Pull Hypothesis on the language pairs Norwegian-Spanish and English-Spanish. In *Corpus Methodologies Explained. An Empirical Approach to Translation Studies*, Meng Ji, Michael Oakes, Li Defeng & Lidun Hareide (eds), 188–231. London: Routledge.

Helbig, Gerhard. 1979. Probleme der Beschreibung von Funktionsverbgefügen im Deutschen. *Deutsch als Fremdsprache* 16: 273–285.

Langacker, Ronald. 2008. *Cognitive Grammar: A Basic Introduction*. Oxford: OUP.

Lefer, Marie-Aude & De Sutter, Gert. 2022. Using the Gravitational Pull Hypothesis to explain patterns in interpreting and translation: The case of concatenated nouns in mediated European Parliament discourse. In *Mediated Discourse at the European Parliament: Empirical Investigations*, Marta Kajzer-Wietrzny, Adriano Ferraresi, Ilmari Ivaska & Silvia Bernardini (eds), 133–159. Berlin: Language Science Press.

López-Campos Bodineau, Rafael. 1997. Las estructuras con verbos de función en lengua alemana: Limitaciones en torno a su productividad y formación. *Revista de Filología Alemana* 5: 303–316.

Marco, Josep. 2021. Testing the Gravitational Pull Hypothesis on modal verbs expressing obligation and necessity in Catalan through the COVALT corpus. In *Empirical Studies in Translation and Discourse*, Mario Bisiada (ed.), 27–52. Berlin: Language Science Press.

Marzouk, Shaimaa. 2021. German light verb construction in the course of the development of machine translation. In *Translation, Interpreting, Cognition: The Way Out of the Box*, Tra&Co Group (ed.), 47–66. Berlin: Language Science Press.

Rabadán, Rosa. 2023. Light Verb constructions in English-Spanish translation. What corpora can tell us. Paper given at the III PaCor Symposium (Parallel Corpora: Creation and Applications), University of the Basque Country, 23–25 June 2021.

Ronan, Patricia & Schneider, Gerold. 2015. Determining Light Verb Constructions in contemporary British and Irish English. *International Journal of Corpus Linguistics* 20(3): 326–354.

Vandevoorde, Lore. 2020. *Semantic differences in translation: Exploring the feld of inchoativity* [Translation and Multilingual Natural Language Processing 13]. Berlin: Language Science Press.

Vendler, Zeno. 1967. *Linguistics and Philosophy*. Ithaca NY: Cornell University Press.

Wittenberg-Kuypers, Eva. 2014. With Light Verb Constructions from Syntax to Concepts. PhD dissertation, University of Potsdam.

CHAPTER 2

Light Verb Constructions in English-Spanish translation

What corpora can tell us

Rosa Rabadán
University of León

Light Verb Constructions (LVCs) are combinations of a partially delexicalized verb and a noun indicating an action or an event (e. g., *give a description*). Studies modelled on the Meaning-Text theory and qualia roles of the Generative Lexicon model propose that LVCs combine nouns and verbs according to shared underlying, underspecified semantic features. This paper explores these features' role in translating English LVCs into Spanish. Data come from the parallel corpus P-ACTRES 2.0, including fiction and nonfiction materials. Results indicate that translation choices for LVCs with *have, take, make/do*, and *give* are governed by the same notions of transference, inception, and volition that determine their combinatorial compatibility. Register also seems to influence the choice. This information may prove significant to machine translation, bi/multilingual writing support, and post-editing.

Keywords: Light Verb Constructions, parallel corpus, semantic compatibility, semantic underspecification, translation solutions

1. Introduction

Light Verb Constructions (LVCs) are complex predicates involving a verb of general meaning (the so-called light verb) like *make/hacer* or *take/tomar* plus an abstract, generally eventive noun phrase (NP), which may also include a modifier, often an article (Bosque 2001; Alonso Ramos 2004; Butt 2010; Sanromán Vilas 2015). Grammatically, LVCs are just like any other V+NP pattern; the light verb is considered semantically weak, serving only as a verbal marker with most of the meaning supplied by the NP (Leech, 2006; Spencer, 2013). LVCs can be rephrased and viewed as equivalent to their single correlated verb, e.g., *make a decision* > *decide, take a rest* > *rest* (Nenonen et al. 2017). Lexically, LVCs are considered

https://doi.org/10.1075/scl.113.02rab

multiword expressions (MWE) and treated as fixed dictionary collocations. However, only some combinatorial dictionaries list them consistently as LVCs (e. g., Spanish REDES, Bosque 2004b, 2006). Databases such as UCREL's USAS do so haphazardly, e. g. *make a mistake* make_A5.3-[i1.2.1 a_Z5 mistake_A5.3-[i1.2.2 is marked as an MWE, whereas *make a decision* [make_A1.1.1 a_Z5 decision_X6 +] is treated as a list of independent elements (Piao, Rayson, Archer & McEnery 2005).[1]

NLP research has shown that it is feasible to detect LVCs automatically and distinguish them from other complex predicates, focusing on contextual information (Nagy, Rácz & Vincze 2020; Vincze, Nagy & Berend 2011 and 2013). However, available research data generally do not include this degree of granularity, particularly when it comes to translation.

Linguistic research has shown that LVCs constitute a semi-productive category, and efforts have focused mainly on the underlying semantic features that govern light verb-noun combinatorial preferences and their generative capabilities (De Miguel 2013, 2011 and 2008, Sanromán Vilas 2017). However, to our knowledge, it has not been explored whether these underlying features also influence, maybe even determine, translation choices.

This paper examines whether translation solutions adopted in Spanish relate to the LVC features of semantic compatibility. Additionally, I will analyze how these solutions behave and correlate in two different registers, fiction and nonfiction.

Section 2 briefly reviews LVCs' relevant literature, focusing on English and Spanish; Section 3 presents the corpus data and method, and Section 4 focuses on the results. The discussion is in Section 5. Section 6 submits the conclusions, future research, and the applied potential of the results.

2. Light Verb Constructions

As a research topic, LVCs have received considerable attention from different theoretical approaches, which conventionally accept that these constructions share some characteristics that keep them separate from other complex predicates (Gross & De Pontonx 2004).[2]

A light verb (e.g., *make* in *make a donation)* is formally not different from a 'heavy' lexical verb (*make a dress*). Both have the same syntax but different semantic structures (Butt 2003, 2010). An LVC combines a semantically 'emptied'

1. For quick reference, see < https://ucrel.lancs.ac.uk/usas/ > and < ucrel-api.lancaster.ac.uk/usas /tagger.html >

2. Bruening (2016: 52) considers LVCs regular verb-complement combinations, thus dispensing with the need for a specific category.

yet grammatically meaningful verb with a host noun that contributes semantic features (Mel'čuk 2004; Sanromán Vilas 2013); together, they constitute a single predicate. Within the same language, the LVC often (but not always, nor in all languages) has a correlate full verb, which has led to considering the LVC as a periphrasis of the latter (*take a bath, bathe*). LVCs are semi-productive, as they have intra- and interlingual restrictions concerning their ability to generate new constructions, e. g., *have a break > hacer un descanso, descansar, hacer cola (*make queue) > queue (*colar)* (Mel'čuk 1996; Koike 2001; Sanromán Vilas 2017).

This minimal common ground points out underlying formal and semantic properties to which exceptions can be found (Langer 2005: 171). However, it seems suited to establishing a baseline on what an LVC is, irrespective of the analysis model.

Among the theoretical approaches, the Meaning – Text Theory considers LVCs a type of collocation where the collocate selection is somewhat arbitrary (Mel'čuk 1997; 2004). In this view, the verb has suffered a semantic bleaching process from its "heavy" verb (HV). The verb retains some grammatical information, e. g. tense, the semantic meaning provided by the noun in the construction (Alonso Ramos 2004: 24, 2007).

By contrast, lexical-functional models (Butt 2010) consider that the light verb has lexical meaning, which derives from the polysemic relations between light and heavy verbs.[3] The analyses focus on identifying the semantic features that the light verb contributes to the LVC, among them volition and aspect (Butt 2003: 18–23).

Other views concentrate on the shared semantics of the light verb and the noun, which happen at a general, *underspecified* level. *Underspecification* allows these lexical items to combine in different syntactic structures and, consequently, to acquire different semantic interpretations (Pustejovsky 1995, 1998). The underlying assumption is that verbs and nouns can combine because of semantic feature agreement, which entails a kind of semantic redundancy (Bosque 2004a).

This idea is key to De Miguel's approach (2008, 2011, 2013), which takes Pustejovsky's Generative Lexicon model (1995), particularly its *qualia* structure, to outline noun-verb combinatorial selections in LVCs. In this view, the new meanings are not derived arbitrarily; rather, they are a possibility already contained in the underspecified definition of the item in the lexicon. In other words, the *underspecified* semantic features have the power to determine the noun-light verb pairing on the grounds of shared abstract meanings.

3. Some cognitivists (Brugman 2001) defend that light verbs are not totally devoid of semantic content, retaining part of the semantics of the corresponding heavy verb.

This sharing of common meanings is also the core notion informing the *hypothesis of semantic compatibility* formulated by Sanromán Vilas (2009, 2012a, 2012b, 2013, 2014, 2017). It maintains that lexical units, among them LVCs, do not combine arbitrarily but rely on shared meaning features that favour particular selections to the detriment of others. In her formulation, light verbs are paradigmatically connected to their polysemic HV, the shared features acting as semantic links between the different senses of the verb.

Additionally, the light verb-noun choice in an LVC is syntagmatically determined by the underlying meaning features they share, e.g. 'creation' in HV *make (a dress)* and LV *make (arrangements)*. However, LV **make (a walk)* does not show semantic agreement and therefore is not a valid combination (see below in this section). The semantic compatibility postulate constitutes the basis for the noun-LV combinatorial capabilities, which are built on shared features by the light verb and its HV and by the noun and its chosen verb in any LVC, respectively.[4]

I capitalize on this position to formulate our working hypothesis: the choice of translation solution also operates on the grounds of light verb-noun combinatorial capabilities and may be determined by the register. My next step is to characterize the shared semantic ground exhibited by the constituents of my chosen LVCs. Most authors tend to cite aspectuality (Bosque 2004b) and volitionality (as an instance of causality) (Piera & Valera 1999: 4416; Butt 2003) as semantic features underlying LVCs. Nevertheless, my aim requires a more granular distribution of the underlying combinatorial triggers for each light verb to test their bearing on translation choices.

Give contributes the core feature of transference, linked to displaced (transferred, already existent) objects. *Give* combines with communication nouns such as *give a lecture, a description, information,* or *advice,* all of which entail a benefactive reading (Butt 2003).

Make and *do* share the core feature of creation with their host nouns and are associated with effected objects, i. e., with no previous existence, created by verbal action, e. g. *make arrangements, mistakes,* or *do the experiment, do business.*

Take (Sanromán Vilas 2017) includes three shared features: (a) (non)volition, which involves the subject, e. g., take possession > *tomar posesión/ hacer(se) cargo*; (b) deixis, signalling the subject as the reference point of movement, e. g. take a beating > recibir una paliza /*encajar pérdidas, una derrota* (figuratively, assume a

4. It can be argued that specific nouns can and do combine with different light verbs, as in take/ have a shower > *tomar/ dar una ducha*, but the verb is always selected according to the noun's highlighted feature, e.g. *dar* (agentive) vs *tomar* (beneficiary) (Sanromán Vilas 2017: 258).

bad result/ be badly beaten). And (c) inchoative aspect, as *take* LVCs tend to focus on the initial part of a process, e. g. take power (over) > *asumir el poder.*

Finally, *have* is aspectually neutral and can occupy the slot of practically any other light verb, e. g., *have/take a bath.* More specifically, *have* shares the features of possession, control or entitlement by cognitive agents, e. g., *have a choice, a row.*

Next, corpus data are described and sampled to test our hypothesis that translation solutions are related to the light verb-noun combinatorial properties and, maybe, to register.

3. Data and method

To obtain empirical data on the different translation solutions for LVCs, I use P-ACTRES 2.0; a PoS annotated English-Spanish bidirectional parallel corpus containing 5,720,319 words, as the source for empirical data (Sanjurjo-González & Izquierdo 2019).[5] The English-into-Spanish subcorpus comprises 4,296,733 between F and NF genres. The F subcorpus includes novels and short stories. It comprises 2,634,087 words, of which 1,276,791 correspond to original texts in English and 1,357,296 to their translations into Spanish. The NF subcorpus includes essays, newspaper editorials, magazine articles, and miscellaneous materials such as leaflets and announcements. It contains 1,662,646 words, of which 788,263 correspond to original texts in English and 874.383 to their translations into Spanish.

I start by querying *give, make, do, have* and *take + (det) + N* in P-ACTRES 2.0. My study is restricted to the core LVs leaving out other candidates to be 'lightened' such as *hold* (an opinion), *offer* (an apology), or *pay* (a visit), which combine with a far narrower range of nouns (Huddleston & Pullum 2002: 296). They are frequently considered phraseological units and tend to have functional equivalents. Another reason for this decision is to take advantage of the cross-linguistic correspondence between those verbs, i.e. *dar*-give, *hacer*- do/make, *tener*- have and *tomar*- take.

I obtained 2,950 concordances, which were sampled and manually screened, leaving us with 1,510 English LVCs after filtering. The sample to be analyzed came to 575 concordances, 350 from the fiction and 217 from the nonfiction subcorpus. Table 1 shows the distribution of the concordances to ensure that all the verbs and registers are represented in the sample.

Next, corpus data are analyzed regarding: first, translation patterns, depending on whether LVCs are kept in the target text, i.e., there exist LVCs in Spanish, as in (take a walk > *dar un paseo*). Alternatively, a single- verb option is favoured, such

5. For quick reference, see <https://actres.unileon.es/wp/parallel-corpora/>

Table 1. LVCs analyzed

LV+(det)+N	**+**	**Fiction**	**Nonfiction**
give		40	23
make		100	52
do		21	14
have		52	28
take		145	100
Totals		358	217

as the single correlated verb (take a walk>*pasear* – walk) or a semantically related full verb (make conversation>*charlar* – chat). Additionally, idiomatic, lexicalized solutions are also considered as in give a hoot>*importar un carajo* – could not care less. These patterns may entail stylistic changes, e. g. vulgarity, as in the previous example (see Section 4). Secondly, the semantic features-translation choice association is examined. The features considered in the analysis are (a) *transference*, (give advice>*dar consejo*); (b) *volition* and *creation* of effected objects (make a visit>*hacer una visita*); (c) *spatial deixis*, (take advantage>*aprovecharse*), (d) *inchoative aspect* (take action>*tomar medidas)*; and (e) *cognitive agent's possession, control, or entitlement*, indicating a state, an event, or an attitude (have control>*tener (el) control*). Furthermore, translation trends and relations between translation solutions and the original LVCs are also examined according to the register.

This examination of the data reveals that English LVCs in Spanish translation adopt different patterns depending on the LVC combinatorial features.

4. Results

Corpus findings reveal four recurrent patterns in the translation solutions:

1. Another LVC in Spanish (LVC), as in *make a suggestion>hacer una sugerencia, have a bath>darse un baño* (give oneself a bath),
2. The single correlate verb (CORRELATE) as in *give guidance>guiar* (guide), *take part>participar* (participate), *do the ironing>planchar* (iron),
3. A verb construction using a fuller, more specialized verb (SPX VC), as in *give permission>conceder permiso* (grant permission); *have a row>enfrascarse en una discusión* (get into a discussion)
4. A full lexical verb, different from the single correlate verb (FULL LV), as in *make holes>perforar* (drill), *have a go>intentar* (try, attempt),

5. Other solutions found (OTHER) are generally multiword expressions showing different degrees of lexicalization and slightly different levels of formality, as in *give a damn* > *traer sin cuidado* (*bring without care, not care) or *take care* > *estar atento* (*be vigilant, pay attention).

The overall trend shows that the preferred solution is a full lexical verb (27.13%), followed by single correlate verbs (25.6%). LVCs take the third position (23.3%), while constructions with a more specialized verb come to 19%. Translation solutions classified as *other* constitute 4.87% of the cases analyzed (Figure 1).

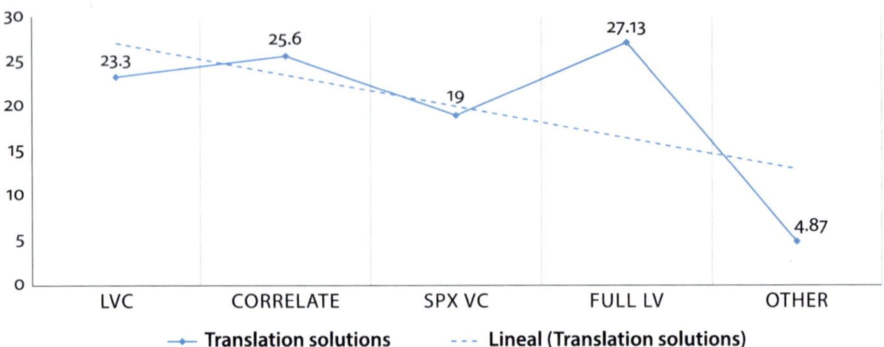

Figure 1. LVCs translated into Spanish: Translation solutions

These results experience register-related variation. In translated fiction, single-verb solutions are also preferred, but the single correlated verb is the first choice in 28.2% of the cases, followed by full lexical verbs other than correlates (25.1%). LVCs are preferred in 23.18% of cases, and constructions with a more specialized verb are 17.3%. Solutions under *other* come up to 5.8% (Figure 2).

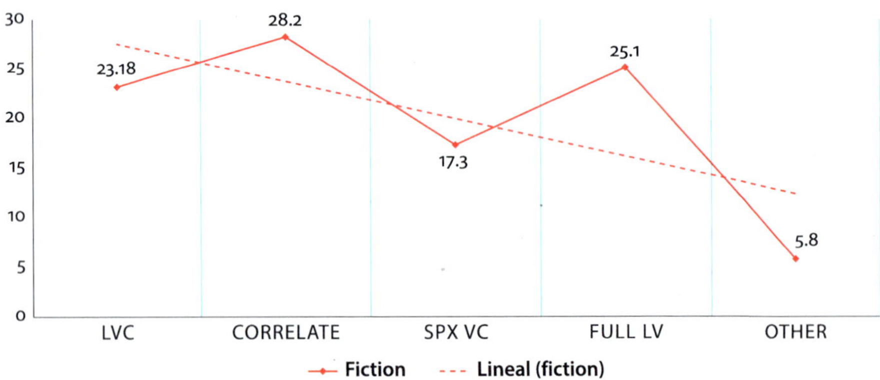

Figure 2. LVCs in translated fiction

However, in translated nonfiction, the preferred solution is a full lexical verb other than the correlate (30.4%), with LVCs taking second place (23.5%). Constructions with a more specialized verb come to 21.6%, while the single correlate verb stands at 21.19%. Solutions labelled *other* constitute 3.22% of all solutions (Figure 3).

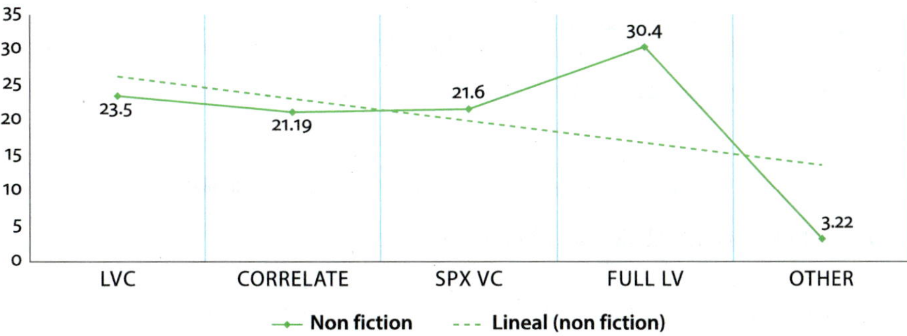

Figure 3. LVCs in translated nonfiction

The following regularities are found when the results are collated in terms of the relation(s) between translation solutions and the LVCs they derive from.

The first solution, another LVC in Spanish, happens with all verb bases, but as shown in Figure 4, it is preferred by *make* (33%) and t*ake* (25.5%) in fiction texts. An LVC is also preferred in nonfiction contexts for *take* (28%) and *give* (26.08%). In all these cases, LVCs constitute over 25% of all solutions. Examples (1) and (2) illustrate this practice.

(1) I'd gladly **make a deal** with ol' Beelzebub just so she might draw one more breath. (FPDR1E.s142)
Yo estaría encantado de ***hacer un trato*** *con el viejo Belcebú si a cambio ella pudiera durar un poco más.* *(FPDR1S.s143)*

(2) That hearing will **take place** in spring next year. (PSTEJ1E.s51)
Este juicio *tendrá lugar* en primavera del año próximo. (PSTEJ1S.s47)

Have, however, does not favor this translation solution in either fiction (9.6%) or nonfiction (10.7%).

As shown in Figure 5, the single correlate verb as a translation solution is favoured by *take* (38.6%) and *have* (32.7%) in fiction (Example 3) and dispreferred in the case of *give* (0%). It is not a preferred choice in nonfiction, except for *take* (27%). For all other verb bases, this option is under 25%.

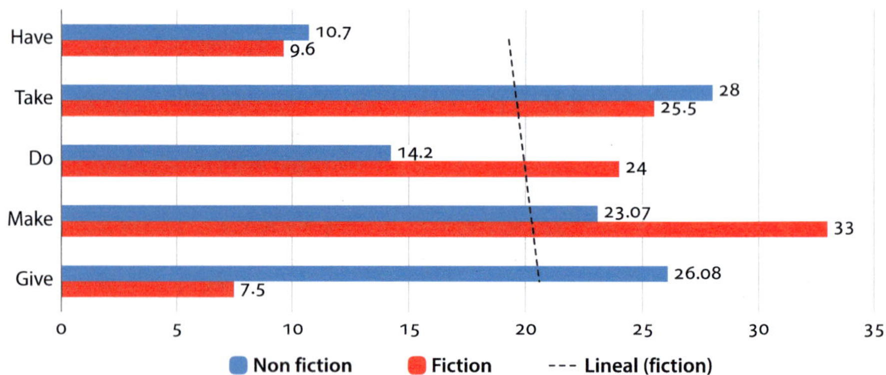

Figure 4. LVCs as a translation solution into Spanish

(3) I could not bring myself to ask her, though, to have her **take part** in my humiliation. (FCT1E.s680)
Sin embargo, no me atreví a pedírselo, a pedirle que ***participara*** *en mi humillación.* *(FCT1S.s672)*

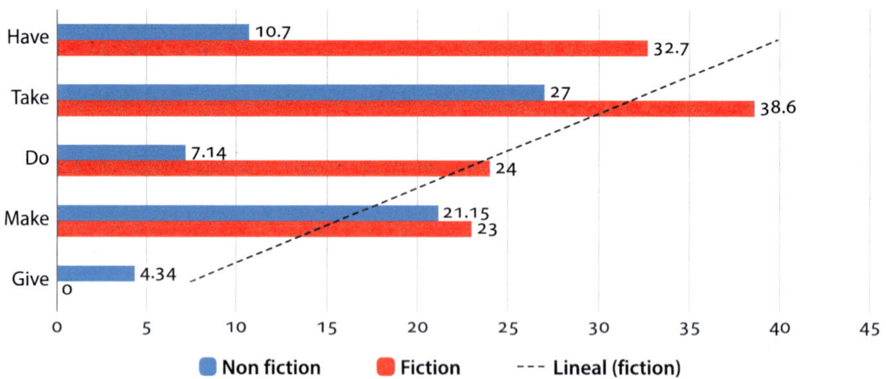

Figure 5. (Single) correlate verb as a translation solution into Spanish

Verb constructions using a more specialized verb (SPX VC) are the preferred solution for *do*-based LVCs in both fiction (38%) and nonfiction (50%), according to corpus data (Figure 6), as in Example 4. *Make* constructions favour this solution in nonfiction (28.8%), as in Example 5.

(4) Cut your losses, **do a deal.** (FCA1E.s2127)
Reduce las pérdidas, ***llega a un acuerdo.*** *(FCA1S.s2069)*

(5) And although we don't have many more genes than apes, just a few hundred extra can **make a** qualitative **difference** in how the brain operates [...]. (EHF1E.s394)
*Y aunque no tenemos muchos más genes que los simios, unos pocos centenares más pueden **marcar una diferencia** cualitativa en la forma de funcionar del cerebro [...].* *(EHF1S.s382)*

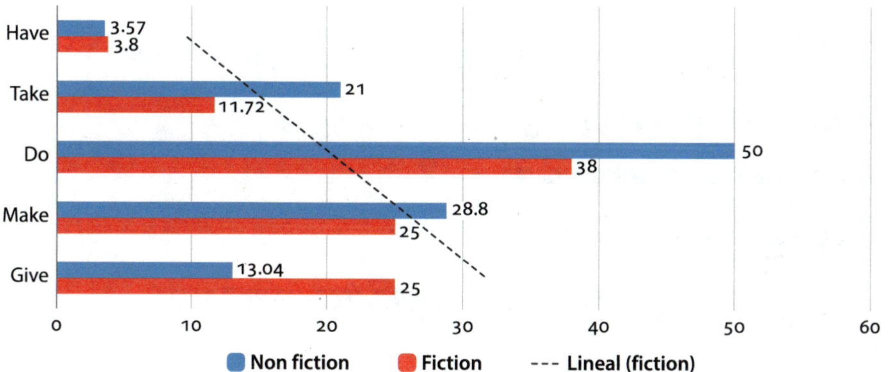

Figure 6. SPX VC using a more specialized verb as a translation solution into Spanish

As shown in Figure 7, other, semantically related, full lexical verbs are preferred by *give* in both registers, fiction (52.5%) and nonfiction (52.17%), as in (6) and (7).

(6) He was so relieved that he wanted to leave now, before Charles could change his mind; but he had to **give an impression** of calm confidence. (FFK7E.s1468)
*Se sentía tan aliviado que deseaba marcharse de inmediato, antes de que Carlos pudiera cambiar de opinión, pero tenía que **transmitir** serenidad y seguridad.* *(FFK7S.s1386)*

(7) Something that is pleasurable at one point might soon **give rise** to indifference, then to displeasure and suffering. (EGD1E.s843)
*Tal vez, algo que resulta placentero en un determinado momento, termine **provocando**, en otro, la indiferencia y, posteriormente, el desagrado y el sufrimiento.* *(EGD1S.s733)*

Have also shows a marked preference for this solution in nonfiction (62.2%) and, to a lesser extent, in fiction (44.2%). *Have* is semantically neutral, and it can easily become any other verb in the target language, as in (8).

(8) I did not want to know details, but I understood that the prayers of my family had persuaded God to **have mercy** on me. (FOJC3E.s975)
*No quise conocer los detalles, pero entendí que las oraciones de mi familia habían convencido a Dios para que **se compadeciera** de mí.* *(FOJC3S.s991)*

Nonfiction *do* constructions, as in (9), come up to 28.6%, while there are no traces of this solution in fiction.

(9) ...component molecules became randomly arrayed to the point where they could no longer **do work**. (EMLSD1E.s652)
*... cuyas moléculas constituyentes terminaban por disponerse aleatoriamente, hasta el punto de no poder seguir **funcionando**.* (EMLSD1S.s620)

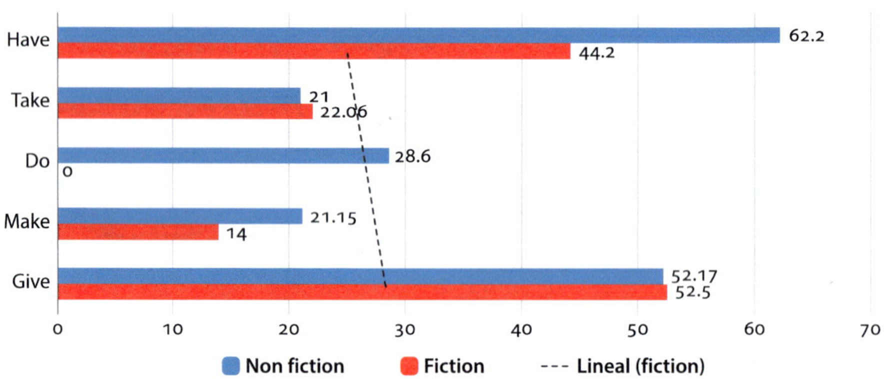

Figure 7. Lexical verb as a translation solution into Spanish

Figure 8 shows the residual, catchall category *other*, a solution better represented in fiction with *do* (14.2%) and *give* (15%). Regarding its neutrality, *have* is a low preference option in both registers, fiction (9.6%) and nonfiction (10.7%). The solutions include idiomatic expressions, paraphrasing, or functional equivalents (Vinay & Dalbernet 1958: 52), as in (10), (11) and (12).

(10) He was gruff, a mass of bristling hair, don't **give a damn** attitude, a confident hunter. (EDB1E.s364)
*Tenía un aspecto bronco, con su mata de pelo erizado y **sus aires de displicencia** que recordaban a los de un cazador profesional.* (EDB1S.s371)

(11) I opened my mouth to protest that I did care, until I realized, with a shock, that actually I didn't **give a damn**. (FKM2E.s434)
*Abrí la boca para replicar que yo me interesaba, pero entonces comprendí, asombrada, que en el fondo **me traía sin cuidado**.* (FKM2S.s426)

(12) "He and his attorney worked to make sure you'd never **have a chance**." (FSA2E.s867)
*Él y su abogado se han asegurado de **ponértelo difícil**.* (FSA2S.s831)

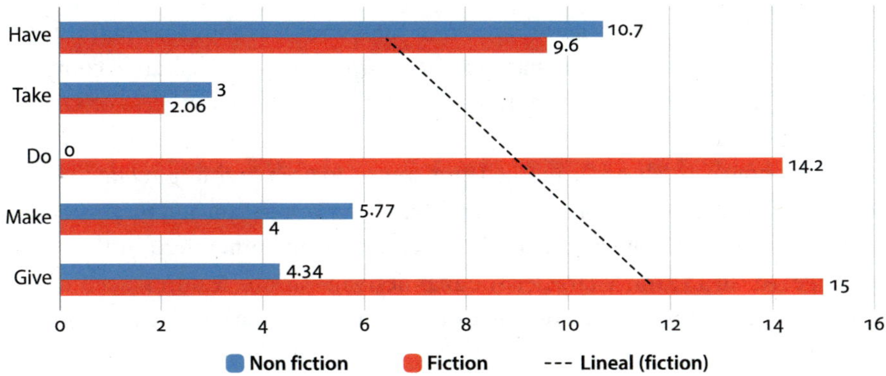

Figure 8. *Other* as a translation solution into Spanish

5. Discussion

My analysis of LVCs in translation shows unitary processing of meaning, indicating awareness of these constructions as semantic units. Translation solutions for these constructions can be summarized in four recurrent patterns: (a) the single correlated verb, (b) a complex verb construction with a more specialized verb, (c) semantically related, alternative, full lexical verbs, and (d) LVCs. A miscellaneous category, dubbed *other*, accounts for idiomatic and more lexicalized expressions.

Overall, in quantitative terms, the preferred solutions are single-verb constructions, either single-verb correlates or lexical verbs semantically related to the source language LVC. Corpus data also reveal that the choice of translation solution relates to the shared semantic features underlying the LVC.

Give LVCs are translated by *a semantically related full lexical verb* other than their single correlates in fiction (52.5%) and nonfiction (52.17%). This choice is based on the underlying feature of *transference*, which results in a change of state of an already existing object through verbal action, as in Examples (6) and (7). According to my results, the semantic compatibility features of *transference* are associated with this translation solution.

Make and *do* alternate two solutions: *LVCs* and constructions including *verbs more specialized (SPX VC)* than those in the original LVC, as in *do the dances* > *ejecutar las danzas* (*execute the dances) or *do work* > *realizar (un) trabajo* (carry out a task). Compatibility features for *make* and *do* are associated with *volition* and *creation* of effected objects, i.e., that exist as a result of verbal action or carrying out a task, as in Examples (4) and (5).

Take constructions favour the *single correlate verb* solution, particularly in fiction contexts (32.7% and 38.6%, respectively). A feature that may influence the selection of this translation solution for *take* LVCs is *spatial deixis*, indicating motion towards the beneficiary (Sanromán Vilas 2009), as shown in *take advantage > aprovechar(se)*. *Take* also has *inchoative aspect* as a core semantic compatibility feature, indicating the inception of the initial phase of a process or change of state, as in Example (3).

Have, however, shows a marked preference for *semantically related lexical verbs* as a translation solution in both registers (44.2% in fiction and 62.2% in nonfiction). *Have* is semantically neutral, and it can be any other verb in the target language. As an LV, this characteristic manifests in various features, such as the cognitive agent's possession, control, or entitlement, indicating a state, an event, or an attitude, as in (8).

The results show the following associations LVC semantic feature(s)- preferred translation solution: Semantically related full lexical verbs are preferred in the case of LVCs that contain transference as a prominent feature. The single correlate verb tends to be associated with inception and spatial deixis. Constructions with more specialized verbs are usually the choice when the original LVCs include the features of volition and creation. Another LVC is a default solution, particularly in aspect-neutral constructions or contexts indicating creation. Results also suggest that a more substantial degree of lexicalization of the corresponding Spanish *tomar* (take) and *dar(se)* (give) constructions point to standardized cross-linguistic equivalents – and translation practices – when the original LVC is clearly perceived as a phraseological unit.

6. Conclusions

The analysis of LVCs in translation corroborates that the choice of translation solution relates to the semantic compatibility features underlying the LVC.

The findings reveal five recurrent patterns in the translation solutions: the single correlate verb, a complex verb construction with a more specialized verb, a semantically related alternative, full lexical verbs, and LVCs. *Other* is an additional category for idiomatic and more lexicalized expressions.

In quantitative terms, the preferred solutions are single-verb constructions, either single-verb correlates or lexical verbs semantically related to the source language LVC. The data also yield information on preference according to the register. Fiction materials show that LVCs are processed as a single semantic unit, which is reflected in a preference for synthetic solutions, i. e., the single correlate verbs (28.2%) and other semantically related, full lexical verbs (25.1%). Results for nonfiction also show a preference for semantically related lexical verbs (30.5%), with the rest of the options below 25%.

Because of this tendency to single-verb solutions, the translations show changes in aspect, mainly inchoative meanings, reduced to a general non-perfective marking. There are also modifications related to register: in fiction, single-verb choices cause a generalized formality boost in the representation of oral speech. In nonfiction, different degrees of grammaticalization point to an attempt at standardization, which may be related to the use of translation technology in nonfiction genres. To better understand the importance of these differences, further work includes contrasting translated and non-translated usage concerning all solutions given to LVCs, to check the bearing of third code practices (Frawley 1984).

This situation suggests that it would be beneficial to include relevant information on LVCs and, by extension, other complex verb constructions in technology used in contrastive linguistics and translation research. It can be done by encoding LVCs information in annotation routines, either as part of already existing layers, as PyMUSAS 0.3.0, a rule-based token and multi-word expression semantic tagger, part of UCREL's semantic analysis system (USAS) (UCREL Research Centre 2022). Another option is an additional grammatical meaning layer encoding more complex meaning (Nagy, Berend, Móra & Vincze 2011; Vincze et al. 2011 & 2013). If these translation trends are programmed into the algorithms, they could also contribute to assigning high-quality, human-like translation options to machine translation. They thus would make it possible for the system to select the most frequent alternatives, for example, give rise>*provocar* vs *dar lugar*. Other computer-aided tools that would also benefit from this information in their algorithms include post-editing aids or authoring support apps in the target language. An example of the former is PETRA© (Ramón & Gutiérrez-Lanza 2018). This statistics-based application locates and calculates significant underuse or overuse of (previously identified through contrastive corpus work) resources in translated texts. Gedire© <https://actres.unileon.es/demos/generadores/demos/GEDIRE> is one of several authoring support apps addressed to Spanish language authors writing in English (Rabadán, Pizarro & Sanjurjo-González 2021). This tool focuses on a particular type of financial report and offers assistance with text construction difficulties concerning the genre structure, associated sentence formulations or genre-specific vocabulary. It guides authors through syntactic and grammatical resources conventionally associated with each rhetorical unit and domain- or genre-specific lexical and phraseological options. So the reviewer or writer can quickly make informed decisions, leading to improved workflow and cost performance and helping to make more acceptable translation or writing decisions in hybrid human-machine environments.

Funding

Research for this paper is part of I+D+i project PID2020-114064RB-I00, funded by MCIN/AEI/10.13039/501100011033.

References

Alonso Ramos, Margarita. 2004. *Las construcciones con verbos de apoyo*. Madrid: Visor.

Alonso Ramos, Margarita. 2007. Towards the synthesis of support verb constructions. In *Selected Lexical and Grammatical Issues in the Meaning – Text Theory. In honour of Igor Mel'čuk* [Studies in Language Companion Series 84], Leon Wanner (ed.), 139–166. Amsterdam: John Benjamins.

Bosque, Ignacio. 2001. On the weight of light predicates. In *Features and Interfaces in Romance. Essays in honor of Heles Contreras* [Current Issues in Linguistic Theory 222], Julia Herschensohn, Enrique Mallén & Karen Zagona (eds), 23–38. Amsterdam: John Benjamins.

Bosque, Ignacio. 2004a. La direccionalidad en los diccionarios combinatorios y el problema de la selección léxica. In *Lingüística teórica. Análisi i perspectives*, Teresa Cabré (ed.), 13–58. Barcelona: Universitat Autònoma de Barcelona.

Bosque, Ignacio (ed.). 2004b. *Redes. Diccionario combinatorio del español contemporáneo*. Madrid: SM.

Bosque, Ignacio (ed.). 2006. *Diccionario práctico combinatorio del español contemporáneo*. Madrid: SM.

Bruening, Benjamin. 2016. Light verbs are just regular verbs. *University of Pennsylvania Working Papers in Linguistics* 22(1): 51–60. https://repository.upenn.edu/pwpl/vol22/iss1/7

Brugman, Claudia, 2001. Light verbs and polysemy, *Language Sciences* 23(4): 551–578.

Butt, Miriam. 2003. The light verb jungle. *Harvard Working Papers in Linguistics* 9: 1–9.

Butt, Miriam. 2010. The light verb jungle: Still hacking away. In *Complex Predicates: Cross-linguistic Perspectives on Event Structure*, Mengistu Amberber, Brett Baker & Mark Harvey (eds), 48–78. Cambridge: CUP.

De Miguel, Elena. 2011. En qué consiste ser verbo de apoyo. In *60 problemas de gramática dedicados a Ignacio Bosque*, M. Victoria Escandell Vidal, Manuel Leonetti & Cristina Sánchez López (eds), 139–147. Madrid: Akal.

De Miguel, Elena. 2008. Construcciones con verbos de apoyo en español. De cómo entran los nombres en la órbita de los verbos. In *Actas del XXXVII Simposio Internacional de la Sociedad Española de Lingüística (SEL)*, Inés Olza Moreno, Manuel Casado Velarde & Ramón González Ruiz (eds), 567–578. Pamplona: Servicio de Publicaciones de la Universidad de Navarra.

De Miguel, Elena. 2013. La polisemia de los verbos soporte. Propuesta de definición mínima. In *Los verbos en los diccionarios*, Sergi Torner Castells & Elisenda Bernal Gallén (eds). *Anexos Revista de Lexicografía* 20: 67–109.

Frawley, William. 1984. Prolegomenon to a theory of translation. In *Translation: Literary, Linguistic and Philosophical Perspectives*, William Frawley (ed.), 159–175. University of Delaware Press.

Gross, Gaston & De Pontonx, Sophie (eds). 2004. Verbes supports. Special issue of *Lingvisticae Investigationes* 27(2).

Koike, Kazumi. 2001. *Colocaciones léxicas en el español actual: Estudio formal y léxicosemántico*. Alcalá de Henares: Universidad de Alcalá/Takushoku University.

Langer, Stefan. 2005. A linguistic test battery for support verb constructions. *Lingvisticae Investigationes* 27(2): 171–184.

Leech, Geoffrey. 2006. *A Glossary of English Grammar*. Edinburgh: EUP.

Mel'čuk, Igor A. 1996. Lexical functions. A tool for the description of lexical relations in a lexicon. In *Lexical Functions in Lexicography and Natural Language Processing* [Studies in Language Companion Series 31], Leo Wanner (ed.), 37–102. Amsterdam: John Benjamins.

Mel'čuk, Igor A. 1997. *Vers une linguistique Sens-Texte*. Paris: Collègue de France.

Mel'čuk, Igor A. 2004. Verbes supports sans peine. *Lingvisticae Investigationes* 27(2): 203–221.

Nagy, István, Berend, Gábor, Móra, György & Vincze, Veronika. 2011. Domain-dependent detection of light verb constructions. In *Proceedings of the Student Research Workshop associated with RANLP 2011*, 1–8. Hissar, Bulgaria, 13 September 2011. <https://aclanthology.org/R11-2001.pdf> (26 May 2023).

Nagy, István T., Rácz, Anita & Vincze, Veronika. 2020. Detecting light verb constructions across languages. *Natural Language Engineering* 26(3), 319–348.

Nenonen, Marja Juha Mulli, Nikolaev, Alexandre & Penttilä, Esa. 2017. How light can a light verb be? Predication patterns in V + NP constructions in English, Finnish, German and Russian. In *Empirical Approaches to Cognitive Linguistics: Analyzing Real-Life Data*, Milla Luodonpää-Manni, Esa Penttilä & Johanna Viimaranta (eds), 75–106. Newcastle upon Tyne: Cambridge Scholars.

Piao, Scott S., Rayson, Paul, Archer, Dawn & McEnery, Tony. 2005. Comparing and combining a semantic tagger and a statistical tool for MWE extraction. *Computer Speech & Language* 19(4): 378–397.

Piera, Carlos & Varela, Soledad. 1999. Relaciones entre morfología y sintaxis. In *Gramática descriptiva de la lengua española*, Ignacio Bosque & Violeta Demonte (eds), 4367–4422. Madrid: Real Academia Española/ Espasa-Calpe.

Pustejovsky, James. 1995. *The Generative Lexicon*. Cambridge MA: The MIT Press.

Pustejovsky, James. 1998. The semantics of lexical underspecification. *Folia Linguistica* 32(3–4): 323–348.

Rabadán, Rosa, Pizarro, Isabel & Sanjurjo-González, Hugo. 2021. Authoring support for Spanish language writers: A genre-restricted case study. *Revista Española de Lingüística Aplicada* 34(2): 671–711.

Ramón, Noelia & Gutiérrez-Lanza, Camino. 2018. Translation description for assessment and post-editing. The case of personal pronouns in translated Spanish. *Target* 30(1): 112–136.

Sanjurjo-González, Hugo & Izquierdo, Marlén. 2019. P-ACTRES 2.0: A parallel corpus for cross-linguistic research. In *Parallel Corpora for Contrastive and Translation Studies: New Resources and Applications* [Studies in Corpus Linguistics 90], Irene Doval & M. Teresa Sánchez Nieto (eds), 215–232. Amsterdam: John Benjamins.

Sanromán Vilas, Begoña. 2009. Diferencias semánticas entre construcciones con verbo de apoyo y sus correlatos verbales simples. *ELUA. Estudios de Lingüística de la Universidad de Alicante* 23: 289–314.

Sanromán Vilas, Begoña. 2012a. La hipótesis de la compatibilidad semántica en la selección de los verbos de apoyo. In *Tradición y progreso en la lingüística general*, Emilio Ridruejo Alonso, Teresa Solías Arís, Nieves Mendizábal de la Cruz & Sara Alonso Calvo (eds), 355–372. Valladolid: Universidad de Valladolid.

Sanromán Vilas, Begoña. 2012b. La representación de las relaciones espaciales en la descripción de los verbos de apoyo. In *Meaning, Texts and other Exciting Things. A Festschrift to Commemorate the 80th Anniversary of Professor Igor Alexandrovic Mel'cuk (Studia Philologica)*, Jurij Apresjan, Igor Boguslavsky, Marie-Claude L'Homme, Leonid Iomdin, Jasmina Milicevic, Alain Polguère & Leo Wanner (eds), 538–553. Moscow: Jazyki slajanskoj kultury. <https://www.ruslang.ru/doc/melchuk_festschrift2012/Sanroman.pdf> (26 May 2023).

Sanromán Vilas, Begoña. 2013. In search of semantic links between nouns and light verbs. Some evidence from Spanish. In Proceedings of the 6th International Conference on Meaning-Text Theory (MTT2013), Valentina Apresjan, Boris Iomdin & Ekaterina Ageeva (eds), 163–175. Prague.

doi Sanromán Vilas, Begoña. 2014. La alternancia *dar/hacer* en construcciones con verbo de apoyo y nombre de comunicación. *Borealis: An International Journal of Hispanic Linguistics* 3(2): 185–222.

doi Sanromán Vilas, Begoña. 2015. The role of determiners in Spanish light verb constructions. *Word* 61(2): 178–200.

doi Sanromán Vilas, Begoña. 2017. From the heavy to the light verb: *An analysis* of *tomar* 'to take.' *Lingvistica Investigationes* 40(2): 228–273.

doi Spencer, Andrew. 2013. *Lexical Relatedness: A Paradigm-Based Model.* Oxford: OUP.

UCREL Research Centre. 2022. PyMUSAS 0.3.0 <https://pypi.org/project/pymusas/> (26 May 2023).

Vinay, Jean-Paul & Dalbernet, Jean. 1958. *Stylistique comparée du français et de l'anglais: Méthode de traduction.* Paris: Didier.

Vincze, Veronika, Nagy, István & Berend, Gábor. 2011. Detecting noun compounds and light verb constructions: A contrastive study. In *Proceedings of the Workshop on Multiword Expressions: From Parsing and Generation to the Real World (MWE 2011)*, 116–121, Portland OR: Association for Computational Linguistics.

Vincze, Veronika, Nagy, István & Berend, Gábor. 2013. Full-coverage identification of English light verb constructions. In *Proceedings of the Sixth International Joint Conference on Natural Language Processing*, Ruslan Mitkov & Jong C. Park (eds), 329–337. Nagoya: Asian Federation of Natural Language Processing.

CHAPTER 3

Reporting direct speech in Spanish and German

Manner-of-speaking and thinking-for-translating

Teresa Molés-Cases
Universitat Politècnica de València

This chapter focuses on the translation of manner-of-speaking expressions in a Spanish to German translation corpus of narrative texts, the translation unit examined being reporting verbs introducing direct speech. It aims, first, to identify translation techniques and, second, to explore whether there are any differences in translators' behavior when facing the domains of motion and speech in written narratives. The results suggest, on the one hand, that manner-of-speaking is mostly maintained in the translation process. On the other hand, in the case of the general verb *decir*|say, inclusion of several frame elements has been identified in translated versions (mainly intention, but also manner and turns in fictional dialogue). I conclude that the consequences for the translation of manner in narrative texts are different for motion and speech events.

Keywords: manner-of-speaking, reporting verbs, narrative texts, direct speech, thinking-for-translating

1. Introduction

According to Talmy's theory of lexicalization patterns (1985: 62–74; 1991: 486), the Spanish and German languages belong to different typological groups (the former is a verb-framed language, while the latter is a satellite-framed language), and therefore their users (e.g., writers, translators) diverge in the way they structure reality through language: in the specific domain of motion, whereas speakers of German usually focus more on manner, speakers of Spanish tend to grant more importance to path, sometimes at the expense of manner. It has also been confirmed that satellite-framed languages have a richer and more varied lexicon of manner-of-motion than verb-framed languages (cf. Slobin 1997: 459). Slobin (1996: 209, 2000: 123) was one of the first to prove that those differences have

https://doi.org/10.1075/scl.113.03mol

some stylistic consequences in the translation of narrative texts, and he proposed the Thinking-for-translating hypothesis. According to this, translators tend to distance themselves from the source text in order to conform to the rhetorical style of the target language. The hypothesis has been extensively examined in the domain of motion through several linguistic combinations and in both inter- and intratypological studies (e.g., Filipović 1999, 2008; Ibarretxe-Antuñano 2003; Cifuentes-Férez 2006, 2013; Lewandowski & Mateu 2016; Alonso Alonso 2018; Labrador 2018). In the specific linguistic combination studied here (Spanish > German), addition of manner-of-motion has been observed in between 23 and 50% of occasions in narrative texts (around 50% in Lübke & Vázquez Rozas 2011: 121; 23.39% in Molés-Cases 2019: 162) (e.g., *La joven entró en su casa* | "The girl entered into her house" > *Das Mädchen stürmte ins Haus* | "The girl stormed into the house").

However, fewer studies have dealt with the domain of speech, and more specifically with the translation of manner-of-speaking (e.g., Rojo & Valenzuela 2001; Klaudy & Károly 2005; Caballero 2015). My research was thus prompted by the fact that this phenomenon has not yet been examined in narrative corpora having Spanish as source language and German as target language. The results of this study will be compared with data from previous works, since I intend to identify any similarities and/or differences between the motion and speech domains (i.e. translation techniques, lexical diversity).[1] Section 2 presents some theoretical underpinnings of the translation of speech events in narrative texts. Section 3 outlines my aim and research questions, and describes the corpus-based methodology. Section 4 details my results (both quantitative and qualitative). This is followed by a brief conclusion.

2. Translation of speech events in written narratives

In this section I summarize a selection of studies on the translation of speech events performed in several linguistic combinations and in various narrative corpora. As will be highlighted, some of them, drawing on the theories of Talmy (1985) and Slobin (1996, 2000), contrast their cognitive-based results with those provided in the previous literature on motion expressions.

To the best of my knowledge, the very first piece of research dealing with the translation of speech events from a cognitive perspective (e.g., Talmy 1985; Slobin

1. Since there is some controversy in the literature about the use of the terms *strategy* and *technique* (see Molina & Hurtado 2002; Ibarretxe-Antuñano 2003) I will use both *strategy* and *technique* indiscriminately to describe "the actual steps taken by the translators in each textual micro-unit", which allow us to obtain "clear data about the general methodological option chosen" (Molina & Hurtado 2002: 49).

1996, 2000) is the study by Rojo and Valenzuela (2001). The authors examine the translation of 400 English verbs of saying in an English > Spanish corpus of novels.[2] They identify the following translation strategies: transference (both of general information, e.g., say > *decir*|say, and of specific information, e.g., confess > *confesar*|confess; in 55% and 22.25% of cases respectively), specification (e.g., talk > *explicar*|explain, in 20.75% of cases) and generalization (e.g., discuss > *hablar*|speak, in 2% of cases). By contrasting their results with those from previous research on motion events, Rojo and Valenzuela point out that Spanish translators grant more importance to the description of ways of saying than to the description of ways of moving. Besides, in translations into Spanish they observe that the avoidance of repetition is frequent (in comparison with the English tendency to use the verb 'say'), and additional information is often specified for stylistic reasons. They also identify a larger diversity of specific verbs of saying in the Spanish translations than in the original English texts (cf. Slobin 1997: 459). The work of Rojo and Valenzuela (2001) triggered subsequent contributions, like those included in Shi (2008) (a Chinese > English study) and Mastrofini (2015) (an English > Italian study).

Bourne (2002) examines the translation of directive speech acts in the same linguistic combination. He studies the original novel *The Men and the Girls* (Trollope 1992) in English and its translation into Spanish, *Un amante joven* (by Margarita Cavándoli). In particular, this author focuses on the first 100 translations of impositive directive speech acts observed in the novel. He also identifies a wider lexical array of reporting verbs in Spanish than in English, and concludes that verbs of reporting are affected by translation for both stylistic and pragmatic effects, "to provide variety, to convey precision and to specify the illocutionary force of an utterance" (2002: 252).

Winters (2007) presents a contribution on the translation of reporting verbs introducing direct speech. Here the original English novel *The Beautiful and Damned* (Fitzgerald 1922) and its two translations into German (both entitled *Die Schönen und die Verdammten*, by Renate Orth-Guttmann and Hans-Christian Oeser) are studied from a stylistic perspective. She uses WordSmith Tools and Multiconcord for corpus analysis, examining a total of 518 occurrences of speech-act reporting verbs (19 verbs). In general terms, Winters observes that Orth-Guttmann translates with more variety, while Oeser uses more repetition; also Orth-Guttmann uses obvious translations (literal solutions found in the bilingual dictionary *Pons* 2001) more frequently than Oeser; Oeser stays closer to the

2. The originals studied are the following: *The Buddha of Suburbia*, Kureishi 1990; *Small World*, Lodge 1984; *Leviathan*, Auster 1992; *Money*, Amis 1984. The translations examined correspond to: *El Buda de los suburbios*, Mónica Martín Berdagué; *El mundo es un pañuelo*, Esteban Riambau Saurí; *Leviatán*, Maribel de Juan; *Dinero*, Enrique Murillo.

source text than Orth-Guttmann and Orth-Guttmann tends to explicitate. Echoing the conclusions reached in previous studies on this issue (cf. Bourne 2002), Winters concludes that the use of varied speech-act reporting verbs emphasizes characters' emotional state and influences the reader's attitude to them. Another interesting observation is that, while the verb 'say' is abundant in English, its German equivalent (*sagen*) is not so present in translations (cf. Orth-Guttmann's 2005 in Winters 2007: 424, where she argues that German readers dislike the repetition of *sagen*). These results are striking because, while English and German are both satellite-framed languages, their users seem to devote divergent attention to the description of speech events.

The thorough and broad analysis included in Caballero (2015) focuses on the translation of verbs introducing direct speech in narrative texts. Caballero examines twelve English fiction narratives and their corresponding translations into Spanish, using 1,585,120 and 1,713,986 tokens, respectively.[3] Her results indicate that the differences between English and Spanish regarding direct speech are mainly discursive (i.e. while English authors tend to use manner verbs, Spanish translators seem to prefer illocutionary and turn-taking verbs, for example "Berger said, 'I think I'd disagree with that" > *– Me parece que no estoy de acuerdo con eso – le interrumpió Berger –* | "I think I disagree with that', interrupted Berger", Caballero 2015: 1412). She also concludes that the typological divergences between these two languages observed in the case of motion events (cf. Slobin 1997: 459) are not detected in the case of speaking events (i.e. there is greater lexical diversity of verbs of saying in Spanish).

Ruano San Segundo (2017) examines the translation of reporting verbs (with the exception of 'say') into four Spanish translations of Charles Dickens's 1854 novel *Hard Times* (by J. Ribera 1972; Lázaro Ros 1992; Víctor Pozanco 1995; and Ángel Melendo 2005). He hypothesizes that the translation of reporting verbs contributes significantly to the characterization of Dickens's characters. His data, extracted from a corpus analyzed with WordSmith Tools, show that none of the translations completely preserves the original value with regard to the specific verbs of reporting, and that this has stylistic consequences in the way readers perceive Dickens's characters. Although his results diverge from those of previous studies dealing with the translation of speech verbs in the English > Spanish

3. Caballero's (2015) sources of data include diverse genres: romance (*My dearest enemy*, Brockway 1998; *Bet me*, Crusie 2004; *Outlander*, Gabaldon 1991), fantasy (*On the edge*, Andrews 2009; *The magicians' guild*, Canavan 2001; *The name of the wind*, Rothfuss 2007), thriller-mystery (*The bone collector*, Deaver 1997; *Mourn not your dead*, Crombie 1996; *The library of the dead*, Cooper 2009), and steampunk (*Soulless*, Carriger 2009; *Clockwork angel*, Clare 2010; *Leviathan*, Westerfeld 2009).

combination, it must be considered that this study focuses on just one novel, and specifically on Dickens's style.

Mastropierro (2020) studies the translation into Italian of reporting verbs in the seven books of J.K. Rowling's Harry Potter series (specifically, those verbs attributed to the three main characters, Harry, Ron and Hermione), analyzing a total of 7,842 bilingual concordance lines. The results of the study indicate that repeated neutral verbs of reporting in English (e.g., 'say', 'tell') are translated into a more diverse lexicon in Italian – in particular, structuring (e.g., *chiese*|asked), metapropositional (e.g., *decretò*|decreed) and signalling discourse verbs (e.g., *interruppe*|interrupted; Caldas-Coulthard's 1987 reporting verb taxonomy is considered by this author). Further, this tendency is observed in the versions translated by two different translators (in Italian the first two books are translated by Marina Astrologo, and the others are translated by Beatrice Masini). Mastropierro concludes that the Italian preference for variety over repetition has stylistic implications and affects the characterization process. He recommends further empirical exploration of this key characterization device in different language combinations.

In a previous study (Molés-Cases 2022) I examine the translation of manner-of-speaking (i.e. reporting verbs introducing direct speech) in narrative texts in a section of the PaGeS corpus (Parallel Corpus German Spanish),[4] and more specifically in the subcorpus including novels originally written in German and their translations into Spanish.[5] The results suggest that transference is the most common translation technique encountered for manner-of-speaking; further, in the case of the original verb *sagen*|say, more varied alternatives (including the frame elements of intention, manner, time and topic length) are found in the Spanish translations in around 30% of cases, probably for stylistic reasons (i.e. a tendency to avoid repetition of the general verb *decir* in narrative texts in Spanish; the use of specific reporting verbs can contribute to the definition of characters' personalities and to scene-setting). Here a higher number of manner-of-speaking verbs were encountered in the Spanish translations than in the German originals. In line with the conclusions reached by Rojo and Valenzuela (2001: 473), my preliminary

4. The PaGeS corpus was compiled by the research group SpatiAlEs (Universidade de Santiago de Compostela, Spain) in a research project funded by the Spanish Ministry of Science, Innovation and Universities, and aimed at the study of spatial relations in both German and Spanish (e.g. Althoff 2017; Krause 2019; Sánchez Nieto 2019; Szumlakowski Morodo 2019). It is a bilingual parallel corpus (German < > Spanish) with part-of-speech tagging. It includes mostly works of fiction (novels and short stories), but also works of non-fiction (essays and popular science texts). At the time of this investigation the corpus amounts to 37,856,102 tokens. It is available at: < https://www.corpuspages.eu >

5. A total of 53 pairs of source and target novels was examined here. A random selection of the results was considered for the analysis.

conclusion was that the domains of manner-of-motion and manner-of-speaking are usually treated differently by translators (i.e. it seems that Spanish translators afford more importance to the description of ways of speaking than to the characterization of motion events).

3. Methodology

3.1 Aim and research questions

This chapter aims to explore further the translation of manner-of-speaking – particularly that expressed by reporting verbs introducing direct speech – in narrative texts within the Thinking-for-translating hypothesis. The study addresses the following research questions, specifically for a verb-framed language > satellite-framed language translation scenario (in this case, Spanish > German):

1. Is manner-of-speaking affected by translation?
2. Are the consequences for the translation of manner in narrative texts different when dealing with motion and speech events?

The first research question emerges from the growing consensus in the literature that manner-of-motion is affected by translation (e.g., Filipović 1999: 20, 2008: 32; Ibarretxe-Antuñano 2003: 154; Cifuentes-Férez 2006: 88, 2013: 10; Alonso Alonso 2018: 365), mainly because of typological differences between source and target language, and because translators tend to comply with the stylistic conventions of the target language. Since manner-of-motion is usually transferred (or even added) in Spanish > German translation scenarios of narrative texts (cf. Molés-Cases 2019: 156), here the translation of manner-of-speaking will be examined using a similar approach, with the aim of identifying any possible consequences of typological divergences and linguistic directionality for translation. By way of illustration of the importance of directionality, in previous studies using narrative corpora in the inverse combination (German > Spanish), reduction/omission of manner-of-motion was observed in 26.27% of occasions (Molés-Cases 2018: 174), whereas manner-of-speaking was in general transferred (Molés-Cases 2022).

The rationale for the second research question stems from the observation of several phenomena. On the one hand, previous studies dealing with the translation of manner-of-motion in the typological combination verb-framed language > satellite-framed language have confirmed that addition and specification of manner are observed in translation of written narratives. For instance, Lübke and Vázquez Rozas (2011: 121) found that manner-of-motion was added in nearly half of all cases in a Spanish > German corpus; in Molés-Cases (2019: 162) addition of manner-of-motion is observed in around 23% of cases in a Spanish > German narrative corpus; Slobin (1996: 212; 1997: 459) identified approximately 25% of specification/addition of manner-of-motion in translations from verb-framed languages into satellite-framed languages. On the other hand, although comparable studies on speech events (i.e. with a verb-framed language as source language and a satellite-framed language as target language) are still not available in the literature, similar studies dealing with the inverse typological combination (satellite-framed language > verb-framed language) (cf. Rojo & Valenzuela 2001; Caballero 2015; Mastrofini 2015; Molés-Cases 2022) have concluded that the main results of the Thinking-for-translating motion frame do not apply in the case of the communication frame. That is, translators into Spanish seem to afford more importance to the description of ways of speaking than to the characterization of motion events, and there seems to be an associated stylistic tendency to avoid the repetition of the general Spanish verb *decir* in translations into Spanish. The paucity of such studies prompted my interest in providing an answer to the second research question for the specific case of the linguistic combination specified.

3.2 Corpus analysis

In this research the PaGeS corpus (Parallel Corpus German Spanish) was used. More specifically, within the subcorpus of works of fiction a selection was made of 10 contemporary novels aimed at a general audience originally written in Spanish and their corresponding translations into German, representing the contributions of 10 authors and 9 translators (the number of tokens examined cannot be indicated here, since tokens per novel are not shown in PaGeS).[6] Here, following the method adopted by Rojo and Valenzuela (2001: 469), the examined verbs were classified into two categories: a series of manner-of-speaking verbs (i.e. a classification of 55 manner verbs of speech in Spanish included in Caballero 2015: 1402)

6. The original and translated novels analyzed were *Azul marino* (Rosa Ribas 2016), *Auf der anderen Seite der Ramblas* (translated by Sabine Hoffmann), *El ángel perdido* (Javier Sierra 2011), *Die Rache der Engel* (translated by Stefanie Karg), *El enredo de la bolsa y la vida* (Eduardo Mendoza 2012), *Der Friseur und die Kanzlerin* (translated by Peter Schwaar), *Inés y la alegría* (Almudena Grandes 2010), *Inés und die* Freude (translated by Roberto de Hollanda), *La hermandad de la sábana santa* (Julia Navarro 2004), *Die stumme Bruderschaft* (translated by Sabine Giersberg), *La reina del sur* (Arturo Pérez-Reverte 2002), *Die Königin des Südens* (translated by Angelica Ammar), *Los enamoramientos* (Javier Marías 2011), *Die sterblich Verliebten* (translated by Susanne Lange), *Ojos de agua* (Domingo Villar 2006), *Wasserblaue Augen* (translated by Peter Kultzen), *Patria* (Fernando Aramburu 2016), *Patria* (translated by Will Zurbrüggen), *Soldados de Salamina* (Javier Cercas 2001), *Soldaten von Salamis* (translated by Will Zurbrüggen).

and the Spanish general verb *decir*|say.[7] After the corpus queries and the selection of those cases reporting direct speech, a total of 1,571 bilingual concordances were considered for the analysis:

a. 621 pairs of source fragments, including the 55 manner verbs (those cases not appearing as direct speech were excluded from the analysis) and their corresponding target fragments.
b. 950 pairs of source fragments including the verb *decir* and their corresponding target fragments (since the 10-novel corpus studied includes 5,089 occurrences of this verb in novels originally written in Spanish, which was too much for a manual qualitative analysis, 95 occurrences introducing direct speech per novel were selected randomly, cf. Slobin 1996: 207).

3.3 Resources

With the aim of identifying possible divergent (or similar) nuances between the source and target texts examined, the following resources were considered: Caballero's (2015: 1401–1403) classification of manner verbs of speech in Spanish, Snell-Hornby's (1983: 170–173) classification of German verbs of talking and uttering, *Diccionario de la Real Academia de la Lengua Española, Digitales Wörterbuch der Deutschen Sprache* (DWDS), and *Duden online*.

4. Results

This section is divided in three parts. The first presents the results regarding the translation of the original fragments including a manner verb of speech. The second part presents the translation results from those including the general verb *decir*. These two parts deal specifically with translation techniques. The third subsection is devoted to the manner-of-speaking verb lexicon.

7. Caballero's (2015: 1402) classification includes the following verbs of speech (subcategories: manner, human): *balbucear*|babble, *balbucir*|slur, *bromear*|joke, *burlarse*|mock, *cantar*|sing, *canturrear*|sing softly, *cecear*|lisp, *chillar*|shout, *clamar*|cry out, *cuchichear*|whisper, *declamar*|recite, *decretar*|decree, *entonar*|sing, *escupir*|spit, *espetar*|blurt out, *exclamar*|exclaim, *fanfarronear*|boast, *farfullar*|mumble, *gemir*|moan, *gimotear*|whine, *gritar*|shout, *gruñir*|groan, *imitar*|imitate, *increpar*|tell off, *jadear*|pant, *lamentar(se)*|grumble, *llamar*|call, *llorar*|cry, *maldecir*|curse, *mascullar*|mumble, *mofarse*|mock, *murmurar*|mutter, *musitar*|mutter, *pontificar*|pontificate, *presumir*|brag, *proclamar*|proclaim, *quejarse*|complain, *recitar*|recite, *refunfuñar*|grumble, *reír*|laugh, *resollar*|pant, *resoplar*|pant, *rezongar*|grumble, *rumiar*|chew, *sentenciar*|sentence, *sisear*|shush, *sollozar*|sob, *soltar*|let out, *suspirar*|sigh, *susurrar*|whisper, *tartamudear*|stutter, *titubear*|hesitate, *vacilar*|hesitate, *vociferar*|shout, *zanjar*|resolve.

4.1 Analysis of manner-of-speaking verbs

In the analysis of manner verbs of speech, I encountered four main translation techniques in the corpus: transference, omission of manner-of-speaking, omission of speech event, and modulation. Transference is the most frequent translation technique identified in the data, with an overall prevalence of 91.79%. This phenomenon is well illustrated in Examples (1) and (2), where the source information on speech (*balbucir*|slur and *exclamar*|cry out, respectively) is translated through an equivalent in German (*stammeln*|slur and *rufen*|cry out, respectively).

(1) – *Es el fin* – balbució –.
["It is the end", he slurred.]
»Das ist das Ende«, *stammelte* *er.*
["It is the end," he slurred.]
(Source: *El enredo de la bolsa y la vida / Der Friseur und die Kanzlerin*)

(2) *¿Qué hacéis aquí?* – *exclamó* *el obispo.*
["What are you doing here?", the bishop cried out.]
»Was macht Ihr hier?«, *rief* *der Bischof.*
["What are you doing here?", the bishop cried out.]
(Source: *La hermandad de la sábana santa / Die stumme Bruderschaft*)

Besides transference, omission of manner-of-speaking was also observed, but to a much lesser extent (4.03%). For instance, in Example (3) the manner information incorporated in the verb *suspirar*|sigh is missing in the translation, where only general information on the speech domain is maintained through the verb *sagen*|say.

(3) –*Excelente* – *suspiró*.
["Excellent", he sighed.]
»Hervorragend«, *sagte* *der Kapitän.*
["Excellent", the captain said.]
(Source: *El ángel perdido / Die Rache der Engel*)

Within the technique of omission of manner-of-speaking, the inclusion of pragmatic force was identified in 1.29% of cases (see Example (4)).[8] Although this percentage is very low, it is assumed here that the inclusion of this nuance (*fragen*|ask) may have a means of compensating for the manner information omitted (*gritar*|yell).

---

8. Drawing on Rojo & Valenzuela (2001: 474), pragmatic force is understood here as the speaker's intention (e.g., *aclarar*|clarify, *preguntar*|ask).

(4) *–¿Qué ha pasado? – gritéa Dujok.*
["What is going on?", I yelled at Dujok.]
»Was ist passiert?«, fragte ich Dujok.
["What is going on?", I asked Dujok.]
(Source: *El ángel perdido / Die Rache der Engel*)

Omission of speech event also appears in the corpus, but on only a few occasions (3.22%). This phenomenon is evident in Examples (5) and (6). Here, any reference to speech (except for quotation marks) is missing in the translation, in contrast to the source fragment, where *resoplar*|pant (Example 5) and *responder*|answer and *reír*|laugh (Example (6)) are included.

(5) *–Yo ... – resoplé –, no tengo tiempo para darte explicaciones [...]*
["I ..." I panted "I don't have time to give you explanations ..."]
»Ich habe keine Zeit für großartige Erklärungen [...]«.
["I don't have time for great explanations ...."]
(Source: *Inés y la alegría / Inés und die Freude*)

(6) *– [...] que [...] murió cristianamente – respondió Ana riendo.*
["... that ... [he] died in a Christian manner", answered Ana, laughing.]
»... dass er einen christlichen Tod gestorben ist«.
["... that he died in a Christian manner"]
(Source: *Azul marino / Auf der anderen Seite der Ramblas*)

Finally, the technique of modulation is rarely observed (0.97%). An instance of this is shown in Example (7), where the original speech information includes a specific manner-of-speaking verb (*exclamar*|exclaim), which mainly expresses loud speech, and the target information is represented by *stöhnen*|moan, a manner-of-speaking verb indicating anger or disagreement.

(7) *–¡Me agota la vida social! – exclamó Marco.*
["Social life exhausts me", he exclaimed.]
»Das gesellschaftliche Leben macht mich fertig!«, stöhnte Marco.
["Social life exhausts me", he moaned.]
(Source: *La hermandad de la sábana santa / Die stumme Bruderschaft*)

4.2 Analysis of the general verb decir

The results of the translation analysis of the verb *decir*|say allow three translation techniques to be identified: transference, specification and omission.

Transference is the most observed translation technique in the corpus (82.42%). This is illustrated in Examples (8) and (9), where the German equivalent of this general verb (*sagen*) was used by the translators.

(8) – *Me temo que tendremos que dividirnos* – dijo –.
["I'm afraid we'll have to separate", he said.]
»Ich fürchte, wir müssen uns trennen«, sagte *er.*
["I'm afraid we'll have to separate", he said.]
(Source: *El ángel perdido / Die Rache der Engel*)

(9) – *Ésa es una buena pregunta* – dijo Pati.
["That is a good question", Pati said.]
»Das ist eine gute Frage«, sagte *Pati.*
["That is a good question", Pati said.]
(Source: *La reina del sur / Die Königin des Südens*)

Some cases of specification of the speech event have been identified too (10.11%). Here three main frame elements were introduced in translations: pragmatic force or intention (77.76%), manner (7.68%) and turns in the fictional dialogue (5.76%).[9] In Example (10), an illocutionary verb (*antworten*|answer) is included in the target fragment, adding pragmatic force or intention. Another specification is illustrated in Example (11), where manner-of-speaking is highlighted in the translation through the verb *knurren*|growl. In Example (12), a turn in the fictional dialogue is introduced in the target fragment through the verb *beginnen*|begin.

(10) – *Lo intentaré* – dijo *al fin [...].*
["I will try", she said finally ...]
»Ich werde es versuchen«, antwortete *sie schließlich [...].*
["I will try", she answered finally ...]
(Source: *La reina del sur / Die Königin des Südens*)

(11) *¿No me ha oído?* – dijo *el operador.*
["Have you not heard me?", said the cameraman.]
»Haben Sie mich nicht verstanden?«, knurrte *der Kameramann.*
["Have you not understood me?", growled the cameraman.]
(Source: *El ángel perdido / Die Rache der Engel*)

(12) – *¿Sabe una cosa, gobernador?* – dijo –.
["You know what, governor?" he said.]
»Wissen Sie was, Governor?«, begann *er.*
["You know what, governor?" he began.]
(Source: *El ángel perdido / Die Rache der Engel*)

9. Manner is understood here as the specific way of pronouncing the message (e.g. *bromear*|joke, *clamar*|cry out, Rojo & Valenzuela 2001: 474). Turns in the fictional dialogue refer to the recreation of the distribution of turns in the fictional dialogue (e.g. *empezar*|start, *concluir*|conclude, Caballero 2015: 1410).

These data (and chiefly the low percentage of specification of manner: 8 cases out of a total of 96 cases of specification) seem to confirm that typological differences are not so consequential in the translation of the domain of speech in narrative texts as in the domain of motion.

Finally, omission is also present in the data, with a frequency of 7.47%. For instance, in Examples (13) and (14) indication of speech is absent in the translation (except through quotation marks).

(13) – *Hablamos después, inspector* – *dijo ella* –.
["We'll talk later, inspector", she said.]
»Nachher unterhalten wir uns, Inspektor.«
["We'll talk later, inspector."] (Source: *Ojos de agua / Wasserblaue Augen*)

(14) – *¿Lo ve?* – *dije [...].*
["See?", I said ....]
»Sehen Sie? [...]«
["See?"]
(Source: *El enredo de la bolsa y la vida / Der Friseur und die Kanzlerin*)

4.3 Manner-of-speaking verb lexicon

As I have noted, previous empirical studies on the translation of written narratives have concluded that some verb-framed languages present a richer and more varied verb lexicon of speaking than some satellite-framed languages (e.g., Rojo & Valenzuela 2001: 472; Bourne 2002: 248; Caballero 2015: 1423, for English > Spanish; Mastropierro 2020: 255, for English > Italian; Molés-Cases 2022, for German > Spanish, and specifically manner-of-speaking). This contradicts the main findings in the literature on the manner-of-motion verb lexicon (e.g., Slobin 1997: 459). The resulting data from this study, however, point to a similar degree of verb-granularity of manner-of-speaking in Spanish and German original and translated versions, respectively (cf. Klaudy & Károly 2005: 22, on the asymmetry hypothesis). After considering Caballero's (2015) classification of 55 manner verbs of speech in source texts, I identified 54 manner-of-speaking verbs and multiword expressions in German target versions. These are included in Table 1.

There are several possible causes for the divergences regarding the manner-verb lexicon of speaking between this piece of research and previous literature. This study presents a new typological configuration: it examines source texts in a verb-framed language (Spanish) and target texts in a satellite-framed language (German). The starting point for my analysis was a limited series of verbs of speech in Spanish (Caballero 2015: 1402). Besides, it seems that German and English differ regarding lexical diversity of verb of speaking, in that, while both are

Table 1. Manner-of-speaking verbs and multi-word expressions identified in the German subcorpus

abrupt beenden, brüllen, brummen, deklamieren, fauchen, fluchen, flüstern, flüsternd antworten/singen, frohlocken, grummeln, hauchen, herausplatzen, in Lachen ausbringen, keuchen, kichern, knurren, krähen, kreischen, lachen, lachend antworten/erwidern/fragen/meinen/verraten, leise sagen, maulen, mit brüchiger Stimme sagen, murmeln, murren, rufen, säuseln, scherzen, scherzend sagen, scherzhaft sagen, schimpfen, schluchzen, schnauben, schnaufen, schreien, seufzen, seufzend antworten/zur Antworte geben, singen, speien, spucken, stammeln, stöhnen, stottern, summen, werfen, wimmern, wispern, witzeln, zaudern, zischen, zögerlich ansetzen/fragen/hervorbringen/sagen, zögern, zögernd sagen.

satellite-framed languages, German does not resort to the general verb *sagen* as frequently as English does in the case of the verb 'say' (cf. Winters 2007: 424) – probably to preserve the original characters' style of speech and for reasons of scene-setting (cf. Ruano San Segundo 2017; Mastropierro 2020).

5. Conclusions

This chapter presented a translation study on the phenomenon of manner-of-speaking through the analysis of a Spanish > German corpus of written narratives. The results suggest that manner-of-speaking is mostly maintained in translation, with only a few cases of omission and modulation. In the case of the general verb *decir*, inclusion of several frame elements has been identified in translations on 10.11% of occasions: mainly intention or pragmatic force, but also manner and turns in the fictional dialogue (cf. Winters 2007 and Caballero 2015, which find comparable results in English).

The data presented here allow three main conclusions. First, manner-of-speaking is rarely affected by translation. Second, consequences for the translation of manner differ when dealing with motion and speech events: while manner-of-motion is often added in translations into German (from Spanish) (Lübke & Vázquez Rozas 2011: 121; Molés-Cases 2019: 162), this tendency is observed only occasionally in the case of manner-of-speaking. In other words, typological differences do not in general seem to affect the translation of the domain of speech in narrative texts. Third, the Spanish and German versions examined present similar diversity of manner-of-speaking verbs. This may indicate a particular behavior of the German language in the case of the verb lexicon of speech within satellite-framed languages (cf. Winters 2007, for English and a comparison with Spanish), and the preference of German translators for the maintenance of manner-of-speaking verbs instead of the use of the general verb *sagen*. The resulting data are conditioned by the configuration of this study (e.g., linguistic directionality, corpus size, narrative genre), and further research – mainly regarding diversity of the verb lexicon – will be required to settle the matter conclusively. Finally, the research presented here could be exploited in pedagogical scenarios, since it would be highly desirable for translation students to receive formal instruction on these contrastive issues between Spanish and German, mainly in specialized courses (e.g., narrative translation).

References

Alonso Alonso, Rosa. 2018. Translating motion events into typologically distinct languages. *Perspectives* 26(3): 357–376.

Althoff, Roswitha. 2017. La correspondencia entre los adverbios alemanes y los verbos españoles y su posible aprovechamiento para la enseñanza. *Estudios Interlingüísticos* 5: 13–30.

Bourne, Julian. 2002. He said, she said. Controlling illocutionary force in the translation of literary dialogue. *Target* 14(2): 241–261.

Caballero, Rosario. 2015. Reconstructing speech events: Comparing English and Spanish. *Linguistics* 53(6): 1391–1461. .

Caldas-Coulthard, Carmen Rosa. 1987. Reported speech in written narrative texts. In *Discussing Discourse*, Malcolm Coulthard (ed.), 149–167. Birmingham: University of Birmingham.

Cifuentes-Férez, Paula. 2006. La expresión de los dominios de movimiento y visión en inglés y en español desde la perspectiva de la lingüística cognitiva. Master dissertation, Universidad de Murcia.

Cifuentes-Férez, Paula. 2013. El tratamiento de los verbos de manera de movimiento y de los caminos en la traducción inglés-español de textos narrativos. *Miscelánea: A Journal of English and American Studies* 47: 53–80.

Diccionario de la Real Academia de la Lengua Española (23rd online edn). <https://dle.rae.es> (15 June 2021).

Duden online. <https://www.duden.de> (20 November 2021).

Digitales Wörterbuch der Deutschen Sprache, Berlin-Brandenburgischen Akademie der Wissenschaften. <https://www.dwds.de> (23 November 2021).

Filipović, Luna. 1999. Language-specific Expression of Motion and its Use in Narrative Texts. PhD dissertation, Cambridge University.

Filipović, Luna. 2008. Typology in action: Applying typological insights in the study of translation. *International Journal of Applied Linguistics* 18(1): 23–40.

Ibarretxe-Antuñano, Iraide. 2003. What translation tells us about motion: A contrastive study of typologically different languages. *IJES, International Journal of English Studies* 3(2): 151–175.

Klaudy, Kinga & Károly, Kriztina. 2005. Implicitation in translation: Empirical evidence for operational asymmetry in translation. *Across Languages and Cultures* 6(1): 13–28.

Krause, Maxi. 2019. Über die Schwierigkeiten, Verbalpartikeln in die kontrastive Beschreibung spatialer Relationen zu integrieren. In *Raumrelationen im Deutschen: Kontrast, Erwerb und Übersetzung*, Barbara Lübke & Elsa Liste Lamas (eds), 129–145. Tübingen: Stauffenburg.

Labrador, Belén. 2018. Crossed transposition in a corpus-based study of motion in English and Spanish. *Languages in Contrast* 18(2): 207–229.

Lewandowski, Wojciech & Mateu, Jaume. 2016. Thinking for translating and intra-typological variation in satellite-framed languages. *Review of Cognitive Linguistics* 14(1): 185–208.

Lübke, Barbara & Vázquez Rozas, Victoria. 2011. Construcciones de "entrar" y "salir" y sus equivalentes en alemán. In *Tiempo, espacio y relaciones espacio-temporales*, Carsten Sinner, Elia Hernández Socas & Christian Bahr (eds), 115–129. Frankfurt: Peter Lang.

Mastrofini, Roberta. 2015. English manner of speaking verbs and their Italian translations: A cross-linguistic comparison. *Athens Journal of Philology* 1(2): 83–98.

Mastropierro, Lorenzo. 2020. The translation of reporting verbs in Italian. *International Journal of Corpus Linguistics* 25(3): 241–269.

Molés-Cases, Teresa. 2018. Some advances in the study of the translation of manner of motion events: Integrating key concepts of Descriptive Translation Studies and 'Thinking for Translating.' *Review of Cognitive Linguistics* 16(1): 153–191.

Molés-Cases, Teresa. 2019. Der Ausdruck von Bewegungsereignissen in Übersetzungen vom Spanischen ins Deutsche. In *Raumrelationen im Deutschen: Kontrast, Erwerb und Übersetzung*, Barbara Lübke & Elsa Liste Lamas (eds), 143–162. Tübingen: Stauffenburg.

Molés-Cases, Teresa. 2022. Manner-of-speaking in a corpus-based translation study of narrative texts. *Meta: Journal Des Traducteurs* 67(2): 431–460.

Molina, Lucía & Hurtado, Amparo. 2002. Translation techniques revisited: A dynamic and functionalist approach. *Meta: Journal Des Traducteurs* 47(4): 498–512.

Rojo, Ana & Valenzuela, Javier. 2001. How to say things with words: Ways of saying in English and Spanish. *Meta: Journal Des Traducteurs* 46(3): 467–477.

Ruano Sansegundo, Pablo. 2017. Corpus methodologies in literary translation studies: An analysis of speech verbs in four Spanish translations of Hard Times. *Meta: Journal Des Traducteurs* 62(1): 94–113.

Sánchez Nieto, María Teresa. 2019. Spatiale Relationen und evaluative Bedeutungen deutscher Verbalkomposita mit dem adverbialen Präverb "herum-." In *Raumrelationen im Deutschen: Kontrast, Erwerb und Übersetzung*, Barbara Lübke & Elsa Liste Lamas (eds), 177–195. Tübingen: Stauffenburg.

Shi, Dongqin. 2008. Communication verbs in Chinese and English: A contrastive analysis. *Languages in Contrast* 8(2): 181–207.

Slobin, Dan. 1996. Two ways to travel: Verbs of motion in English and Spanish. In *Grammatical Constructions: Their Form and Meaning*, Masayoshi Shibatani & Sandra A. Thompson (eds), 195–220. Oxford: Clarendon Press.

Slobin, Dan. 1997. Mind, code and text. In *Essays on Language Function and Language Type. Dedicated to T. Givón*, Joan L. Bybee, John Haiman & Sandra A. Thompson (eds), 436–467. Amsterdam: John Benjamins.

Slobin, Dan. 2000. Verbalized events: A dynamic approach to linguistic relativity and determinism. In *Evidence for Linguistic Relativity*, Susanne Niemeier & René Dirven (eds), 107–138. Berlin: Mouton de Gruyter.

Snell-Hornby, Mary. 1983. *Verb-descriptivity in German and English*. Heidelberg: Carl Winter.

Szumlakowski Morodo, Irene. 2019. Redundanz in der Beschreibung von Fortbewegung in der vertikalen Achse im Deutschen und im Spanischen. In *Germanistik im Umbruch – Linguistik, Übersetzung und DaF*, Irene Doval & Elsa Liste Lamas (eds), 115–125. Berlin: Frank & Timme.

Talmy, Leonard. 1985. Lexicalization patterns: Semantic structures in lexical forms. In *Language Typology and Syntactic Description, Vol. 3: Grammatical Categories and the Lexicon*, Timothy Shopen (ed.), 57–149. Cambridge: CUP.

Talmy, Leonard. 1991. Path to realization: A typology of event conflation. In *Proceedings of the Berkeley Linguistics Society* 17, 480–519. Berkeley CA: BLS.

Winters, Marion. 2007. F. Scott Fitzgerald's *Die Schönen und Verdammten*: A corpus-based study of translators' style. *Meta* 52(3): 412–425.

CHAPTER 4

"Ich bekomme es erklärt"

The dative passive in translation between German and Spanish: A study based on data from the *PaGeS* corpus

María Teresa Sánchez Nieto
University of Valladolid

Spanish lacks a construction that parallels the German dative passive, which presents the process from the recipient perspective while often leaving the agent implicit. The main aim of this chapter is to elucidate as to what extent the recipient perspective is maintained, and which voice resources (*genus verbi*) and translation techniques are involved in the translation of German passive constructions between German and Spanish. The evidence for the study is taken from the Parallel Corpus of German and Spanish (PaGeS). When translating sentences which include the *bekommen/kriegen* variants of the dative passive, translators into Spanish do not maintain the recipient perspective, but opt for, mainly, the agent perspective in about 40% of the examples under scrutiny. In these cases, simplification comes into play as a translation technique.

Keywords: dative passive, German, Spanish, translation techniques

1. Introduction: Focus, conceptual frame, and state of the art

In both Romance and Germanic languages, speakers/writers make use of the passive semantic-functional category in order to present a situation from a process point of view. Each linguistic system has several lexical-grammatical resources linked to the passive category, and users of different languages prioritize some of these depending on textual and contextual factors – cf., for example, the reflections of authors like García Yebra (1997), Reisinger (1999) or Clarós (2006) on the use of the passive voice when translating from French, German or English into Spanish.

https://doi.org/10.1075/scl.113.04san

Spanish speakers can foreground the process point of view of the action by hiding the agent or leaving it in the background using different formulas. Firstly, by means of the periphrastic passive structure *ser*+participle (Sp. *El incendio fue extinguido en pocas horas* / Engl. [lit.] *'The fire was extinguished within a few hours'*), also through the passive-reflexive voice (*pasiva refleja*), formed by the pronoun *se*+the 3rd person of the verb (Sp. *Allí se sirve buen vino* / Engl. [lit.] *'There good wine is served'*) – see Cartagena & Gauger (1989: 359–360). The process point of view can also be foregrounded through the 3rd person plural of the active voice (Sp. *Allí sirven buen vino/* Engl. [lit.] *'There they serve good wine'*), termed by Cartagena and Gauger (1989: 359) as 'unpersönliches Konstrukt' (*impersonal construction*).[1] Other mechanisms include (i) lexical devices such as the auxiliaries *quedar(se)* (lit. *'remain'*)+past participle (Sp. *El corredor quedó relegado al cuarto puesto* / Engl. *'The runner was relegated to fourth place'*) or *resultar* (lit. *'result'*)+past participle (*En el accidente resultaron heridas tres personas* / Engl. *'Three people were injured in the accident'*), both of which stress the result of the process targeted by the verb; (ii) the use of indefinite pronouns such as *alguien* (somebody), *nadie* (nobody), *uno* (one) (Sp. *Alguien ha destrozado los bancos del parque* / Engl. *'Someone has vandalized the park benches'; Aparentemente, nadie había robado el dinero* / Engl. *'Apparently, no one had stolen the money'*; Sp. – *¿Cómo se hace? – Uno coge esta palanca y la gira en esta dirección / Engl '"How is it done?" "You take this lever and turn it in this direction"'*), and (iii) nouns with an indefinite reference like *la gente* (people), etc. (Sp. *Hoy en día, la gente no paga por leer periódicos* / Engl. *'Nowadays, people do not pay to read newspapers'*).

On their part, German speakers/writers have the so-called *werden-Passiv* (i.e., the process passive, Ger. *Die Tür wurde geöffnet* / Engl. *'The door was opened'*) and the *sein-Passiv* (i.e., the statal passive, Ger. *Die Tür ist geöffnet* / Engl. *'The door is open'*) at their disposal to stress the process while leaving the agent in the background. This can be accomplished as well by means of other alternative lexical and syntactic resources, such as the indefinite pronoun *man* (Ger. *Hier darf man nicht rauchen* / Engl. *'You are not allowed to smoke here'*), constructions such as *sein*+*zu*+ infinitive (Ger. *Diese Aufgaben sind noch zu erledigen* / Engl. [lit.]*'These tasks are still to be completed'*), *sich lassen*+infinitive (Ger. *Das Buch lässt sich gut lesen* / Engl. *'The book reads well'*), reflexive verbs (Ger. *Das Buch liest sich gut* / Engl. *'The book reads well'*), and the attributive *zu*+ present participle construction (Ger. *die zu erledigende Aufgabe* / Engl. [lit] *'the task to be done'*), among others, see Eggelte (2020: 151–52). Besides the *werden* passive, and its alternatives, the German language has a further processual passive form: the dative passive.

1. All the examples offered in this paragraph are my own and have been specifically built to show the patterns under discussion.

Known also as *bekommen-Passiv*, the dative passive consists of a set of structures in which the partially desemantized verbs *bekommen/kriegen/erhalten* act as auxiliaries for the past participle of the main verb. This main verb typically selects an agent, a primary object (a direct object in the accusative case acting in theme role) and a secondary object (an indirect object in the dative case, showing mostly – but not always – the recipient role, see below). The recipient role is emphasised and moves to the first position in the sentence, adopting the syntactic role of the subject and the nominative case. Thus, this construction allows the speaker/writer to present the situation from the point of view of the recipient (s. 1a and 1b).

(1) a. Der Vater erzählt dem Kind eine
the-NOM.SG father-nom.sg tell-PRS.1SG the-DAT.SG child-DAT.SG a-ACC.SG
Geschichte.[2]
story-ACC.SG
'The father tells the child a story'

b. Das Kind bekommt vom Vater
the-NOM.SG child-NOM.SG get-PRS.1SG by;the-DAT.SG father-DAT.SG
eine Geschichte erzählt.
a-AKK.SG story-ACC.SG tell-PTCP.PRF
'The child gets a story told by the father'

Two questions make the dative passive especially interesting for a more in-depth study, with the aid of corpus evidence in the context of translation between German and Spanish.

Firstly, when translating from German into Spanish, it may sometimes be observed how the active voice is selected for translating dative passive sentences that do not mention any agent, as a result of the tendency to avoid the structure *ser*+past participle in familiar and/or colloquial language use, see Cartagena & Gauger (1989: 359), cf. 4.3 below, and García Yebra (1997: 348). This might jeopardize the semantic function of the passive (i.e., stressing the process while leaving the agent in the background), as the active voice typically selects agent subjects. But in these cases, it can also be noted how translators find options for leaving the agent in the background as much as possible. This can be accomplished by filling the agent role in the subject function with lexical devices such as an indefinite pronoun (s. *alguien* in 2b); which is but one of a series of translation solutions observed in practice.

2. Examples (1a) and (1b) are my own.

(2) a. Ich würde es gerne völlig
I-NOM.SG.RECIP AUX.COND-1SG it-ACC.SG.TH gladly-ADV totally-ADV
neu erzählt bekommen.[3]
afresh-ADV tell-PTCP.PRF get-INF
'I would like to get it told totally afresh'

b. Quiero que alguien me lo
want-PRS.1SG CONJ somebody-AG to me-RECIP.1SG it-TH.3SG
cuente. todo de nuevo.
tell-PRS.SBJV.3SG everything DIR.OBJ again-ADV
'I want somebody to tell everything to me again'

Secondly, the German dative passive is an intricate usage-related phenomenon: each of the eligible auxiliary verbs (*bekommen, kriegen* and *erhalten*) indicates a different register. In Sánchez Nieto (2017), testimonies from monolingual corpora referred to the use of the *erhalten* passive in texts dealing with economic and especially with financial issues in written contexts, whereas the Duden grammar (1995: 178) stresses the strong bond that the *kriegen* passive has with spoken colloquial language. Bader's (2012) data evidences this relationship of the *kriegen* passive with colloquial language use as well.

The dative passive deserves attention in German-Spanish translation-applied contrastive studies. On the one hand, this passive (both in its *bekommen* and *kriegen* variants) appear frequently in day-to-day language. On the other hand, in my experience, the semi-grammaticalised status of the constructions (Szatamari 2006: 140), with the auxiliaries *bekommen, kriegen* and *erhalten* retaining part of its lexical meaning, prevent prospective translators who simultaneously learn German as a foreign language from fully grasping the 'grammatical' meaning of the dative passive, at least when they are faced with these constructions for the first time. Excluding Sánchez Nieto (2017), to date, and to the best of my knowledge, only Cartagena & Gauger (1989: 422–423) have specifically addressed the dative passive, although from a purely contrastive point of view. In their comprehensive comparison of the grammars of the German and the Spanish languages, they devote some paragraphs to the "*bekommen / kriegen / erhalten*-Fügung". Gauger (1978: 310) had already mentioned the construction *bekommen* + past participle, in order to term it *pasiva perifrástica 1* (*'periphrastic passive 1'*) and identify

3. Examples (2a) and (2b), as well as Examples (3) to (18) have been extracted from the PaGeS corpus, freely available at < www.corpuspages.eu > (see Section 3). Due to space constraints, the specific bibliographical data of the works to which those testimonies belong will not be provided, as these can be recalled by querying the example text directly in the search window in PaGeS (between inverted comas) and subsequently clicking on the bibliographical link provided on the results page.

it as one of the linguistic resources (*recursos lingüísticos*) for "expressing [in German] the action simply without naming the agent" (Gauger, id, my translation).

The scarcity of specific studies might be due to the fact that Spanish lacks a construction which parallels the German dative passive. Indeed, Cartagena and Gauger (1989: 422) admit that the Spanish language "does not have a construction that can be equated" with it. Because of this, the authors continue, translators "will probably have to make do with the same correspondences of the *werden* passive" (id., my translation). Nevertheless, the authors show how none of the Spanish correspondences of the *werden* passive "reproduces all the [semantic] characteristics" of the *bekommen* passive (ibid, 423). They also explain accurately this lack of total correspondence by analysing all possible Spanish translations of the German sentence *Die Briefe bekam ich später (von einem Freund) zugesandt* (Engl. '*I later got the letters sent by a friend*').

As a Spanish scholar in the field of German Studies, Elena García (1990) signals the need to pay due attention to the periphery of the semantic category of the passive – including the constructions *haben* and *bekommen* + past participle – and describes the semantic features of both constructions. In order to compensate for the scarcity of DE/ES comparative literature, a brief state of the art is sketched below, pointing out studies which focus on the German dative passive mainly from a monolingual perspective.

A comprehensive state of the art as regards the dative passive can be found in Lenz (2013: 66 ff.). The author summarizes the previous linguistic research on what she terms "the German GET passive" (ibid., 63). In doing so, she delves into "the syntactic, semantic/pragmatic, dialect and sociolinguistic characteristics" of the *bekommen, kriegen* and *erhalten* constructions.

Szatmari (2006: 140) posits a grammaticalisation continuum along which the various readings of the *bekommen* + participle II constructions can be lined up. The closer to the "minus" pole, the more faded the possession relation between dative and accusative complements is and the more grammaticalised the *bekommen* passive construction is. According to the author, the use of the *bekommen* passive is located in a transitional zone, as the sentences in Figure 1 show (Szatmari, id.).[4]

In order to go some steps further and to raise the semantic issues behind the grammaticalisation of the dative passive, several scholars have addressed the case of the (in)compatibility of the dative passive with specific verbs – or, in other words, with verbs that select specific semantic roles for their complements. Cook (2006: 145–46) shows that the semantic role contained in the dative object must be a BENEFICIARY/MALEFICIARY. The BENEFICIARY enjoys positive results of the

4. Engl. 'She gets the boards cut.' = > 'She gets the catalogue sent to her.' = > 'She gets "Rollmops" called after her.'

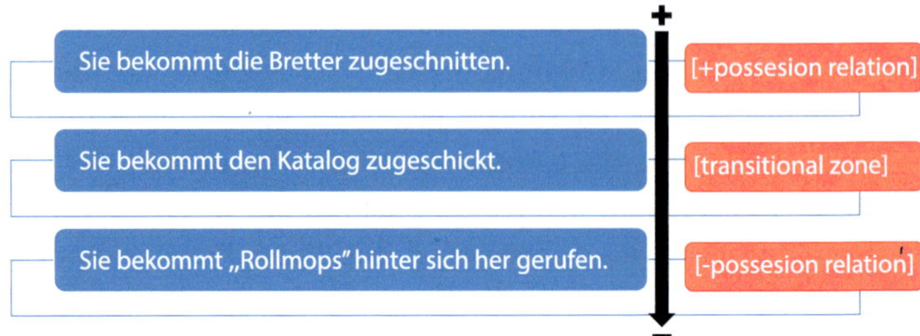

Figure 1. Continuum of possession relation in sentences with the *bekommen* passive (after Szatmari, 2006: 140)

agentive situation (typically an achievement or an accomplishment) denoted by the main verb, whereas the MALEFICIARY suffers the negative consequences of the situation. Thus, Ger. *Die Mutter setzt das Kind der Kälte aus* (Engl. '*The mother exposes the child to the cold*') can be transformed into a *werden* passive sentence with *Kind* ('*child*') in the role of patient (Ger. *Das Kind wurde der Kälte ausgesetzt* / Engl. '*The child was exposed to the cold*'), but not into a dative passive sentence such as Ger. **Die Kälte bekam/kriegte das Kind ausgesetzt* (Engl. '**The cold got the child exposed*'). Nevertheless, a sentence like Ger. *Man entzog ihm den Führerschein* (Engl. '*Someone took his driving licence from him*') can be transformed into a dative passive sentence such as Ger. *Er kriegte den Führerschein enzogen* (Engl. '*He got his driving licence taken from him*'). This occurs, as Cook (2006) proposes, because *Die Kälte* ('*the cold*') is semantically a GOAL, but not a BENEFICIARY/MALEFICIARY, whereas *ihm/er* (him/he) is.[5] Similarly, a dative passive sentence such as Ger. **Das Buch bekam ein Zitat entnommen* (Engl. '**The book got a quote taken from it*') is not acceptable because *das Buch* ('*the book*') acts as a LOCATIVE, but not as a MALEFICIARY.

In a study based on the deWac corpus, Bader (2012) found that ditransitive verbs whose dative complement is not a recipient (that is, where the possession relation is more faded) had lower observed-to-expected ratios, while other verbs with typical recipients – such as Ger. *überreichen* ('*to hand over*') – had higher values in this scale. Taking this line of research a step further, Bader and Häussler (2013: 134–35) ask themselves "whether the German *bekommen* passive still shows semantic traces of the lexical verb *bekommen*". The authors show that, although "the meaning of the lexical verb *bekommen* still constrains the *bekommen* passive in certain ways" – see Bader & Häussler (2013: 135 ff) for a summary of the main findings to this respect –, "the Recipient Constraint", i. e., that the dative object must always be a recipient, does not always govern this construction. This leads

5. These examples are Cook's (2006).

the authors to agree with previous research which rejects the term *recipient passive* for this construction and adopt the more neutral term *bekommen passive*. As for the present chapter, the more general term *dative passive* is adopted, since all three variants (the *bekommen*, the *kriegen* and the *erhalten* passive) are dealt with here.

These insights are much in line with the interesting changes that Lenz (2013: 69) detects as to the way in which different versions of the Duden Grammar before and after 2005 deal with these constructions. While the editions of the Duden Grammar prior to 2005 classify the *bekommen, kriegen* and *erhalten* passives as alternatives to the *werden* passive, the 2005 and 2009 editions list the *bekommen* passive and its variants "as an independent passive construction" (Lenz, id., citing the Duden Grammar, 2005: 555 ff). So does Eggelte (2020: 150–52) in her German grammar for Spanish university students and specialists of German as a foreign language. Moreover, in the respective citations selected by Lenz (id.) from the 1984 and 2005 versions of the Duden Grammar, an additional difference can be observed: whereas the 1984 version takes a normative stance, the 2005 version concentrates rather on acceptability issues, such as the less acceptable combination of the *bekommen* passive with intransitive dative verbs like "*helfen* ('to help'), *applaudieren* ('to applaud'), *danken* ('to thank'), *drohen* ('to threaten)" – see Duden Grammar (2005: 556 ff, cited in Lenz 2013: 69).

2. Aims of the study

The main purpose of this study is thus a descriptive one. Its first aim is to approach, both quantitatively and qualitatively, the so-called German dative passive and (1) to observe how Spanish professional translators render this construction into Spanish; (2) to observe in which contexts and registers German translators are prone to use the German dative passive when translating from Spanish (see Sections 4.2 to 4.4). As I proceed inductively and do not try to demonstrate with corpus data any previously given correspondences of the German dative passive in the Spanish language, the present study follows a corpus-driven approach (s. Saldanha 2009: 4). By doing so, the present study contributes to the descriptive branch of Translation Studies.

The following two aims in this chapter derive from one another and are (a) to complement my previous corpus-driven study on the *bekommen* passive (Sánchez Nieto 2017) by incorporating new evidence on the dative passive obtained from version 2.0 of the PaGeS corpus, and (b) to get to know the PaGeS corpus better and to show the potential of its current version for translation and contrastive research by contrasting the figures of the evidence obtained in version 2.0 with those of the evidence obtained in former versions of the PaGeS corpus (see Section 4.1).

The last aim of the study is to highlight, if only briefly, how the results of this study can be incorporated into teaching programs in order to stimulate the contrastive competence of trainee translators in the DE/ES language pair (see Section 5).

Our research questions (RQs) are the following:

> RQ 1: For each of the three stylistic variants of the dative passive (*bekommen/kriegen/erhalten* passive), to what extent is the recipient perspective maintained in DE > ES and maintained or incorporated into ES > DE translation? Which voice resources (*genus verbi*) and which translation techniques are involved when translating dative passive constructions from German into Spanish and from Spanish into German? And how is the usage-related meaning of the *kriegen* and the *erhalten* passives accounted for in DE > ES and ES > DE translation?
>
> RQs 2a and 2b: How does the distribution of *bekommen, kriegen* and *erhalten* passives across the different versions of the PaGeS corpus and subcorpora of PaGeS' version 2.0 look like and what does this distribution tell us about PaGeS itself?

3. Methodology

In this section, the design for the specific procedure which allowed us to approach the phenomenon of the dative passive in DE < > ES translation in a corpus-driven manner (RQ 1) will be explained. In doing so, the suitability of the PaGeS corpus as the best source to date of DE/ES bilingual data will be stressed. It will also emphasize the PaGeS' current technical shortomings (such as the impossibility of getting access to POS-tagging information stored with PaGeS' textual data). This shortcut makes it necessary to complement the procedure with other corpus analysis tools such as SketchEngine. Thus, the next paragraphs are devoted to the extraction, filtering, and tagging of the data in order to prepare them for analysis.

Firstly, a secondary sample corpus (s. Sánchez Nieto 2018 for a definition) was extracted from PaGeS <www.corpuspages.eu>, a free online available corpus in German and Spanish. Version 2.0 of PaGeS (published 01 May 2020) consisted of a core corpus and the Europarl supplement. The core corpus is mainly made up of fictional texts, comprised of both Spanish and German originals and their respective translations into the other language (in version 2.0 about 13.5 million tokens in each language, half of which pertain to originals and the other half to translations), plus a small amount of German and Spanish aligned translations of third language originals.[6] The Europarl supplement comprises the German and Spanish part of the CoStEP Corpus (Graën, Batinic & Volk 2014), a cleaned version of the Europarl v7 release, and includes some 35 million German and some 39 million Spanish tokens. Both the core corpus and the Europarl supplement are aligned at sentence level and lemmatized, but version 2.0 was not POS tagged – see Doval et al. (2019) for further details about the corpus. To extract the relevant examples, three very simple searches with the respective chains "bekommen", "erhalten" and "kriegen" were performed separately in the core corpus and in the Europarl supplement, both in original German and in translated German.[7] The results were downloaded and saved in 12 separate Excel files.

Secondly, the data in each of the files containing the raw PaGeS results were uploaded to Sketch Engine as small corpora. There, up to four different CQL queries were run on these corpora so as to locate the specific paragraphs which included examples of the three variants of the dative passive. The CQL queries were designed so that they could recognize the different syntactic patterns in which the dative passive appears, but the results still included some noise and had to be cleaned manually. At the end, 155 valid examples of the *bekommen* and the *kriegen* passives were obtained, but there was no single occurrence of the *erhalten* passive. The CQL queries for the *kriegen* variant are exemplified below.

1. [lemma="kriegen" & tag="VFIN.*"][]{0,8}[tag="VPP.*"]=>auxiliary *kriegen* appears in *Indikativ Präsens* or *Präteritum*; the past participle of the main verb appears at the end of the sentence, thus separated by up to 8 words from the auxiliary (*kriegt [...] gesagt*);
2. [lemma="kriegen" & tag="V.*"][tag="VPP.*"]=>auxiliary *kriegen* appears right before the past participle of the main verb (*kriegt gesagt; kriegte gesagt*);
3. [tag="VPP.*"] [lemma="kriegen" & tag="V.*"]=>auxiliary *kriegen* appears right after the past participle of the main verb, as in subordinate sentences, be it in simple tenses (*geregelt kriegt, gelegt kriegte*), compound tenses (*hat gesagt*

6. This part of the core corpus was excluded from the searches performed for this study.

7. The CoStEP Corpus includes the language codes of the speakers' contributions, i.e., the Members of the European Parliament (MEPs) as metadata (Graën, Batinic & Volk 2014:3). These metadata have been indexed into PaGeS, thus allowing to filter out corpus texts by this criterion. To date, the procedure to do so is the following. (i) selecting the checkbox "Europarl" and (ii) typing either *dede* or *eses* in the "Dialectal v." (Dialectal version) field to obtain examples found in speeches issued either in German or in Spanish, along with their aligned translations into the other language. To obtain examples of, for example, translated German, the user will type a German expression and then make sure that s/he types "eses" in the "Dialectal v." field.

gekriegt) or as infinitive in different verb complexes (*[kann ...]gesagt kriegen; [wird...] gesagt kriegen*, etc.);

4. [tag="VPP.*"][word="zu"][lemma="kriegen" & tag="V.*"] = > the past participle of the main verb appears right before the *zu*-infinitive of the auxiliary *kriegen* (*gesagt zu kriegen*).

Figure 2 shows the functionality of SketchEngine to build CQL queries, in this occasion to search for testimonies of the *bekommen* passive in certain constructions in the secondary sample corpus of original German obtained from the Europarl supplement at PaGeS).

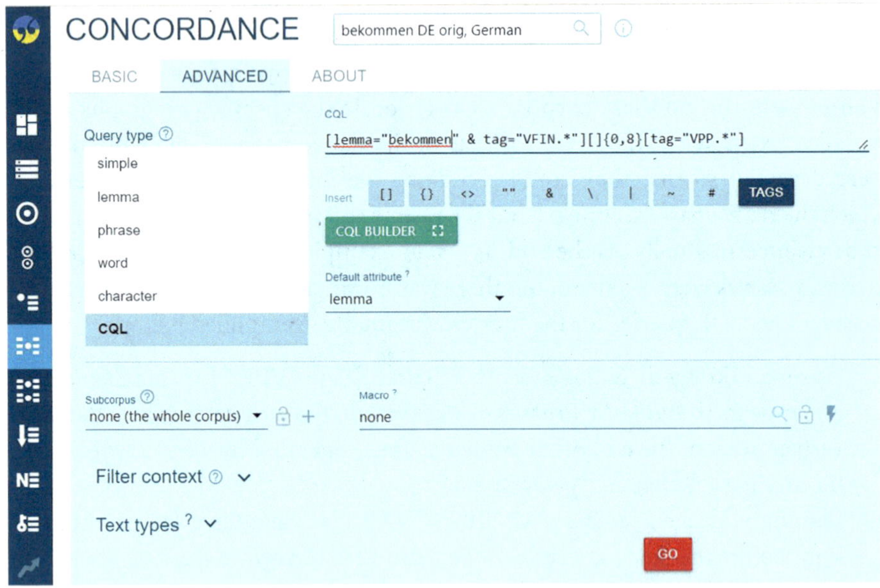

Figure 2. CQL query to obtain examples of the *bekommen* passive in *Indikativ Präsens* or *Präteritum*

Thirdly, the manually cleaned results were organized in four Microsoft Word documents (core corpus: original German; core corpus: translated German; Europarl supplement: original German; Europarl supplement: translated German) and the Word documents were added to an ATLAS.ti project[8] for further,

8. Atlas.ti is a software for qualitative analysis. This kind of software allows the researcher to mark up data of very different nature (be it in form of texts, audios, videos, images, or even geographical data) and code the data to create user-labelled categories that can be then subject to further analysis by quantifying, relating and graphically representing those categories. Thus, with the aid of the software, the researcher creates a second layer of information *from* de data, which s/he then interprets.

qualitative analysis. This involved marking the examples in the Word documents with labels (codes) for the phenomena under scrutiny. Thus, the secondary sample corpus obtained from PaGeS was enriched with the following metadata: kind of dative passive (*bekommen* passive, *kriegen* passive), subcorpus of origin (core corpus, Europarl), semantic roles (s. 4.2), perspective (s. 4.2), type of recipient (s. 4.2), translation technique (s. 4.3), and expression of voice (s. 4.3). These codes allowed us to carry out a minimum quantification of the phenomena they labelled.

4. Results and discussion

In Section 4.1, frequencies found for the three variants of the dative passive are discussed in relation to earlier versions of the PaGeS corpus, one of which served as a basis for my first approach to this issue (Sánchez Nieto 2017). Subsection 4.2 deals with the specific semantics of the entity behind the subject of a sentence whose predicate revolves around a form of the dative passive. Subsections 4.3 and 4.4 approach respectively the *bekommen* passive and the *kriegen* passive in translation. There, attention is paid to the techniques observed (1) in the translation into Spanish of the German sentences containing a form of these passives; (2) in the translation of those Spanish sentences that result in a German sentence containing a form of these passives. Attention is paid to shifts in voice in translation as well.

4.1 Overall presence of the three passive variants in PaGeS across versions

Table 1 shows the distribution of the examples of the *bekommen, kriegen* and *erhalten* passives throughout the different versions of the PaGeS corpus (v. 1.0, 1.1 and 2.0), as well as in the subcorpora of version 2.0: the core corpus and the supplement Europarl v7.

There is an increase of 3 points per million in the presence of the *bekommen* passive between the PaGeS 1.0 and the core corpus of PaGeS 2.0 (release: May 2020): 1.84 words per million versus 4.84 wpm. Secondly, PaGeS 1.0 did not feature any example of the *kriegen* passive, whereas in PaGeS 2.0 at least several examples can be found.

Focusing now on the overall data obtained from version 2.0, it is worth noticing that the normalised frequency (wpm) of the *kriegen* passive is seven times lower than that of the *bekommen* passive in the corpus.

Subsequently, looking at the data obtained from version 2.0 subcorpora (core corpus and Europarl supplement), it can be seen that dative passive use is overall

Table 1. Distribution of the examples of the dative passive throughout the different PaGeS versions and subcorpora

	***bekommen* passive (orig. DE+trans. DE<ES)**	**norm. freq.**	***kriegen* passive (orig. DE+trans. DE<ES)**	**norm. freq.**	***erhalten* passive (orig. DE+trans. DE<ES)**
PaGeS v. 1.0	9	1.84	0	-	0
PaGeS v. 1.1	28		?	-	?
PaGeS v. 2.0 (May 2020)	**146**		**9**		**0**
PaGeS v. 2.0 **core corpus** [comparable to v. 1.0]	64	4.84	9	0.68	0
PaGeS v. 2.0 **Europarl v.7 supplement**	82	2.32	0	0	0

quite lower in the Europarl supplement than in the core corpus. Firstly, the wpm rate of the *bekommen* passive in Europarl is 2.52 points lower than in the core corpus. Secondly, the *kriegen* passive is not at all represented in the Europarl supplement. The absence of the *kriegen* passive in version 1.0 and its low wpm rate in version 2.0 emphasizes the peripheral character of the *kriegen* passive which, as stressed by the Duden grammar (1995: 178), belongs to colloquial language use.

Surprisingly, no example of the *erhalten* passive can be found throughout the different versions of PaGeS' (1.0, 1.1 and 2.0). I had expected to find some testimonies of this variant of the dative passive at least in the Europarl supplement of PaGeS 2.0, since – following Duden again – the *erhalten* passive can be ascribed to an elevated language style (Duden-Grammar, *id.*). This usage could be expected to be represented in the language use of the German Members of Parliament (MPs) at the European Parliament. Let us here remember that the Europarl supplement includes an alignment of meeting protocols where the speeches of the MPs are transcribed. From all the transcribed speeches, PaGeS features the ones issued in original German, in addition to those issued in original Spanish, and those translated into Spanish or German. The absence of the *erhalten* passive in PaGeS 2.0 leads to the conclusion that this variant of the dative passive is even more peripheral than the *kriegen* variant, at least in the language use featured in PaGeS (modern fiction, essay, and Europarl debates).

Finally, coming down to translation direction, the figures obtained after querying PaGeS clearly evidence a much more frequent use in original German than in translated German.

Table 2. Presence of the variants of the dative passive in original and translated German in PaGeS

	bekommen passive	*kriegen* passive
Original German	110	6
Translated German	36	3
Total	146	9

The *bekommen* passive was found to be more unbalanced with regard to translation direction in the Europarl supplement (76 testimonies in DE > ES but only six in ES > DE translation) than in the core corpus (34 testimonies in DE > ES and 30 in ES > DE translation). The more formal register used in Europarl debates might have prevented German translators from using the *bekommen* passive. Another explanation for these low figures might lie in certain translation norms that could operate at European institutions: these norms might be pushing translators towards relying more often on literal translation, with translation memories offering those more literal solutions to translators in subsequent translation situations. That would also explain why in DE > ES translation the recipient perspective has been found to be maintained more frequently in testimonies from the Europarl supplement than in those of the core corpus, which is made up of mainly literary texts.

4.2 Semantic roles in subject function in the dative passive and their prevalence in DE <> ES translation

Here the focus will be placed on the most frequent semantic roles that appear in subject function in the German examples using the dative passive. In a first step the difference between RECIPIENTS and EXPERIENCERS could be distinguished. I define EXPERIENCERS as human entities in whose mind a psychological event takes place, as is shown in (3) below. The data show that RECIPIENTS (88 examples) outnumber EXPERIENCERS by far (12 examples).[9]

9. As this part of the analysis is of a qualitative nature, the emerging categories (here: the semantic roles) attempt to describe the data as accurately as possible. Thus, I have not bound myself to a particular role classification (such as the thematic roles listed in Cook 2006: 164 in the context of Lexical Functional Grammar) but have taken some of them from Cook (id.), defining others anew (like RECEIVER or POSSESSOR below).

(3) **Wir** wollen gemeinsam die Entsorgungswege und deren Sicherheit **detailliert und fundiert nachgewiesen bekommen** [...]
Queremos trabajar conjuntamente para garantizar que **contemos con** pruebas detalladas y fiables de las rutas de gestión de los residuos y su seguridad [...]

A closer look at the testimonies of the dative passive obtained from PaGeS allows a further classification of what I first termed RECIPIENTS into finer categories: BENEFICIARIES (4), MALEFICIARIES (5), and RECEIVERS.[10] The RECEIVER should be interpreted here as the destination of a communicative transaction, typically involving a communicative object (message), cf. Example (6).

(4) Ich habe nur eine Woche Urlaub bewilligt bekommen.
Solo me han concedido una semana de vacaciones, [...]

(5) Willst du noch Handschellen angelegt kriegen?
¿Quieres que te pongamos las esposas?

(6) "Sie hat im Verlag angerufen und gesagt gekriegt, daß du heute abend nach Hause kommst."
– Ha llamado a la editorial y le han comunicado que regresabas esta noche.

In the secondary sample corpus under scrutiny, the number of RECEIVERS (46 examples) slightly outnumbers the sum of BENEFICIARIES (27 examples) and MALEFICIARIES (16 examples), pointing to the conclusion that the semantic subcategory RECEIVER might have a central status in the use of the dative passive, at least in the genres analysed in this study.

The *bekommen* and *kriegen* passives in DE<>ES translation undergo processes (notably voice change, see 4.3 and 4.4 below) which carry with them a change in their semantic roles. As a result, BENEFICIARIES, MALEFICIARIES, RECEIVERS and/or EXPERIENCERS sometimes become AGENTS or POSSESSORS. This role change will be labelled here as the 'perspective change' phenomenon. This is due to the fact that, for example, a BENEFICIARY becoming an AGENT implies a change in the point of view from which the situation is presented.

AGENTS are animated (whereas FORCES are non-animated) entities that cause a change in another entity (typically an object or THEME). POSSESSORS indicate entities that access the property of an object as a result of the agentive situation suggested by the verb. Both AGENTS and POSSESSORS appear only in the examples translated into Spanish. In (7) a BENEFICIARY becomes an AGENT, in (3) (cf. above) an EXPERIENCER becomes a POSSESSOR, and in (8) a BENEFICIARY becomes a POSSESSOR as well.

10. See Section 1 for a definition of BENEFICIARY and MALEFICIARY.

(7) **Sie** möchte von äußerlich anzuwendenden Hilfsmitteln Verantwortlichkeiten **abgenommen kriegen.**
Quiere **quitarse** toda responsabilidad en la elección de los instrumentos que se usen.

(8) Haben wir den Mut, dafür zu sorgen, und schaffen **wir** es, ausreichend Finanzmittel **zur Verfügung gestellt zu bekommen** ?
¿Tenemos la valentía de garantizar que lo haremos y que **conseguiremos** disponer de los recursos financieros adecuados?

The frequency with which the particular recipient perspective typical of the *bekommen* and the *kriegen* passive changes or remains unchanged in DE>ES translation can be seen on Table 3. In most cases, the recipient perspective is maintained. Interestingly, though, nearly one out of four examples in the data show that translators faced with the German dative passives switched to the agent perspective in Spanish. I will come back to these data in Sections 4.3.1 and 4.4.1.

Table 3. *Bekommen* and *kriegen* passive: perspective change DE>ES translation

	No. of testimonies
Perspective of the recipient is maintained	69 (60%)
Change to agent perspective	30 (26.09%)
Change to experiencer perspective	5 (4.35%)
Change to possessor perspective	5 (4.35%)
Change to theme perspective	5 (4.35%)
Change to force perspective	1 (0.87%)
Total	115

Being PaGeS a bilingual and bidirectional corpus, it was possible to collect data in order to look at the dative passive from the opposite translation direction, i.e., ES>DE translation. The results are synthesized in Table 4. This data shows that the *bekommen* and/or *kriegen* passives were to a large extent (68.29%) motivated in an original Spanish expression which was already formulated from the perspective of the recipient, so that the *bekommen* and/or *kriegen* passive maintain that perspective. Nevertheless, a few testimonies could be found where the original Spanish structure implied a situation presented from a different perspective (that of an agent, an experiencer, or a theme), with the German structures implying a change to the recipient perspective. Examples of all these cases will be discussed in Sections 4.3.2 and 4.4.2.

Table 4. *Bekommen* and *kriegen* passive: perspective change ES > DE translation

	Examples
Perspective of the recipient is maintained	28 (68.29%)
Change from theme perspective	1 (2.44%)
Change from experiencer perspective	4 (9.76%)
Change from agent perspective	6 (14.63%)
Total	**39**

4.3 Bekommen passive in translation: Translation techniques applied and changes in voice

4.3.1 *Bekommen passive in DE > ES translation*

In DE > ES translation, translators handling the *bekommen* passive maintain the recipient perspective in 65 out of 110 examples (59.1%). In such cases, linguistic compression (Molina & Hurtado Albir 2002: 510) can be observed to a large extent in translated Spanish (66% of the testimonies, as in Example 9), followed at a great distance by modulations (Molina and Hurtado Albir id.), present in 8.7% of the testimonies (see Example 9) and by other residual techniques. It can be further observed that, when professional translators maintain the recipient perspective while rendering the *bekommen* passive into Spanish, they often use the active voice (60% of the available testimonies in PaGeS, see Example 10). The passive-reflexive voice (*pasiva refleja*) is used, however, in 33% of the testimonies. Most of the latter, interestingly, originate in the Europarl supplement, i.e., testifying the activity of those professionals who translate into Spanish transcriptions of the speeches issued by German-speaking MPs at the European Parliament (Example 11).

(9) **Wer** das "Bekenntnis zur deutschen Kultur- und Schicksalsgemeinschaft" verletze, solle das Staatsbürgerrecht **entzogen bekommen**.
A quien atentase contra la «adhesión a la comunidad de cultura y de destino alemanas» se le debía **arrebatar** sus derechos como ciudadano.

(10) ein Gegenspieler ist das Über-Ich. Es verkörpert die Normen, Ideale, Rollen, die Leit- und Weltbilder, die **der Mensch** durch seine Erziehung **beigebracht bekommt.**
[...] el hambre, el instinto sexual, la envidia, el odio, la confianza, el amor, etc. El superyó es la parte que contrarresta el ello: representa las normas, los ideales, los roles, los ideales e imágenes del mundo que **el ser humano adquiere** mediante la educación.

(11) Für solche Gelegenheiten **habe ich** einen Dienstwagen **zur Verfügung gestellt bekommen.**
Para tales ocasiones **se ha puesto a mi disposición** un coche oficial.

The very limited use of the Spanish passive voice in the DE > ES translated testimonies confirms a tendency stressed by several authors for the Spanish and, from a contrastive point of view, for the Spanish-German language pair as well. Referring to the Spanish *ser* passive constructions as a possible equivalent of the German *werden* passive, Cartagena and Gauger (1989) state:

> At the diaphasic level, it must be noted that their frequency is generally very low. In written language, especially in journalistic style, passive *ser* constructions are not uncommon, but they hardly occur in spoken language. Here, active structures are generally preferred. This tendency is even more pronounced when there is no indication of an agent; in such cases, an impersonal or reflexive construction regularly appears, e.g. not *Ahora todo es vendido a mitad de precio*, but *Ahora venden todo a mitad de precio* or *Ahora todo se vende a mitad de precio.*
>
> Cartagena & Gauger (1989, 359 [my translation])

See also Fernández (2009: 132) on the use of impersonal *se* in Spanish and its German counterparts.

On the other hand, interestingly, in 30 testimonies out of 110 (27.3%), the Spanish translator chose not to maintain the recipient perspective typical of the *bekommen* passive, but rather to present the situation in Spanish from the point of view of the agent. In those cases, the figures are quite similar to the cases in which the recipient perspective is maintained, with linguistic compression as the preferred translation technique (in 70% of the testimonies, see Example 12), followed by slightly more frequent modulations (13.3%, see Example 13), and a somewhat clearer tendency to use the active (66.6%) rather than the passive-reflexive voice (23.3%). Among the modulations, however, there are interesting testimonies of translations which have formed the *bekommen* passive using a verbless expression (nominalisations), as is shown in (14).

(12) Anders die allgemeine, natürliche Religion, die der Knabe von anderen Lehrern **mitgeteilt bekam** und die wohl auch die Religion des Vaters war.
Es distinta la «religión general, natural», que otros maestros **transmitieron** al muchacho y que era también la religión de su padre.

(13) Würden wir einer solchen Idee Rechnung tragen –[...]– dann könnte jeder Mitgliedstaat kommen und sagen, **wir** möchten einen Exportzuschuß **genehmigt bekommen**
si aceptásemos esa idea – [...] –, **cualquier Estado miembro** podría **solicitar** la autorización de una subvención a la exportación.

(14) So, lieber Alexander, kann man die Redezeit auch verlängern, indem **man** viele Fragen **gestellt bekommt.**
[...] señor Álvaro, acaba de demostrar usted cómo se puede alargar el tiempo de intervención mediante **la aceptación** [Ø] de tantas preguntas.[11]

4.3.2 *Bekommen passive in ES > DE translation*

In ES > DE translation, translators make use of the *bekommen* passive to maintain the recipient perspective in 28 examples out of 36 (77.78%, see Example 15), most of them (25 out of 36) originating in the core corpus. In those cases, linguistic amplification (Molina & Hurtado Albir 2002: 510) is the most represented translation technique in translated German (61.13% of the examples), followed by modulations (12.7%, see Example 16). Moreover, in this constellation – that is, when German translators use the *bekommen* passive to translate an original Spanish expression that points out a situation formulated from the perspective of the recipient – a Spanish verb form in the active voice was to be found in most original Spanish expressions (90.1% of the testimonies). In a few testimonies, nevertheless, forms of the passive-reflexive voice (6.44%) were found in the original texts, followed by isolated uses of the Spanish periphrastic passive (3.4%, Example 17).

(15) Nos alojamos en una suite del hotel más lujoso, donde cada noche nos **dejaban** una escultura de chocolate con temas autóctonos, como el cacique [...].
Wir bewohnten eine Suite im besten Hotel am Platz, und **bekamen** dort jeden Abend eine Skulptur aus Schokolade **serviert**, in der einheimische Themen dargestellt waren, etwa der Kazike Caupolicán [...].

(16) [...] aclarando que mi intención era que me **sacara** el Tarot y aceptara desde luego un pago por la consulta.
Gleichzeitig erklärte ich, dass ich noch einmal die Karten von ihr **gelegt bekommen** wollte und die Einladung gewissermaßen als Gegenleistung zu verstehen sei.

(17) Era por entonces de buen tono que **las hijas** de familias asentadas **fueran** instruidas en las artes sociales y **salpicadas** con el don de la música de salón, donde la polonesa era menos peligrosa que la conversación o las lecturas cuestionables.
Damals gehörte es zum guten Ton, daß **Töchter** angesehener Familien in Gesellschaftskünsten unterrichtet wurden und das nötige Rüstzeug für Salonmusik **verabreicht bekamen** – im Salon war die Polonaise weniger riskant als das Gespräch oder eine zweifelhafte Lektüre.

---

11. As the noun *aceptación* is a nominalization of the agentive verb *aceptar*, it can be understood that the underlying situation (13) is issued from the point of view of the agent, which remains implicit. The transposition observed in (14) might be due to de possible indirect character of the translations in the Europarl corpus, as MPs' speeches are usually translated into English and then subsequently translated into the other languages of the Member States.

It should be stressed here, though, that almost one out of four examples of the *bekommen* passive in ES > DE translation originates in sentences formulated from perspectives other than the RECIPIENT, like the AGENT in (18) – featuring an amplification – or the EXPERIMENTER in (19) – with the use of the *bekommen* passive resulting in a modulation –:

(18) –[...] La gente se pelea por recuperar su dinero.
– ¿**Pagan**? – intervino Genis.
– De momento, sí, [...].
Die Leute prügeln sich darum, ihr Geld zurückzubekommen." „**Bekommen** sie denn **etwas ausgezahlt**?", fragte Genis. „Im Moment schon, [...]."

(19) Señor Presidente, la mejor muestra de la buena voluntad que tenemos son las mil enmiendas que estamos **viendo** desde la comisión hasta el Pleno.Herr Präsident, die Tausend Änderungsanträge des Ausschusses, die **wir** im Parlament **vorgelegt bekommen**, sind der beste Beweis unseres guten Willens.

These perspective shifts will be discussed in 4.4.2 together with a similar shift found for the *kriegen* passive in ES > DE translation.

4.4 Kriegen passive in translation: Translation techniques applied and changes in voice

In the following two subsections, the nine examples found in version 2.0 of the PaGeS Corpus (all of them pertaining to the core corpus, and, more specifically, to fiction books) will be analysed.

4.4.1 *Kriegen passive in DE > ES translation*

The few testimonies of the *kriegen* passive in DE > ES translation obtained from PaGeS 2.0 are quite interesting. Spanish translators handling the *kriegen* passive maintain the recipient perspective in four examples out of six (66.6%), i.e., 6 points more frequently than when translating the *bekommen* passive. The Spanish active voice is employed across all the available testimonies, see Example 4, shown here again as (20):

(20[4]) Willst du noch Handschellen **angelegt kriegen**?
¿Quieres que te **pongamos** las esposas?

4.4.2 *Kriegen passive in ES > DE translation*

In ES > DE translation, again, the active voice was present in all three original Spanish testimonies. There are two interesting facts here. First, the recipient perspective was already present in two out of three available original testimonies, but these two

Spanish originals contained idiomatic expressions (resolved by German translators with equivalent idioms) that indicate agentive situations which include physical violence against the recipient (i.e., the latter is a MALEFICIARY, see Examples 21 and 22). The combination of the *kriegen* passive with predicates of physical violence that contributes to a negative semantic prosody had been previously described in Sánchez Nieto (2017) basing on original German data. The translated German data in the present study fit as well in the latter description. In Szatmari's (2006) terms, the *kriegen* passive seems to be highly grammaticalised here, as the possession relation underlying the verb *kriegen* has completely disappeared.

(21) Y a quien intenta venirme con verdulerías **le suelto un soplamocos** y santas pascuas.
Und wer mir mit Zoten kommt, der **kriegt eine geklebt**, und damit basta.

(22) – Tú calla, desgraciado, a ver si **te pego una leche** que te mando a La Rioja.
„Halt bloß das Maul, du elender Wicht, sonst **kriegst du eine geschmiert**, dass du in der Rioja landest."

Second, in the third available original Spanish testimony, the situation was formulated from the perspective of the THEME (cf. Example 23), a perspective which, at first sight, would not trigger the use of the *kriegen* passive:

(23) –[...] Los cascos cuestan dinero, ya lo sabes.
„[...] Wir kriegen ja diese Pfandflaschen nicht geschenkt."

The modulation associated to this perspective shift (from THEME to RECIPIENT) bears some similarity with that found for the *bekommen* passive in ES > DE translation and exemplified in 4.3.2, cf. (19). Both, together with the other EXPERIENCER-to-RECIPIENT and AGENT-to-RECIPIENT perspective shifts found for the *bekommen* passive in ES > DE translation, might be explained by means of the thinking-for-translating hypothesis (Slobin 1996, cited in Molés-Cases 2020). This hypothesis predicts that

> translators codify different pieces of information depending on the mechanisms and limitations of the target language (usually their mother tongue) and, as a result, tend to distance themselves from the source text, in order to conform to the rhetorical style of the target language. (Molés-Cases 2020: 143)

The use of both the *kriegen* and the *bekommen* passive might be considered part of the "rhetorical style" in registers like the ones portrayed: face-to-face communication, symmetrical relation between the communication partners in the case of the *bekommen* passive, and familiar communication – maybe with a less symmetrical relation between the communication partners in the case of the *kriegen* passive, like Example (23) and the threatens uttered in (21) and (22) seem to suggest.

5. Conclusion

The Parallel Corpus of German and Spanish (PaGeS) available online has enabled us to study the phenomenon of the dative passive in DE<>ES translation. The enlargement of the textual base that led to version 2.0 has proved critical in approaching this translation phenomenon. This only underlines the importance of an ongoing project like PaGeS: it offers scholars access to bilingual data that allow for the study of not commonly studied specific phenomena in the DE/ES language pair. PaGeS is the only free available parallel corpus involving German and Spanish existing up to date, something remarkable bearing in mind the vast number of corpora that involve English.

In DE>ES translation, as is shown in Section 4, translators maintain the recipient perspective typical of the German constructions in about 2/3 of the available testimonies, the rest of these favouring other perspectives, notably that of the agent. This means that, when translating from German into Spanish, it is not always easy to maintain the semantic function of these passives, i.e., to move the pronouns or lexical units referring to the recipient to the first position of the sentence, thus stressing the recipient role in the situation presented. When translating from Spanish into German, the use of the dative passive was found to be triggered in slightly more than three out of four examples by syntactic-semantic contexts where the perspective of the recipient was already present in the Spanish source text. Those examples with perspectives other than the recipient are very interesting and have been discussed in Section 4.4.2 in the light of the thinking-for-translating hypothesis.

The three variants of the dative passive show very different figures in the data obtained from PaGeS. While the *bekommen* passive is much more frequent than the *kriegen* passive, the *erhalten* passive is not at all represented in the data. PaGeS probably does not include samples of the written registers where the *erhalten* passive would be more likely to occur. It must be borne in mind that the Europarl supplement, although it includes testimonies of specialized language, reflects a genre which is rooted in the spoken mode. Speeches are per se texts that are written-to-be-spoken, when not spoken directly.

Despite the scarcity of bilingual testimonies involving the *kriegen* passive in PaGeS, these are coherent with the monolingual testimonies studied previously in Sánchez Nieto (2017), regarding the negative semantic prosody of the construction, as in Examples (21) and (22). The *kriegen* passive comes into play here to suggest situations of aggression and force exerted on a MALEFICIARY.

Finally, some suggestions for incorporating the findings of this study into the teaching of general DE>ES translation are presented as follows. (1) draw attention to the constructions first; this can best be achieved when dealing with the DE>ES translation of passive meaning and with the linguistic means that German has to focus on the process while leaving the AGENT implicit; (2) have students search in PaGeS corpus for examples of the *bekommen* passive by typing expressions like Ger. "geschenkt bekommen" (Engl. '*receive as gift*') (between inverted comas) and analyse the results as to which syntactic roles (subject, indirect object, direct object) the BENEFICIARY/MALEFICIARY, the THEME and the AGENT (if the latter happens to appear in the German example) have been assigned; (3) have the students translate into German Spanish sentences with ditransitive verbs and implicit AGENTS, such as *Me regalaron este jersey por mi cumpleaños/Me sirvieron el desayuno en la habitación* by explicitly using the *bekommen* passive, and subsequently comparing students' translations with those produced in by professionals in similar syntactic-semantic contexts and accessible through PaGeS; and finally (4) pay special attention to the different registers in which the *kriegen* and *bekommen* passives appear. This can be achieved by having students translate text excerpts like the German bitexts of Examples (21) and (22) – without presenting them as translations, slightly modifying the local references if necessary, and providing a minimal context for them – and subsequently comparing their productions with the Spanish (original) correspondences in PaGeS, while looking for traces of colloquial language present in them and (maybe) in the students' own productions.

Regarding the use of corpora in the translation classroom with German as L2, a note of caution should be sounded. Although authors like Van Lawick stress that "working with parallel corpora can foster a critical and creative approach of the student regarding the reexpression [of the message] in the target language" (2005: 393, my translation), others like Szumlakowski (2021: 130) point to the technical problems that teachers and learners can face when dealing with corpora (for example, lack of knowledge of the querying language used), or rightly point to the importance that age, linguistic competence and, most notably, the way that the teacher facilitates the learning activities have on the success of the data-driven activities with corpora (Soliño, 2021: 116). Regarding linguistic competence, Doval (2018: 80) reminds that, although examples of language use from parallel corpora like PaGeS are especially relevant for foreign language teaching at advanced levels, they are definitely too difficult for beginners. Nevertheless, the teacher can always use materials from parallel corpora as a basis to be adapted to specific learner needs, as shown in Marco and van Lawick (2009).

References

Bader, Markus. 2012. The German bekommen passive: A case study on frequency and grammaticality. *Linguistische Berichte* 231: 249–98.

Bader, Markus & Häussler, Jana. 2013. How much bekommen is there in the German bekommen passive? In *Non-canonical Passives* [Linguistik Aktuell/Linguistik Today Series 205], Artemis Alexiadou & Florian Schäfer (eds), 115–39. Amsterdam: John Benjamins.

Cartagena, Nelson & Hans Martin Gauger. 1989. *Vergleichende Grammatik Spanisch-Deutsch 1*. Mannheim: Dudenverlag.

Claros, M. Gonzalo. 2006. Consejos básicos para mejorar las traducciones de textos científicos del inglés al español (I). *Panace@: Boletín de Medicina y Traducción* 7(23): 89–94.

Cook, Philipa. 2006. The datives that aren’t born equal: Beneficiaries and the dative passive. In *Datives and Similar Cases: Between Argument Structure and Event Structure* [Studies in Language Companion Series 75], Daniel Hole, Andre Meinunger, & Werner Abraham (eds), 141–184. Amsterdam: John Benjamins.

Doval, Irene, Fernández-Lanza, Santiago, Jiménez-Juliá, Tomás, Liste-Lamas, Elsa & Lübke, Barbara. 2019. Corpus PaGeS: A multifunctional resource for language learning, translation and cross-linguistic research. In *Parallel Corpora for Contrastive and Translation Studies: New Resources and Applications* [Studies in Corpus Linguistics Series 90], Irene Doval & María Teresa Sánchez-Nieto (eds), 103–21. Amsterdam: John Benjamins.

Duden. 1995. *Grammatik der deutschen Gegenwartssprache*. Mannheim: Dudenverlag.

Duden. 2005. *Die Grammatik: Unentbehrlich für richtiges Deutsch*, 7 edn. Mannheim: Dudenverlag.

Eggelte, Brigitte. 2020. *Gramática alemana*. Salamanca: Ediciones de la Universidad de Salamanca.

Elena García, Pilar. 1990. Ramificaciones de la diátesis pasiva en alemán: Las construcciones bekommen y haben Partizip II. *Anuari de Filologia* XIII(A/1): 57–64.

Fernández, Francesc. 2009. Das unpersönliche Berichten über Vorgänge im Deutschen und Spanischen: Ergebnisse einer korpusgestützten und kontrastiv binnendifferenzierten Textsortenanalyse. *Lebende Sprachen* 54(3): 131–37.

García Yebra, Valentín. 1997. La voz pasiva francesa y su traducción al español. *Thélème: Revista Complutense de Estudios Franceses* 11: 347–53.

Gauger, Hans Martin. 1978. Problemas de una gramática contrastiva del español y del alemán. un ejemplo: La voz pasiva. *Iberoromania* 7: 18–27.

Graën, Johannes, Batinic, Dolores & Volk, Martin. 2014. Cleaning the Europarl Corpus for linguistic applications. In *Konvens 2014, Hildesheim, 8–10 October 2014*, 1–7. <https://web.archive.org/web/20200228122825id_/https://www.zora.uzh.ch/id/eprint/99005/1/Cleaning_the_Europarl_Corpus_for_Linguistic_Applications.pdf> (26 May 2023).

van Lawick, Heike. 2005. El corpus paralelo bitextual en la enseñanza de traducción: Identificación y soluciones para doch. In *II AIETI. Actas del II Congreso Internacional de la Asociación Ibérica de Estudios de Traducción e Interpretación*, 393–407. Madrid: AIETI.

doi Lenz, Alexandra N. 2013. Three 'competing' auxiliaries of a non-canonical passive: On the German GET passive and its auxiliaries. In *Non-canonical Passives* [Linguistik Aktuell/Linguistik Today Series 205], Artemis Alexiadou & Florian Schäfer (eds), 63–94. Amsterdam: John Benjamins.

doi Marco, Josep & van Lawick, Heike. 2009. Using corpora and retrieval software as a source of materials for the translation classroom. In *Corpus Use and Translating: Corpus Use for Learning to Translate and Learning Corpus Use to Translate* [Benjamins Translation Library 82], Alison Beeby, Patricia Rodríguez-Inés & Pilar Sánchez-Gijón (eds), 9–28. Amsterdam: John Benjamins.

doi Molés-Cases, Teresa. 2020. On the translation of manner-of-motion in comics. *Languages in Contrast* 20(1): 141–65.

doi Molina, Lucía & Hurtado Albir, Amparo. 2002. Translation techniques revisited: A dynamic and functionalist approach. *Meta* 47(4): 498–512.

Reisinger, Hildegard. 1999. Aspectos culturales de la traducción científica en España. *Grenzgänge* 6(11): 82–92.

Saldanha, Gabriela. 2009. Principles of corpus linguistics and their application to translation studies research. *Tradumàtica* 7: 1–7.

doi Sánchez-Nieto, María Teresa. 2017. Wiedergabe der Rezipientenperspektive: Entsprechungen des bekommen-Passivs im Spanischen. *Lebende Sprachen* 62(1): 187–208.

doi Sánchez-Nieto, María Teresa. 2018. Secondary sample corpora in contrastive linguistics and translation studies. *Across Languages and Cultures* 19(1): 121–37.

Slobin, Dan. 1996. From "thought and language" to "thinking for speaking." In *Rethinking Linguistic Relativity*, Stephen C. Levinson & John J. Gumperz (eds), 70–96. Cambridge: CUP.

Soliño Pazó, María Mar. 2021. Corpus PaGeS: Un corpus paralelo bilingüe en el aula de alemán como lengua extranjera. In *Corpus y traducción: Perspectivas lingüísticas, didácticas y literarias*, Julia Lavid López, Estefanía Avilés, Julia Bobkina & Matilde Vivancos (eds), 111–27. Madrid: Guillermo Escolar.

Szatmari, Petra. 2006. Sich-Lassen-Konstruktionen als Konkurrnzformen des bekommen-Passivs. *Deutsch als Fremdsprache* 43(3): 138–43.

Szumlakowski Morodo, Irene. 2021. Aplicación del corpus PaGes en la formación de profesores. In *Corpus y traducción: Perspectivas lingüísticas, didácticas y literarias*, Julia Lavid López, Jelena Bobkina, Estefanía Avilés & Matilde Vivancos (eds), 129–42. Madrid: Guillermo Escolar.

CHAPTER 5

Exploring near-synonyms through translation corpora

A case study on 'begin' and 'start' in the English-Spanish parallel corpus PACTRES

Noelia Ramón
University of León

This chapter explores the Spanish translations of the English ingressive verbs 'begin' and 'start' in the parallel corpus PACTRES. 'Begin' and 'start' are considered near-synonyms and the aim of this paper is to trace any semantic differences between them through an analysis of their Spanish translations. I obtained the translational options in Spanish for 'begin' and 'start' and compared the divergences using statistical significance tests. The findings revealed that the verb 'start' presents a wider range of ingressive verbs as translational options in Spanish, thus pointing towards a larger number of associated sense relations than the verb 'begin'. This study illustrates the usefulness of parallel corpora in highlighting semantic differences between near-synonyms in the source language, here English.

Keywords: near-synonyms, parallel corpora, translation strategies, sense relations

1. Introduction

The present study focuses on the translation solutions found in Spanish for two aspectual verbs in English which are often considered to be near-synonyms: 'begin' and 'start'. These two verbs indicate an ingressive aspect and occur in similar syntactic constructions, including to-infinitive complementation, -ing clause complementation, nominal complementation (transitive) and intransitive patterns. In this study we will analyse the various translational options provided in Spanish for the verbs 'begin' and 'start' to determine whether the translators' choices reflect any semantic differences between these two verbs. The empirical data have been extracted from the PACTRES parallel corpus of English and Spanish.

https://doi.org/10.1075/scl.113.05ram

The aim of this paper is two-fold: (1) to establish the inventory of translational options available in Spanish to cover the semantic field of ingressive aspect expressed lexically by the verbs 'begin' and 'start' in English, and (2) to illustrate how data from a parallel corpus may contribute valuable information with regard to semantic differences between near-synonymous lexical items in the source language.

2. Theoretical framework

2.1 Aspectual verbs: 'Begin' and 'start'

In present-day English, a variety of verbs, including 'begin' and 'start', are used to express temporal distinctions, and are therefore labelled as aspectual verbs. As a temporal distinction "aspects are different ways of viewing the internal temporal constituency of a situation." (Comrie 1976: 3). Traditionally, the different aspectual distinctions include the speaker's choices to refer to an event as completed (perfective aspect), ongoing (imperfective aspect), beginning (ingressive aspect), continuing (continuative aspect), ending (egressive aspect), or repeating (iterative or habitual aspect) (Brinton 1988). The complexity of the actualization in language of this type of temporal meaning has led to a widely accepted distinction between the terms 'aspect' and *Aktionsart*: 'aspect' would be expressed by verbal inflectional morphology (simple, progressive, perfective), whereas *Aktionsart* refers to the intrinsic temporal qualities of a situation, i.e., the lexical meaning of verbs (*begin, start, continue, cease, finish, stop*, etc.).

Aspectual verbs are defined as lexical verbs, "which [are] placed before a non-finite clause and which [express] the situation described by this clause as beginning, ending or ongoing." (Declerck, Reed & Cappelle 2006: 763). These verbs characterize the state of progress of some event or activity, which is normally reported in a complement clause following the verb phrase (Newmeyer 1975; Comrie 1976; Comrie 2001; Declerck et al. 2006). The two verbs analysed in this paper, 'begin' and 'start', are aspectual verbs and can be classified as ingressive.

2.2 Synonymy

The verbs 'begin' and 'start' are generally considered synonyms or near-synonyms in English. The concept of synonymy refers to similarity in meaning between two lexical items and is, therefore, related to semantics. Today, there is a general consensus among linguists to subscribe to the no-synonymy rule. In other words, there must be some type of difference between two existing linguistic items that are considered synonyms or near-synonyms, either in the semantic covering, in the syntactic environment or in the collocational patterns. Complete synonymy is something which could hardly exist over time, as one of the two items would eventually disappear. We will consider here synonymy as a sense relation, as defined by Kreidler (1998: 303): "the relations of meaning between words, as expressed in synonymy, hyponymy, and antonymy." As has been pointed out, "synonyms usually involve a match between some, but not all, of a word's senses." (Murphy 2003: 145).

'Begin' and 'start' share an ingressive meaning, but authors agree on the difficulty to tease out the differences between these two verbs: "In many sentences start and begin may be substituted one for the other with little or no change in meaning" (Dixon 2005: 181). Previous studies have shown that 'begin' and 'start' appear to have different semantic preferences to some extent and are consequently not completely synonymous (Freed 1979; Dixon 1991, 2005; Duffley 1999; Mair 2003; Egan 2008). It has been found that 'start' is significantly more common in spoken registers of English than 'begin' (Egan 2008). Another difference is that the verb 'start' may only indicate an initial phase of the onset of the activity, whereas 'begin' indicates that the event has actually initiated, as described by Freed:

> Only from a sentence with *begin* does it necessarily follow that the nucleus (or characteristic activity) of the event has been initiated; a sentence with *start* followed by a to V complement can have as a consequence that only the onset of the event named in the complement has been initiated. We may conclude, therefore, that *start* refers to the onset of an event while *begin* refers to the initial temporal segment of the nucleus of an event. (Freed 1979: 71)

In this paper exploring the list of translational options found in Spanish for conveying both 'begin' and 'start' will provide us with valuable information regarding the semantic differences implied in the source language, i.e., English.

3. Data and method

3.1 The English-Spanish parallel corpus PACTRES

The empirical data for this study have been extracted from the English-Spanish parallel corpus PACTRES compiled and stored at the University of León, Spain (Sanjurjo-González & Izquierdo 2019). The long-term research group ACTRES (Contrastive Analysis and Translation English-Spanish in its Spanish acronym) compiled this parallel corpus as a means for carrying out contrastive analyses between English and Spanish at all levels. PACTRES is a bi-directional parallel corpus, but this study will focus exclusively on the Spanish translations of the

English forms of 'begin' and 'start'. This corpus currently includes 4.2 million words in the direction English-Spanish, grouped into 5 different subcorpora according to register: fiction, non-fiction, newspapers, magazines, and miscellanea. All the texts included were published in English between 2000 and 2018 and the corresponding translations are in the European variety of Spanish. Table 1 shows the number of words included in each subcorpus.

Table 1. Contents of the English-Spanish parallel corpus PACTRES

	English	Spanish	Total
Books-fiction	1,276,791	1,306,568	2,583,359
Books-nonfiction	514,786	573,523	1,088,309
Newspaper	118,665	129,810	248,475
Magazine	114,634	122,024	236,658
Miscellanea	40,178	49,026	89,204
Total	2,065,054	2,231,679	4,296,733

3.2 The data

All the verb forms of 'begin' and 'start' have been retrieved from PACTRES, with all their possible morphological variants: base forms, -s forms, -ing forms and -ed/-en forms. A number of instances had to be discarded because they were used as nouns ('beginning', 'start', 'starts') or because they were used in fixed expressions with adverbial meanings (*to begin with, to start with*). The final number of concordances analysed was 1,361 instances of the lemma 'begin' and 848 instances of the lemma 'start'. The fact that 'begin' occurs more often in PACTRES is due to the written nature of the texts included. As mentioned above, the verb 'start' is more frequent in oral texts than 'begin' (Egan 2008). For this study the samples were retrieved from the whole corpus, without any restriction according to register.

Once all the concordances with their translations into Spanish had been retrieved, I proceeded to the actual classification. First, all the concordances were classified according to the type of complementation following them: to-infinitive clauses, -ing clauses, in intransitive patterns or in transitive patterns followed by a noun phrase. This enables us to observe grammatical differences between 'begin' and 'start'. Second, the concordances in each group were further classified according to the translations provided in Spanish. Third, the results for each complementation type data in 'begin' and 'start' were compared to observe any differences in the translations that could point towards the semantic similarities or dissimilarities between these two near-synonyms. The results were analysed using a chi-square test (p-value < 0.05) to identify any statistically significant differences. Finally, the complete inventory of ingressive verbs used as Spanish translations was compared to identify the semantic nuances implied by one verb but not by the other.

4. Results and discussion

4.1 Comparing syntactic patterns of 'begin' and 'start'

A first stage of the analysis has focused on the classification of all the concordances of 'begin' and 'start' as verbs according to the syntactic patterns in which they occur in the English subcorpus of PACTRES. Table 2 shows the raw number of cases found in each category for both verbs.

Table 2. Number of tokens found in each syntactic pattern with 'begin' and 'start'

	'BEGIN'	'START'
to-inf. clause	725	211
-ing clause	198	205
intransitive pattern	312	313
transitive pattern	126	119
TOTAL	**1,361**	**848**

Because the corpus contains more instances of 'begin' than of 'start', percentages have been used to compare their frequencies, as shown in Figure 1.

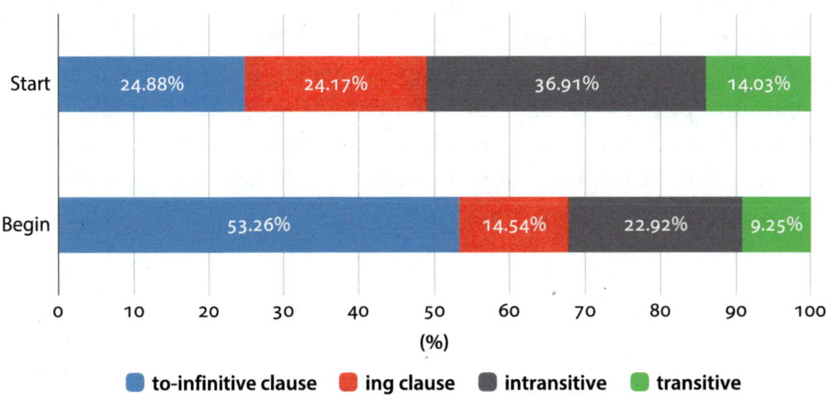

Figure 1. Percentage of occurrence of complementation patterns with 'begin' and 'start'

Figure 1 shows that 'begin' is more than twice more often followed by a to-infinitive clause than 'start,' as illustrated in (1) and (2).

(1) My mind began to clear. (FMJ1E.s22)

(2) Carla started to cry. (FFK5E.s512)

In contrast, -ing clauses occur more frequently after 'start' than after 'begin', ((3) and (4)).

(3) Samantha screamed and began crying. (FGJ4E.s968)

(4) He has to start looking ahead. (FIK1E.s139)

The intransitive pattern is also more frequent in the case of 'start' than in the case of 'begin' ((5) and (6)).

(5) An hour later the contest began. (FFK3E.s1003)

(6) "We won't be allowed near the wall if fighting starts again." (FCT1E.s72)

And finally, the transitive use is the least common one in both verbs, with 14% for 'start' and 9% for 'begin', as in (7) and (8).

(7) Please begin your work as soon as possible. (FCJ1E.s498)

(8) When they disappear inside again it's time to start dinner. (FKUM1E.s46)

It must be noted here that all the morphological forms of these two verbs were considered together. The manual analysis revealed certain trends that suggest that collocational issues contribute to the selection of the complementation pattern. For example, the -ing forms 'beginning' and 'starting' will never be followed by an -ing clause, as there seems to be a "strong aversion to the (immediate) co-occurrence of identical or similar grammatical structures." (Vosberg 2011: 305).

At this stage, only syntactic issues are considered, and it can be seen that 'begin' occurs more often in clause complementation patterns than in transitive or intransitive patterns but 'start' occurs around 50% of cases in clausal patterns and 50% in transitive or intransitive patterns. The analysis of the translations into Spanish in the following sections will shed some light onto the semantic features that do distinguish these two verbs.

4.2 Spanish translations of 'begin'

In this section I summarise the findings related to the translational options in Spanish for all the instances of 'begin' in PACTRES, in all the possible syntactic patterns. All the examples in this paper include both the source text in English and the target text in Spanish, with their corresponding coding and sentence number at the end of each example. Figure 2 shows the main choices taken by the Spanish translators to translate the English ingressive verb 'begin'.

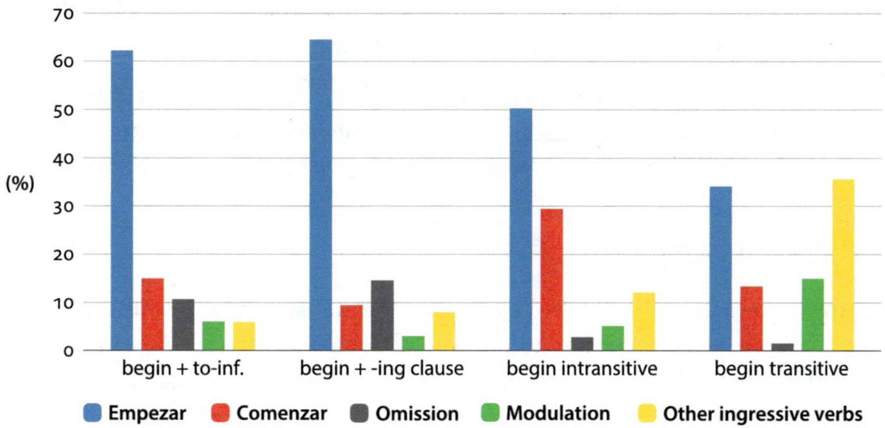

Figure 2. Spanish translations of 'begin' according to the type of complementation

Figure 2 shows that the translations of 'begin' when followed by a clause present a very similar pattern, with a heavy dependence on the verb *empezar* (over 60% of cases, see (9) and (10)). Similar frequencies can also be seen in the less common translations for both to-infinitive clauses and -ing clauses, evenly distributed: the ingressive verb *comenzar*, which is slightly more formal than *empezar*, omission, modulation or other ingressive verbs in Spanish.

(9) Lester begins to awaken. (EHP1E.s731)
Ahí por fin empieza a reaccionar. (EHP1S.s725)

(10) Jake and I will begin gathering wood. (FKS2E.s488)
Jake y yo empezaremos a reunir madera. (FKS2S.s479)

In contrast, in the other two patterns (transitive and intransitive), 'begin' shows less dependence on the common verb *empezar* with 50% in intransitive patterns and 34% in transitive patterns. Much higher percentages are found in other translational options in Spanish, such as the verb *comenzar* (30% in intransitive (11) and 13% in transitive patterns), or other ingressive verbs, especially in transitive patterns (35%) (12).

(11) "It's about to begin." (FSP1E.s222)
Está a punto de comenzar. (FSP1S.s213)

(12) The director began the countdown. (FHM2E.s40)
El realizador inició la cuenta atrás. (FHM2S.s42)

Other minor strategies found in PACTRES for translating the English verb 'begin' into Spanish are omission (13) and modulation (14), all under 15% of cases in all the patterns.

(13) "And I began thinking: 'How do we draw out the principles?" (EBD1E.s282)
Y pensé: "¿Cómo podemos extraer los principios?". (EBD1S.s278b)

(14) If she waited any longer to begin her revenge, it could be too late. (FPA1E.s1118)
Si esperaba más para cobrarse venganza, podría ser demasiado tarde. [If she waited any longer to take revenge, it could be too late.] (FPA1S.s1095)

4.3 Spanish translations of 'start'

Figure 3 shows the choices taken by the Spanish translators when translating the verb 'start' classified according to the type of complementation. We can observe a trend in the Spanish translations similar to the translations listed for the verb 'begin'.

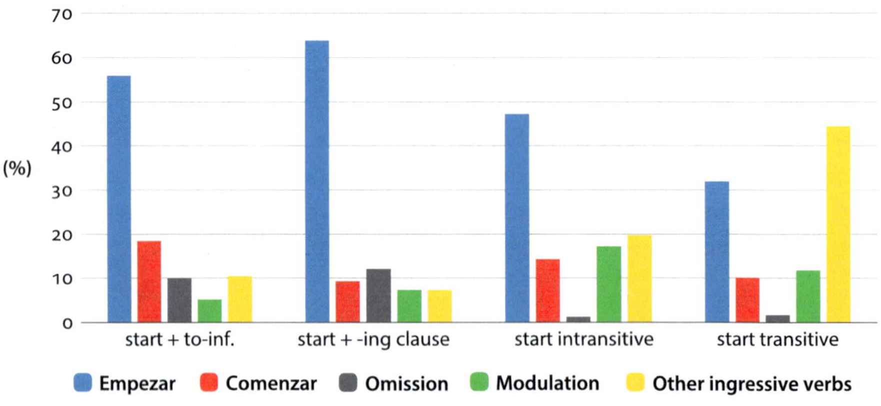

Figure 3. Spanish translations of 'start' according to the type of complementation

The clause complementation patterns again show a heavy dependence on the verb *empezar* (see (15) and (16)) and much lower frequencies of the remaining options. In contrast, the translations of 'start' as an intransitive or a transitive verb present a wider range of options, in particular ingressive verbs other than *empezar* (see (17) and (18)).

(15) He would start to say something and then stop. (EGM1E.s226)
Él empezaba a decir algo, pero se callaba. (EGM1S.s220)

(16) If I am given all the time in the world, then I start daydreaming. (EWS1E.s645)
Si me dan todo el tiempo del mundo, entonces empiezo a soñar despierto. (EWS1S.s638)

(17) I packed my things and started home. (FKO1E.s1191)
Hice las maletas y emprendí el camino de regreso a casa. (FKO1S.s1171)

(18) "They're starting a Duelling Club!" said Seamus. (FRJK1E.s112)
– ¡Van a abrir un club de duelo! – dijo Seamus-. (FRJK1S.s113)

Again, as in the case of the translations of 'begin', omission and modulation are minor strategies for the verb 'start' in its Spanish translations. Omission is more frequent in clause complementation patterns (around 10%) (see (19)) and less common in transitive and intransitive patterns (around 1%). In contrast, modulation occurs more often in transitive and intransitive patterns (10%, see (20)) and less often in clause complementation patterns (5%).

(19) " Just put your hands on his, try to start warming it ". (FHC1E.s678)
– Tú solo cógele las manos y trata de calentárselas. (FHC1S.s654)

(20) " I know, you saw him start the last game. (FWO1E.s447)
– Ya sé que lo viste salir como titular en el último partido. [I know you saw he was a starter in the last game.] (FWO1S.s446)

4.4 Comparing the Spanish translations of 'begin' and 'start'

Figure 4 shows all the translations of the English verbs 'begin' and 'start' grouped according to their Spanish translations found in PACTRES. The verb *empezar* is clearly dominant for the translation of 'begin' and 'start', with over 50% of instances in both cases.

The verb *comenzar* is the second most frequent as the equivalent for 'begin', followed by other ingressive verbs. In contrast, the verb 'start' is more often translated by other ingressive verbs than by *comenzar*, including *iniciar, arrancar, poner en marcha*, etc. This may be related to the fact that 'start' is more closely associated to spoken discourse, whereas *comenzar* is slightly more formal and occurs more often in written discourse in Spanish (Hernández Díaz 2019). Omission and modulation are minor translation strategies for both verbs 'begin' and 'start'. If we compare the translational options of 'begin' and 'start' in Spanish according to the syntactic patterns in which they occur, we find that there are a few statistically significant differences, as shown in Table 3. I have highlighted the cases with p-value < 0.05.

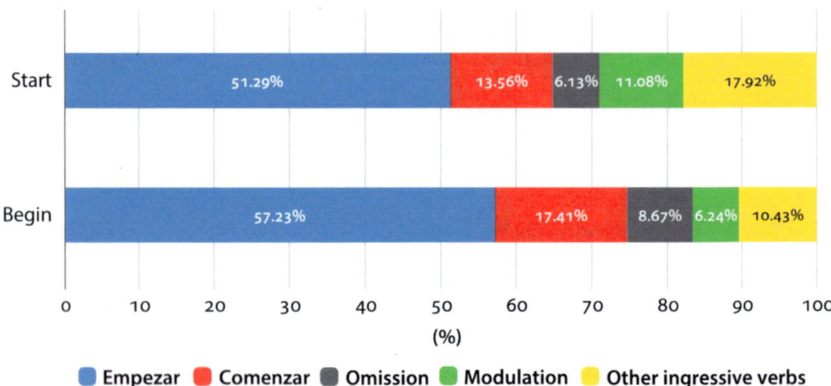

Figure 4. Translations of 'begin' and 'start' into Spanish

Table 3. Statistical analysis of the translations of 'begin' and 'start' into Spanish

	Empezar	*Comenzar*	Omission	Modulation	Other ingressive verbs	Totals
'begin' to-inf	451 (62.2%)	109 (15%)	78 (10.8%)	44 (6.1%)	43 (5.9%)	725
'start' to-inf	118 (55.9%)	39 (18.5%)	21 (9.9%)	11 (5.2%)	22 (10.4%)	211
χ^2 stat.	2.7065	1.4604	0.1123	0.2164	5.1112	
p-value	.099938	.226864	.737587	.64182	.023772	
'begin' -ing	128 (64.6%)	19 (9.6%)	29 (14.6%)	6 (3%)	16 (8.1%)	198
'start' -ing	131 (63.9%)	19 (9.3%)	25 (12.2%)	15 (7.3%)	15 (7.3%)	205
χ^2 stat.	0.0243	0.0127	0.5216	3.7472	0.0827	
p-value	.876176	.910406	.470173	.052897	.773621	
'begin' intrans.	157 (50.3%)	92 (29.5%)	9 (2.9%)	16 (5.1%)	38 (12.1%)	312
'start' intrans.	148 (47.2%)	45 (14.4%)	4 (1.3%)	54 (17.3%)	62 (19.8%)	313
χ^2 stat.	0.5765	20.8439	1.9803	23.0937	6.766	
p-value	.447697	<0.00001	.159358	<0.00001	.009291	
'begin' trans.	43 (34.1%)	17 (13.5%)	2 (1.6%)	19 (15.1%)	45 (35.7%)	126
'start' trans.	38 (31.9%)	12 (10.1%)	2 (1.7%)	14 (11.8%)	53 (44.6%)	119
χ^2 stat.	0.1331	0.6811	0.0033	0.5769	1.9853	
p-value	.715197	.409193	.954036	.447524	.158834	

The results show that when 'begin' and 'start' are followed by a to-infinitive clause, 'start' is more often translated by other ingressive verbs than 'begin', and this difference is statistically significant (p-value: .037045) (21). The other translation strategies show no significant differences in this syntactic pattern.

(21) Then he started to run. (FCU1E.s652)
Y echó a correr. (FCU1S.s629)

When 'begin' and 'start' are followed by an -ing clause, the translation strategies are very similar, with no statistically significant difference in the occurrence of any of the Spanish translational options. No statistically significant difference was found either when 'begin' and 'start' occurred as transitive verbs followed by a nominal object. This syntactic pattern is the least frequent in both cases and the distribution of the translational options in Spanish is very similar, covering the verb *empezar*, the verb *comenzar*, other ingressive verbs, omission and modulation.

The most significant differences are found when 'begin' and 'start' occur in the intransitive pattern. It is in this syntactic environment where several translational options present statistically significant differences, which points towards the fact that the sense relations expressed in this syntactic context are the ones that differ mostly between the two English verbs. The verb 'begin' is clearly much more often translated by *comenzar* than 'start' in Spanish (22). As mentioned above, this is related to the fact that 'start' occurs more often in spoken discourse (Egan 2008), whereas *comenzar* is more closely associated to written discourse (Hernández Díaz 2019).

(22) But the next wave of European transformations is only just beginning. (ELM1E.s358)
Y la siguiente oleada de transformaciones europeas no ha hecho más que comenzar. (ELM1S.s354)

In addition, the English verb 'start' is much more often modulated in the Spanish translations than 'begin', and this may also be related to the fact that it is slightly more informal and allows for this modulation (23).

(23) Vianne felt a smile start. (FHK1E.s364)
Vianne no pudo evitar sonreír. [Vianne couldn't help smile.] (FHK1S.s365)

And, finally, the verb 'start' is much more often translated into Spanish by other ingressive verbs than the verb 'begin', as in (24).

(24) Later, however, when the trouble did start, he simply sat there and watched. (FZM1E.s182)
No obstante, más tarde, cuando llegó el problema, se limitó a quedarse sentado y mirar. (FZM1S.s195)

Because other ingressive verbs are significantly more common as Spanish translations of the verb 'start' than of the verb 'begin', it may be claimed that the verb 'start' includes more sense relations different from the ones triggered by the English verb 'begin'. These other sense relations may be more detailed or precise, not only implying the initiation of the action. Some of these sense relations will be described in Section 4.5 below.

A previous study on the translations of 'begin' and 'start' into Norwegian (Egan 2012) provided interesting findings in this respect. Egan (2012) found that these two verbs are "sense synonyms when they occur with to-infinitive and gerund complements." (Egan 2012: 12). In contrast, in transitive and intransitive patterns this author found significant differences in the translations chosen, which "may point to differences in the semantics of the expression in the original language." (Egan 2012: 12).

In the present chapter, I have found similar results in the translations of 'begin' and 'start' into Spanish when followed by -ing clauses and in intransitive patterns. However, the Spanish translations revealed an additional statistically significant difference as 'start' was translated more often by other ingressive verbs than 'begin' when followed by a to-infinitive clause (see Example 21). As for the translations of 'begin' and 'start' in transitive patterns followed by a nominal object, no statistically significant difference was found in Spanish translations, as was the case in Norwegian. This may be due to the existence of cognates in Norwegian of both English verbs (*begynne* and *starte*); the Norwegian verb *starte* was never used as an equivalent of 'begin'. In Spanish there are no cognates of the English verbs 'begin' and 'start', and for this analysis I have considered separately the two most common translations – the Spanish verbs *empezar* and *comenzar*, none of which presents statistically significant differences as the translation of 'begin' and 'start' in transitive constructions. The findings shown here complement the results in Egan (2012) from the perspective of a Romance language, demonstrating similar trends in some constructions and differences in others.

One of the shared statistically significant differences in Spanish and Norwegian translations is the much wider range of other ingressive verbs as equivalents of 'start' than as equivalents of 'begin'. Therefore, the next section will expand on this issue by analysing the inventory of ingressive verbs other than *empezar* and *comenzar* in the Spanish translations of 'begin' and 'start'.

4.5 Spanish ingressive verbs as translations of 'begin' and 'start'

An exhaustive analysis of all the Spanish translations of 'begin' and 'start' in PACTRES revealed the complete inventory of all the ingressive verbs used as equivalents of these two verbs, including all other verbs apart from *empezar* or *comenzar*. Table 4 shows the complete list of these other ingressive verbs found in the Spanish translations, together with the number of tokens in each pattern. All the types found as equivalents of 'start' but not as equivalents of 'begin' are highlighted.

Table 4. Types and tokens of ingressive verbs used as translations of 'begin' and 'start'

'begin' + to inf	'start' + to inf.	'begin' + ing	'start' + ing
43 cases	22 cases	16 cases	15 cases
ponerse a: 16	ponerse a: 6	ponerse a: 10	ponerse a: 6
echarse a: 14	echarse a: 4	echarse a: 4	echarse a: 3
romper a: 5	ir a: 4	iniciar: 1	ir + gerund: 3
iniciar: 3	disponerse a: 3	emprender: 1	iniciar: 1
emprender: 2	ir + gerund: 2		encaminarse a: 1
disponerse a: 2	estar a punto de: 1		acabar de: 1
pasar a: 1	hacer amago de: 1		
	instar a: 1		
'begin' intransitive	**'start' intransitive**	**'begin' transitive**	**'start' transitive**
38 cases	62 cases	45 cases	53 cases
iniciar: 18	poner en marcha: 9	iniciar: 34	iniciar: 15
dar comienzo: 9	iniciar: 7	dar comienzo: 3	poner en marcha: 9
ponerse a: 2	echar a andar: 7	echar a: 2	encender: 5
disponerse a: 1	arrancar: 5	poner en marcha: 1	arrancar: 4
producirse: 1	ponerse a: 5	disponer: 1	abrir: 3
reanudarse: 1	encaminarse a: 4	lanzar: 1	prender: 2
emprender: 1	salir: 3	dar inicio: 1	constituir: 2
encarar: 1	partir: 2	estrenar: 1	crear: 2
surgir: 1	emprender: 2	inaugurar: 1	reemprender: 1
nacer: 1	ir: 2		acabar de: 1
originar: 1	declarar: 2		formar: 1
acercar: 1	emerger: 1		establecer: 1
	llegar: 1		cobrar: 1
	reanudar: 1		emprender: 1
	reemprender: 1		ponerse manos a la obra: 1
	dirigirse a: 1		trabar: 1
	soltar: 1		enzarzarse: 1
	provocar: 1		entablar: 1
	dar comienzo: 1		montar: 1
	encenderse: 1		
	entrar: 1		
	surgir: 1		
	disponerse a: 1		
	lanzarse a: 1		
	brotar: 1		

Table 4 illustrates that the English verb 'start' presents a much wider range of translation equivalents in Spanish than the verb 'begin', particularly in the transitive and intransitive patterns. Interestingly, all the highlighted equivalents found for 'start' did not occur at all as translations of 'begin' in the corpus. These highlighted lexical verbs in Spanish are the ones that point towards the sense relations covered by 'start' that are not covered by the verb 'begin'. The results have to be interpreted considering separately the clause complementation patterns (to-infinitive and -ing clauses), and the transitive and intransitive patterns:

1. 'begin' and 'start' followed by complement clauses: the highlighted Spanish equivalents for 'start' indicate just the beginning of the onset, but not of the actual action involved, as in (25).

   (25) I started to ask who Helmut Newton was, but then had a better idea. (FTD1E.s329)
   Estaba a punto de preguntar quién era Helmut Newton cuanto tuve una ocurrencia mejor. [I was about to ask who Helmut was, ...]. (FTD1S.s331)

   Other verbs with a similar meaning of 'being about to' in the corpus are: *acabar de, hacer amago de, estar a punto de.* These results demonstrate empirically Freed's (1979) assertion that the action following 'start' may not have taken place yet or might have been interrupted. This sense relation is not present in the verb 'begin'.
2. 'begin' and 'start' as intransitive and transitive verbs: here we find more semantic differences between the translations of the two verbs in Spanish. The list of translation equivalents of 'start' is much longer, and these equivalents represent a wider range of ingressive meanings than the translations of 'begin'. The equivalents of 'start' include semantic fields such as switching on different mechanic/electronic devices, including cars (*arrancar, encender*), references to the initial phases of a trip (*salir, partir, ir, encaminarse a, dirigirse a*) (see (26)), to building or creating something from scratch (*crear, montar, formar, constituir*), or to opening physical objects (*abrir, entrar*). These lexical specializations of the ingressive meaning are not covered by 'begin' in our corpus. Egan (2012) found similar results for the sense relation of 'start' implying the creation of a new participant or process, which was closely associated to the Norwegian translation *oppstå*, which was not used to translate 'begin'.

(26) Put him aboard, and don't leave till the car starts. (FPM1E.s438)
Acomódelo y no se vaya hasta que salga el tranvía. [Put him aboard, and don't leave until the tram leaves.] (FPM1S.s415)

To conclude this section, I may say that this trend towards the use of a much wider range of ingressive verbs other than *empezar* and *comenzar* as translations of 'begin' and 'start', which is statistically significant in intransitive patterns (see Table 3), seems to be spreading to other syntactic environments in Spanish translations, in particular to to-infinitive complements.

5. Conclusions

The present chapter provided a detailed analysis of the Spanish equivalents of the near-synonymous English verbs 'begin' and 'start' as found in the English-Spanish parallel corpus PACTRES. The aim was to provide a complete inventory of the translational options to try and identify any differences between these two verbs via their Spanish equivalents, as "systematic differences in translation equivalents may serve to highlight differences in meaning." (Egan 2012: 13).

Syntactically, the verbs 'begin' and 'start' both occur followed by clause complements in the form of to-infinitive and -ing clauses, or either in intransitive or transitive patterns followed by a nominal object. It was found that 'begin' is more often followed by clausal complements (70%), whereas 'start' shows 50% of cases with clausal complements and 50% of cases in transitive or intransitive patterns.

Semantically, the verbs 'begin' and 'start' share a clear ingressive meaning, and the empirical data analysed reveal that the most common Spanish verbs used for translating both verbs are *empezar* and *comenzar*. Other translational options include modulation, omission and also other ingressive verbs such as, *iniciar, ponerse a, echarse a*, etc. The results show that the list of translational equivalents in the form of other ingressive verbs is much longer for 'start' than for 'begin', illustrating the fact that 'start' has a wider range of meanings within a general ingressive framework.

In sentences where 'start' is followed by a to-infinitive or an -ing clause, several Spanish equivalents exemplify that the action is about to start, but has not started yet, and this sense relation never appears in the translations of 'begin'. In intransitive and transitive patterns, the translations found in PACTRES show that 'start' is translated into Spanish by a much wider range of different ingressive verbs than 'begin'. These Spanish translations identify sense relations covered by 'start', but not by 'begin', including switching on mechanic/electronic devices, initiating a trip, building or creating something from scratch, and opening physical objects.

Because translation corpora "contain the intuitive linguistic responses of competent language users to a series of linguistic prompts" (Egan 2012: 13), the translational solutions provided highlight differences in meanings between near-synonyms in the source language. Identifying different translational solutions does not necessarily mean that there are differences in meaning, but if clear trends can be observed of one particular item as translated by certain equivalents, whereas the near-synonym presents a clearly different trend with different patterns, these trends helps us distinguish different sense relations of near-synonyms in the source language. Unquestionably, other factors might also be at play and not necessarily reflected in the translation equivalents, for example collocational issues in the target language, typological differences between languages, the semantic role of the subject of 'begin' and 'start', etc., but the similarities and differences found in the translation equivalents in a parallel corpus may point towards similarities or differences in the original constructions. Authentic translational options may highlight aspects of the semantics of the items in the source language. Further studies on the near-synonyms 'begin' and 'start' should focus on collocational trends in the target language to provide a clearer picture of the semantic differences identified here.

Funding

This research has been funded by grant PID2020-114064-RB-I00 awarded by the Spanish Ministry for Science and Innovation.

References

Brinton, Laurel. 1988. *The Development of English Aspectual Systems*. Cambridge: CUP.

Comrie, Bernard. 1976. *Aspect*. Cambridge: CUP.

Comrie, Bernard. 2001. Some thoughts on the relation between aspect and Aktionsart. In *Functional Grammar: Aspect and Aspectuality. Tense and Temporality: Essays in Honor of Alexander Bondarko*, Adrian Barentsen & Youri Poupynin (eds), 43–50. Munich: Lincom.

doi Declerck, Renaat, Reed, Susan & Cappelle, Bert. 2006. *The Grammar of the English Tense System: A Comprehensive Analysis*. Berlin: Mouton de Gruyter.

Dixon, Robert. 1991. *A New Approach to English Grammar on Semantic Principles*. Oxford: Clarendon Press.

Dixon, Robert. 2005. *A Semantic Approach to English Grammar*. Oxford: OUP.

doi Duffley, Patrick. 1999. The use of the infinitive and the -ing after verbs denoting the beginning, middle and end of an event. *Folia Linguistica* 33: 295–331.

doi Egan, Thomas. 2008. *Non-finite Complementation: A Usage-based Study of Infinitive and -ing Clauses in English*. Amsterdam: Rodopi.

Egan, Thomas. 2012. Using translation corpora to explore synonymy and polysemy. In *Aspects of Corpus Linguistics: Compilation, Annotation, Analysis* [Varieng. Studies in Variation, Contacts and Change in English 12], Signe Oksefjell Ebelig, Jarle Ebeling & Hilde Hasselgård (eds). <http://www.helsinki.fi/varieng/journal/volumes/12/egan/> (28 May 2023).

Freed, Alice. 1979. *The Semantics of English Aspectual Complementation.* Dordrecht: Reidel.

Hernández Díaz, Axel. 2019. Gramaticalización y diacronía de las perífrasis comenzar a y empezar a + infinitivo. *Boletín de Filología* 54(2): 81–110.

Kreidler, Charles W. 1998. *Introducing English Semantics.* London: Routledge.

Mair, Christian. 2003. Gerundial complements after begin and start: Grammatical and sociolinguistic factors, and how they work against each other. In *Determinants of Grammatical Variation in English*, Günter Rohdenburg & Britta Mondorf (eds), 329–343. Berlin: Mouton de Gruyter.

Murphy, M. Lynne. 2003. *Semantic Relations and the Lexicon.* Cambridge: CUP.

Newmeyer, Frederick J. 1975. *English Aspectual Verbs.* The Hague: Mouton.

Sanjurjo-González, Hugo & Izquierdo, Marlén. 2019. PACTRES 2.0. A parallel corpus for cross-linguistic research. In *Parallel Corpora for Contrastive and Translation Studies* [Studies in Corpus Linguistics 90], Irene Doval & M. Teresa Sánchez Nieto (eds), 215–232. Amsterdam: John Benjamins.

Vosberg, Uwe. 2011. The role of extractions and horror aequi in the evolution of -ing complements in Modern English. In *Determinants of Grammatical Variation in English*, Günter Rohdenburg & Britta Mondorf (eds), 305–328. Berlin: De Gruyter.

CHAPTER 6

RUN away!
Exploring the iceberg of core vocabulary with English-Spanish parallel corpora

Belén Labrador
University of León

Drawing on a previous translation-based study on the manner and path of motion in English and Spanish (Labrador 2018), this paper examines a tier-1 word (Beck et al. 2002), the verb RUN, with the aim of illustrating how parallel corpora can assist in revealing the iceberg underneath the tip of core vocabulary, i.e., in providing the co-text, uses and translations of basic words. The parallel corpus P-ACTRES has been used to analyze all the occurrences of RUN, comparing fiction and non-fiction, identifying the most frequent collocates, and contrasting its use followed by a satellite with the corresponding translations. The results show a more frequent use of this combination in fiction and crosslinguistic differences in terms of patterns and collocates in the expression of motion.

Keywords: parallel corpus, English-Spanish, core vocabulary, motion

1. Introduction

The core vocabulary of English includes approximately the two or three thousand most frequently used words in everyday communication (Nation 1990). As this does not appear to be a large amount of vocabulary, it comes as good news to learners of English. Some other interesting and surprising facts about word frequencies are shown in Table 1, a chart with the number of lemmas and the percentages of content in the Oxford English Corpus, where we can see that (a) the 10 most common words constitute 25% of spoken and written English, which means that one in every four words used in English is one of these words; (b) it is necessary to know 100 words to understand 50% of everything native speakers say and write and 1.000 words to understand 75% of what they say; and (c) native speakers use just 7.000 words for 90% of everything they say and write (Oxford Dictionaries 2021).

https://doi.org/10.1075/scl.113.06lab

Table 1. Number of lemmas and percentages of content in Oxford English Corpus. (Oxford Dictionaries 2011)

Vocabulary size (no. lemmas)	% of content in OEC	Example lemmas
10	25%	the, of, and, to, that, have
100	50%	from, because, go, me, our, well, way
1000	75%	girl, win, decide, huge, difficult, series
7000	90%	tackle, peak, crude, purely, dude, modest
50,000	95%	saboteur, autocracy, calyx, conformist
> 1,000,000	99%	laggardly, endobenthic, pomological

When students learn about these facts, they may be suspicious at first, but also optimistic and confident at the same time, as they tend to associate the learning process with the quantity of data to study. Therefore, studying these numbers of words seems to be an easily achievable task. However, they soon realize that they have jumped to this conclusion too readily, as they have been studying English for a considerable number of years, they think they know more than two or three thousand words, even seven thousand words, which account for 90% of the language (Oxford Dictionaries 2021), but they do not seem to master the language yet.

The reason for this is the fact that the difficulty in learning a foreign language lies not so much in the quantity, or breadth, but the quality, or depth, of vocabulary knowledge. Learning a word involves much more than simply being able to recognize it, grasp its meaning, know how to translate it, or even how to spell and pronounce it (Thornbury 2004). There are different degrees of knowing vocabulary in the same way as there are different degrees of knowing people: first, we meet them, then we get to know them until we finally truly know them. We may understand a word, but we may not be able to use it properly; maybe we can both understand it and use it but only in its main non-idiomatic senses; perhaps we can understand it only in context and use it only if prompted; we may understand it and use it perfectly well with all its different meanings, etc. Vocabulary depth is not a matter of all-or-nothing. It is a matter of granularity, which conveys either or both the productive (or active) and receptive (or passive) knowledge. Words can be seen as coarse-grained materials with few large components (how to spell them, how to pronounce them, and how to translate them) and then we can also need to go deeper, into further detail, to fully understand their uses and nuances and to be able to remember them; "the more one engages with a word (deeper processing), the more likely the word will be remembered for later use" (Schmitt 2000: 120).

The learning process of words involves different degrees of comprehension and production, and corpus-based lexical studies can help L2 teachers and students to gain insight into the use of core vocabulary. Monolingual corpora provide the co-textual information of words or expressions and by using parallel corpora as well, we can also retrieve further information about their meanings and uses in different syntactic structures and collocational patterns, and about their equivalences in the second or foreign language. "Due to the incremental nature of vocabulary acquisition, repeated exposures are necessary to consolidate a new word in the learner's mind" (Schmitt & Carter 2000: 4). An analogy can be made with corpora as submarines, which let us see the part of the iceberg that is beneath the surface, as magnifying glasses, or as microscopes, which enable us to see all these fine-grained aspects, what is hidden, hence not so visible at first sight, and many different types of examples for those repeated exposures.

2. Tier-based approach

When we are dealing with vocabulary teaching, the first important thing is to select the words that will be taught, to decide what to teach, and consequently how to teach it as well. Vocabulary can be divided into three broad categories or tiers, in terms of frequency and difficulty, according to the tier-based approach (Beck et al. 2002).

> The first tier consists of the most basic words, e.g., *warm, dog, tired, run, talk, party, swim, look*, and so on. These are the words that typically appear in oral conversations, and so children are exposed to them at high frequency from a very early stage. (Beck et al. 2002: 9)

The second tier corresponds to high frequency and more complex words, "words that are of high utility for mature language users and are found across a variety of domains. Examples include *contradict, circumstances, precede, auspicious, fervent, and retrospect*" (Beck et al. 2002: 9). The third tier corresponds to low-frequency and usually technical words. "Some examples of Tier Three words might be *filibuster, pantheon* and *epidermis*. In general, a rich understanding of these words would not be of high utility for most learners" (Beck et al. 2002: 9). In line with this approach, Marzano (2012: 31) holds that "not all terms in the English language should receive equal consideration from an instructional perspective since a large proportion of terms are not very frequently encountered".

There are 8.000 tier-1-word families (Beck et al. 2002: 10); these words are common because they appear in everyday life. Thus, it is considered that they do not require instruction. However, these words are familiar only for English native speakers or EOSs (English-Only-Students), not for foreign language learners or ELLs (English Language Learners). Therefore, they do require academic instruction in their case: “Basic words or tier-1 words (Beck, McKeown & Kucan, 2002) are common words that EOS already know. However, ELLs have to be taught these basic words” (Chung 2012: 109).

3. The expression of path and manner of motion

Verbs that belong to the tier-1 group are frequent, which justifies their inclusion in the syllabus, and apparently easy to learn, especially since they tend to be simple from a morphological and lexical perspective. However, their use may render them more complicated from a syntactic point of view, as can be the case with some action verbs used when expressing motion.

The expression of path and manner of motion tends to differ between satellite-framed languages, like English, and verb-framed languages, like Spanish. In satellite-framed languages, the path of motion is typically expressed with a satellite “entity which acts as a spatial reference point for the motion/ location of the figure” (Talmy 2007: 71), usually a preposition e.g., ‘out of’, and the manner is expressed with a verb e.g., ‘ran’, in a sentence like ‘I ran out of the house’. In verb-framed languages, the path is expressed through a verb e.g., *salí,* and the manner through a gerund or a prepositional phrase e.g., *corriendo*, in a sentence like for example, ‘Salí corriendo de la casa’ > *I went out running of the house.*

This typology of languages according to these patterns was first pointed out by Talmy (1985) and has led to a considerable amount of research: some scholars have studied the process of acquisition of these patterns in the expression of motion events in L1 informants; they have elicited narratives in different languages: English, German, Spanish, Hebrew, and Turkish (Berman & Slobin 1994), English and Korean (Choi & Bowerman 1991), English and Spanish (Slobin 1996). Others have analyzed translations of different pairs of languages, for example from English into Spanish (Cifuentes-Férez 2013, Author 2018), or into Spanish and Basque (Ibarretxe-Antuñano 2003), from German into Spanish (Molés-Cases 2018), among others.

Some of the studies on the expression of motion across languages have focused on foreign language teaching, in cases where the learner’s L2 belongs to one of the two main language types and the learner’s L1 or mother tongue to the other, e.g., English and French (Nicoladis & Brisard 2002), English and Spanish (Hochestein et al. 2006), English and Japanese (Stringer 2007), Spanish and German/ French/ Italian (Hijazo 2010). These studies, as well as the present paper, are prompted by the need to deal with the difficulties arising from this contrastive difference in the expression of motion, which sometimes causes L2 learners or translation students to misuse basic verbs, as they tend to reproduce the syntactic pattern of their L1.

In translation, when one of these expressions is translated from one type of language into a language belonging to the other type, there are usually cases of crossed transposition, e.g., He limped across the street>*Il a traversé la rue en boitant* (he has crossed the street limping) (Molina & Hurtado Albir 2002: 499). Crossed transposition implies a double shift of part-of-speech from the source text to the target text. It is called 'crossed' transposition because it is a double case of transposition and the order of the elements involved is reversed. An example of crossed transposition in translation from English into Spanish can be seen in Figure 1, where the English word 'ran', which is a finite verb, is translated as a non-finite verb with the function of a manner adjunct in Spanish (*corriendo*). On the other hand, the meaning conveyed in English by the satellite *out* is expressed in Spanish by the main verb, *salí*.

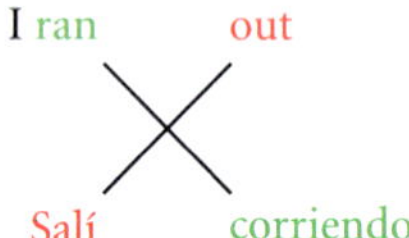

Figure 1. Example of crossed transposition

Although crossed transposition is the expected type of transfer between a satellite-framed language like English and a verb-framed language like Spanish, a previous study shows that, despite being a common translation solution, crossed transposition ranks fourth, after implicitation of either path or manner and compression of both meanings in a verb. In implicitation of path, e.g., 'jumped down'> ... *saltaron*, the path, expressed through 'down' in this example, is lost in translation and in implicitation of manner, for example, 'I climbed down off the scaffold'>*Bajé del andamio*, it is the manner of motion (expressed through 'climbed' in the second example) that is not explicitly translated into Spanish. In the cases of compression, both meanings are retained but expressed condensed in a verb in Spanish, e.g., 'which blew up during the battle'>*que explotó durante la batalla* (Labrador 2018).

4. Analysis

In this corpus-based study, the lexeme RUN has been put under the spotlight. The selection of this lexeme was made on the grounds of (a) frequency, (b) difficulty, and (c) usefulness: RUN is a prototypical tier-1 word, since it is listed as one of the examples of this group of words in Beck et al. (2002), so it is a very frequent word in English; in addition, it was found to be the most frequent verb in the cases of crossed transposition in an English-Spanish contrastive study on the expression of motion (Labrador 2018).

Like many other words belonging to the core vocabulary of English, RUN is apparently easy to learn; most learners of English, even beginners, would claim to know this word. However, they usually fail to use it with other meanings apart from the literal use of *correr* in simple intransitive contexts, which results in the underuse of this common word in English. Sometimes we tend to focus on explaining difficult words to the detriment of easy words with interesting and varied uses. By paying more attention to them, we can prevent our students from making mistakes or unidiomatic sentences like *'he entered the room running', caused by negative transfer from their mother tongue, instead of saying 'he ran into the room'. These types of mistakes found in the students' productions constitute one of the reasons for this piece of research and the selection of the lexeme RUN as the object of study.

The problem with learning core vocabulary is that, at first, students can only see the tip of the iceberg, which is the concept, the spelling, the pronunciation, the equivalent in Spanish, and the different forms of the lexeme. However, there is much more to it than meets the eye, and parallel corpora can help us to explore the bulk, all those aspects that lie underneath, that are less well-known to learners, aspects that have to do with their frequency, connotations, register, derivations, grammatical behavior, combinations, collocations, co-text, etc.

For this paper, the parallel corpus used has been a subcorpus, containing English source texts and their corresponding translations into Spanish of the P-ACTRES corpus (Izquierdo et al. 2008 and Sanjurjo-González & Izquierdo 2019). P-ACTRES 2.0, is a bidirectional parallel corpus which contains over 4 million words (4,179,282), of which 2,523,458 words correspond to the subcorpus of English STs and Spanish TTs (the former P-ACTRES 1.0) – the subcorpus used for the purpose of this paper – and 1,655,824 words to the subcorpus of Spanish STs and English TTs. The repository of textual pairs in this second direction is still under construction. It comprises texts or excerpts of texts from different text-types: fiction books, non-fiction books, newspaper articles, magazine articles and miscellanea. It is a corpus of general language which includes a wide variety of authors, topics and writing styles (for a demo and further information see <http://actres.unileon.es>).

The search yielded 926 occurrences of RUN ('run', 'runs', 'running', 'ran') in the fictional and non-fictional source texts in English. All these aligned concordances were downloaded and analyzed manually. The analysis consisted of two phases: (a) an intralinguistic analysis and classification of the uses found, and (b) an interlinguistic analysis of the translations into Spanish of the group of occurrences expressing path and manner of motion in English, and their subsequent classification applying Pym's typology (2018) of translation solutions. The following section presents the results of these findings.

5. Results

5.1 Intralinguistic stage

The first stage of the process was intralinguistic: I focused on the uses of the different forms of the lexeme RUN: 'run', 'runs', 'ran', and 'running', in the English source texts. As can be seen in Table 2, RUN is used twice as much in fiction as it is in non-fiction. The figures in brackets are the raw numbers of occurrences but the fiction and the non-fiction subcorpora have different sizes so the numbers are also given per million words. The expression of motion is much higher in fiction, and intransitive uses rank second, whereas transitive and intransitive uses are more common in non-fiction. Another common pattern combines a transitive use with the expression of motion and some particular collocates; finally, there are some other minor cases. The blue oval lines indicate the highest figures in each case: the two most important uses in non-fiction are the intransitive and transitive uses and, in fiction, the expression of motion and the intransitive uses.

Table 2. Uses of RUN in the P-ACTRES fiction and non-fiction subcorpora per million words

Uses	Total no. cases (1,791,577 w)	Non-fiction (514,786 w)	Fiction (1,276,791 w)
Expression of motion (verb + satellite)	437	77.70 pmw (40)	310.93 pmw (397)
Intransitive uses	253	114.61 pmw (59)	151.94 pmw (194)
Transitive uses	175	110.72 pmw (57)	92.41 pmw (118)
Transitive use and expression of motion	55	3.88 pmw (2)	41.51 pmw (53)
Others	7	5.82 pmw (3)	3.13 pmw (4)
Total	927	312.75 pmw (161)	599.94 pmw (766)

Regarding the intransitive uses, there are instances of both animate and inanimate subjects, some of them followed by a time or place adjunct e.g., 'home', 'all day and night', 'at 3.30', 'on schedule', 'x times a week'; others by purpose adjuncts like 'for your life/ for their lives', 'for cover', 'for help', 'for comfort', 'for dinner'. The other two common patterns are (a) RUN plus an adjective or adverb like 'run free/ deep/ high/ low (on)/ parallel/ perpendicular/ short of/ late/ unchecked/ counter to/ amok/ unruly' and (b) 'run' followed by a prepositional phrase: 'in the family', especially with diseases or traits that are inherited and, 'in the veins', with the noun 'blood'.

The transitive uses include collocates that have to do with:

a. the distances covered by the action of running, for example, 'race', 'yards', 'miles', 'marathons', 'blocks', 'laps', 'way', 'course', 'bleachers', 'the touchline', 'the bases';
b. something that is organized, maintained, or managed, in a more figurative meaning of RUN, like 'school', 'business', 'farm', 'operations', 'a city', 'a region', 'a country', 'office', 'department', 'empire', 'foundation', 'the police (force)', 'squad', 'place', 'camp', 'factory', 'system', 'training', 'database', 'administration', 'show', 'armies', 'service', 'restaurant', 'workshop', 'tutorial', 'a railroad', 'an ER', 'pool house', 'contest', 'firm', 'companies', 'corporations', 'camp', 'orchard', 'one's life', 'fares', 'a fitness centre', 'kindergarten', 'crew', 'kitchen', 'seminars', 'war', 'simulations', 'magazine', 'cell', 'team';
c. devices or vehicles that are operated, such as 'car', 'aircraft', 'boats', 'heater';
d. 'a test', 'check', 'experiment', 'study', or 'interview' that is conducted.

Some interesting collocations found include 'run errands', 'run a risk', and 'run riot'; finally, three specific uses are worth noticing: newspapers or similar subjects 'run stories' or 'cartoons'; 'to run something by somebody', as in Example (1), and another minor use includes inversion of the subject (usually a noun like 'report', 'mantra', etc.) and the verb, always preceded by direct speech, as in Example (2).

(1) 'Want me to run them by you?'

(2) '"These are extraordinary times" runs the mantra.'

We can also see that some examples combine a transitive use with the expression of motion; in most cases, they include the words 'finger', 'hand', or something similar and then a satellite, as in Example (3); finally, there is an idiomatic expression, where 'running' coordinates with 'up' or 'off': 'up and running' or 'off and running'.

(3) 'running a nervous hand through his dark hair'.

5.2 Interlinguistic stage

The subsequent part of the analysis, which is interlinguistic, describes the translation solutions used for the expression of motion. Drawing on Pym's (2018) typology of translation solutions, we can see, in Table 3, that one of his categories, namely, 'density change', is the most common translation solution found for RUN in expressions of motion, especially in fiction. In density change

> there is a marked change in the amount of information available in a given textual space. Translators can reduce textual density by using solutions that spread information over a greater textual space, using Explicitation, Generalisation, and Multiple Translation, as when the one word Gemeinde is translated as the six words 'Gemeinde, German unit of local government' (Newmark 1981: 31). Using the inverse solutions can increase density. (Pym 2018: 43)

Another category, which includes crossed transposition, ranks second: It is 'perspective change' (Pym 2018); there are also cases of 'modulation' (Vinay & Darbelnet (1972[1958]), where "an object is seen from a different point of view, as in a hotel being *Complet* ('full') in French and has *No Vacancies* in English.". Then we have cases of 'copying structure':

> syntactic or compositional structures are brought across from one language into another, as in *Open mouth and lend voice to tongue* (from the television series Spartacus), where Latin syntactic and metaphorical structures are used in English. (Pym 2018: 43)

Finally, there are just a few cases of 'cultural correspondence', "different elements in different cultures are presented as carrying out similar functions [...] culture-specific items (currency units, measures, etc.)." (Pym 2018: 44) and 'text tailoring', "semantic or performative material in the start text is deleted, updated, or added to on the levels of both form and content" (Pym 2018: 44).

The satellites found are listed in Table 4 in order of frequency. As can be noticed, the path that has to do with getting 'out' or 'into' a place seems to prevail over the others.

Perspective change includes cases of (a) crossed transposition and (b) modulation. As can be seen in Examples (4) to (8), the words that express manner of motion are the verb RUN in English and expressions like *a la carrera, a toda velocidad, corriendo, a toda prisa, a todo correr* in Spanish and those expressing path of motion are a satellite in English: 'across', 'ahead', 'back', 'down', 'in', 'past', etc. and verbs like *cruzar, adelantarse, regresar, bajar, entrar, salir, atravesar, ascender*, etc. in Spanish.

Table 3. Translation solutions found for RUN + satellite in fiction and non-fiction per million words

Translation solution	Total no. cases	Non-fiction	Fiction
Density change	260	54.39 pmw (28)	181.70 pmw (232)
Perspective change	96	13.59 pmw (7)	69.70 pmw (89)
Copying structure	69	3.88 pmw (2)	52.47 pmw (67)
Cultural correspondence	11	1.94 pmw (1)	7.83 pmw (10)
Text tailoring	1	1.94 pmw (1)	0
Total	437	75.75 pmw (39)	311.71 pmw (398)

Table 4. Satellites found in combination with RUN

Satellite	Hits	Satellite	Hits	Satellite	Hits
out	52	from	13	at	3
into	44	over	13	beside	3
away	38	toward/s	11	about	2
down	36	on	9	overhead	2
through	33	for	6	aboard	1
to	29	in	6	alongside	1
back	21	after	5	behind	1
up	20	upstairs	5	beneath	1
across	16	downstairs	4	beyond	1
along	16	forward	4	outside	1
off	16	past	4	round	1
around	14	ahead	3	underneath	1

(4) 'Simon ran across the street.'
Simon cruzó la calle a la carrera.
Simon crossed the street hurriedly.

(5) 'The older one, a boy, probably four, ran ahead'.
El mayor, un chico probablemente de unos cuatro años, se adelantó corriendo.
The older, a boy probably four-years-old, went ahead running.

(6) 'He ran back to his work station.'
Regresó a toda velocidad a su puesto de trabajo.
He went back at full speed to his work station.

(7) 'They ran through the City Hall garage'.
Atravesaron a todo correr el garaje del edificio municipal.
They went through at full speed the garage of the City Hall.

(8) 'ran up the grand stairs of Italian marble'
ascendió la majestuosa escalinata de mármol italiano a toda prisa.
went up the grand stairs of marble Italian in a hurry.

Examples (9) to (12) are cases of modulation; the words underlined in Spanish are the translations of the expression of motion, but they do not express only path or manner specifically. As can be seen, the perspective is slightly different (the subject becomes the object and vice versa); however, the meaning stays the same.

(9) 'A chill ran down my spine'.
Sentí un escalofrío a lo largo de la columna vertebral.
I felt a chill all along my spine.

(10) 'Garbo's famous quote often ran through Delaney's mind'.
Delaney recordaba la famosa frase de la actriz.
Delaney remembered the famous sentence of the actress.

(11) 'the money ran out'.
se quedó sin dinero.
Was left without money.

(12) 'to let the juices run out'.
para que suelten jugo.
So that they let go juice.

In the cases of density change, which is the most frequent translation solution found (59.49% of all the occurrences), a single verb is used in Spanish, so the expression is reduced from two elements to one, sometimes to convey both meanings, manner, and path (compression, as in Examples (13) and (14)) and some others just to express one of them, because the other is left implicit – implicitation of path (Examples (15) and (16)) or implicitation of manner (Examples (17) and (18)). In both cases, the information is "spread over [...] less textual space" (Pym 2018: 57).

(13) 'She ran along the corridor'.
Recorrió el pasillo.
S/he ran along the corridor.

(14) 'I ran around'
correteaba
I ran around

(15) 'I ought to run away but I can't'.
Debería correr pero no puedo.
I ought to run but I can't.

(16) 'he and Schramm ran out to buy pencils'.
él y Schramm corrieron a comprar lapiceros.
he and Schramm ran to buy pencils.

(17) 'grab them as you run out the door'.
cójalos cuando salga.
grab them when you go out.

(18) 'somebody ran to a drugstore'.
alguien fue al supermercado.
somebody went to the supermarket.

Some other times, however, the same structure used in English is kept in the translation: these are cases of copying structure, where the verb is used to express manner and a satellite to express path, as in Examples (19) to (21).

(19) 'He left the window and ran downstairs'
Se apartó de la ventana y corrió escalera abajo
ran stairs down

(20) 'Lowell ran through some market stands'.
Lowell corrió a través de algunos puestos del mercado.
Lowell ran through some stands of the market.

(21) '... who fell down in horse manure running after a posse'
... que cayó al suelo cubierto de estiércol de caballo cuando corría en pos de un grupo armado
who fell onto the ground covered in manure when she ran after an armed group

And some minor cases include instances of cultural correspondence, with idiomatic expressions to translate the expressions of motion (Examples (22) and (23)) and of text tailoring, where part of the text has been deleted in the translation.

(22) 'Juices ran in his mouth'.
la boca se le hacía agua.
the mouth was done water.

(23) 'the rumor had run out of gas'.
el rumor había perdido fuelle.
the rumor had lost breath.

The results have revealed that, although crossed transposition (or perspective change in Pym's terms) is frequent, RUN follows the general tendency in Spanish for density change – using only a verb either encompassing both meanings, path, and manner or making one of them implicit. After them comes copying structure – expressing manner through a verb and path through a satellite; finally, other minor translation solutions are cultural correspondence and text tailoring.

6. Discussion and pedagogical implications

The particular rhetorical style typical of a verb-framed language or a satellite-framed language is developed at an early age and once established, difficult to change (Berman & Slobin 1994); therefore, if the particular rhetorical style of English as a satellite-framed language is not acquired soon, it may lead to the production of unidiomatic sentences expressing motion even by advanced learners of English (Hijazo-Gascon 2010: 2–3). Therefore, this type of expressions should be taught at an early stage, for young Spanish learners of English to acquire this pattern as soon and as naturally as possible.

There are different kinds of activities that can be used to implement this learning process in the classroom, both through direct methods, like the data-driven learning (DDL) approach (Johns 1991) or the corpus-aided discovery learning (CADL) approach (Gavioli 2000) and through indirect methods, using teaching resources and classroom tasks based on the findings of corpus research (Boulton 2010). As examples of the former, some aligned concordance lines from a parallel corpus can be selected and even edited for simplification purposes, so that students can discover which elements express path and which elements express manner of motion in each language. As examples of the latter, genre-based activities can be used, for instance, story-telling activities, as the expression of motion seems "to be an important feature of children's short stories (they occur significantly more frequently in this genre than in general language)" (Labrador 2018). Stories can be read or told, by the teacher or by the learners; these stories would have been selected to ensure they include good examples of expressions of movement, e.g., 'and Gretel <u>pushed</u> the witch <u>into</u> the boiling water', 'the wolf <u>blew</u> the straw and stick houses <u>down</u>', 'the ugly duckling decided to <u>run away</u>', etc.

Other narrative texts, pictures, flashcards, songs, or videos can be used which give rise to descriptions of situations where characters move in a particular way. The teacher provides controlled exposure to these expressions in receptive activities (students read or listen to a text where these expressions occur) or elicits them in productive activities (students are prompted to use these expressions of motion). In the productive activities, teachers can offer corrective feedback rephrasing or reformulating (one of the possible responses to give corrective feedback suggested by Thornbury 1999: 117–119) an unidiomatic phrase uttered by a pupil who has translated literally from Spanish, e.g., Student: *'he entered the room running' – Teacher: 'Ok, he ran into the room'.

7. Conclusions

In this corpus-based study, a tier-1 word, the lexeme RUN, and its translations into Spanish have been analyzed, with teaching purposes in mind, to provide an intralinguistic and interlinguistic perspective on its wide range of meanings, nuances, grammatical and collocational behaviors, and cross-linguistic correspondences. When we are dealing with vocabulary in foreign language teaching, it is important to consider not only what words to teach but also their key collocations and patterns. This focus on the co-text and collocational behavior of tier-1 words is intended not only to increase learners' passive knowledge, that is, for them to understand the different meanings and uses of these words, but also to increase their active knowledge, i.e., for them to produce language that includes these other less-known uses. The fact that the word RUN is more commonly found in fiction and especially in a particular pattern expressing motion indicates that the primary meaning of this action verb prevails; however, other frequent uses (e.g., transitive uses in non-fiction) seem to reflect other metaphorical meanings and common collocations.

Additionally, by providing Spanish learners of English with crosslinguistic equivalences in explicit grammar teaching exercises, DDL activities with selected concordance lines or communicative lessons including these patterns, they can be more aware of the differences in the expression of motion between the two languages. Therefore, they will tend to use the idiomatic pattern in English rather than (a) simply using a single verb (without a particle), thus failing to notice that there is often density change in the transfer between English and Spanish or (b) keeping the same pattern as in Spanish, thus failing to notice that there is often perspective change between these two languages.

The preference for density change as a translation solution in the translations into Spanish of the expression of motion in English may be connected to the linguistic economy, as, in general, the English satellites (mostly prepositions) are considerably shorter than the Spanish complements expressing manner (mostly non-finite verb forms and prepositional phrases). In addition, as Spanish verbs tend to be morphologically and semantically more complex, they can more easily convey both the meaning of path and the meaning of manner without the need for other words: "An attempt to express both meanings outside the verb at all costs might result in long and awkward sentences in Spanish" (Labrador 2018: 225).

The final aim of this research into the complex aspects of a basic little word like RUN is to show how parallel corpora can assist in giving a bigger picture of the iceberg underneath core vocabulary. The results can have a positive impact on contrastive analysis, by raising awareness of the different uses and key collocations of common words in each language, on error analysis, in the prediction of mistakes, and, consequently, on the instruction of both translator trainees and learners of English, fostering an increase in their use of frequent and idiomatic uses of basic words. By increasing the exposure to varied utterances with RUN, students are more likely to reuse them in their productions, thus enhancing their linguistic and communicative competencies.

References

Beck, Isabel, McKeown, Margaret, & Kucan, Linda. 2002. *Bringing Words to Life: Robust Vocabulary Instruction*. New York NY: Guilford.

Berman, Ruth A. & Slobin, Dan Isaac. 1994. *Relating Events in Narrative: A Crosslinguistic Developmental Study*. Hillsdale NJ: Lawrence Erlbaum Associates.

doi Boulton, Alex. 2010. Data-driven learning: Taking the computer out of the equation. *Language Learning* 60(3): 534–572.

doi Choi, Soonja & Bowerman, Melissa. 1991. Learning to express motion events in English and Korean: The influence of language-specific lexicalization patterns. *Cognition* 41: 83–121..

Chung, Stephanie F. 2012. Research-based vocabulary instruction for English language learners. *The Reading Matrix* 12(2): 105–120.

Cifuentes-Férez, Paula. 2013. El tratamiento de los verbos de manera de movimiento y de los caminos en la traducción Inglés-Español de textos narrativos. *Miscelánea: A Journal of English and American Studies* 47: 53–80.

Gavioli, Laura. 2000. The learner as researcher: Introducing corpus concordancing in the classroom. In *Learning with Corpora*, Guy Aston (ed.), 108–137. Houston TX: Athelstan.

Hijazo-Gascon, Alberto. 2010. La adquisición de eventos de movimiento en segundas lenguas. *Interlingüística* 20. UEA repository.

doi Hochestein, Jill, Eisenberg, Ann & Naigles, Letitia. 2006. Is he floating across or crossing afloat? Cross-influence of L1 and L2 in Spanish-English bilingual adults. *Language and Cognition* 9(3): 249–61.

Ibarretxe-Antuñano, Iraide. 2003. What translation tells us about motion: A contrastive study of typologically different languages. *IJES: International Journal of English Studies* 3(2): 151–175.

doi Izquierdo, Marlén, Hofland, Knut & Reigem, Øystein. 2008. The ACTRES Parallel Corpus: An English-Spanish translation corpus. *Corpora* 3(1): 31–41.

Johns, Tim. 1991. Should you be persuaded: Two examples of data-driven learning. *Classroom Concordancing. English Language Research Journal* 4: 1–16.

Labrador, Belén. 2018. Crossed transposition in a corpus-based study of motion in English and Spanish. *Languages in Contrast* 18(2): 207–229.

Marzano, Robert. 2012. A comprehensive approach to vocabulary instruction. *Voices from the Middle* 20(1): 31–35.

Molés-Cases, Teresa. 2018. Some advances in the study of the translation of manner of motion events. Integrating key concepts of Descriptive Translation Studies and 'Thinking for Translating'. *Review of Cognitive Linguistics* 16(1): 153–191.

Molina, Lucía & Hurtado Albir, Amparo. 2002. Translation techniques revisited: A dynamic and functionalistic approach. *Meta* 47(4): 498–512.

Nation, Ian. 1990. *Teaching and Learning Vocabulary*. New York NY: Newbury House.

Newmark, Peter. 1981. *Approaches to Translation*. Oxford: Pergamon Press.

Nicoladis, Elena & Brisard, Frank. 2002. Encoding motion in gestures and speech: Are there differences in bilingual children's French and English? In *Space in Language: Location, Motion, Path and Manner. Proceedings of the 31st Stanford Child Research Forum*, Eve V. Clark (ed.), 60–68. Stanford CA: CSLI.

Oxford Dictionaries. 2011. The OEC: Facts about the language. 26 Dec 2011. <https://web.archive.org/web/20111226085859/http://oxforddictionaries.com/words/the-oec-facts-about-the-language> (15 April 2021).

Pym, Anthony. 2018. A typology of translation solutions. *The Journal of Specialised Translation* 30: 41–65.

Sanjurjo-González, Hugo & Izquierdo, Marlén. 2019. PACTRES 2.0. A parallel corpus for cross-linguistic research. In *Parallel Corpora for Contrastive and Translation Studies* [Studies in Corpus Linguistics 90], Irene Doval & M. Teresa Sánchez Nieto (eds), 215–232. Amsterdam: John Benjamins.

Schmitt, Norbert. 2000. *Vocabulary in Language Teaching*. Cambridge: CUP.

Schmitt, Norbert & Carter, Ronald. 2000. The lexical advantages of narrow reading for second language learners, *TESOL Journal* 9(1): 4–9.

Slobin, Dan Isaac. 1996. Two ways to travel: Verbs of motion in English and Spanish. In *Grammatical Constructions: Their Form and Meaning*, Masayoshi Shibatani & Sandra Thompson (eds), 195–220. Oxford: Clarendon Press.

Stringer, David. 2007. Motion events in L2 acquisition: A lexicalist account. In *BUCLD 31: Proceedings of the 31st annual Boston University Conference on Language Development*, Vol. II, Heather Cauntnulton, Samantha Kulatilake & I-hao Woo (eds), 585–96. Somerville MA: Cascadilla Press.

Talmy, Leonard. 1985. Lexicalization patterns: Semantic structure in lexical forms. In *Language Typology and Lexical Descriptions, Vol. 3: Grammatical Categories and the Lexicon*, Timothy Shopen (ed.), 36–149. Cambridge: CUP.

Talmy, Leonard. 2007. Lexical typologies. In *Language Typology and Syntactic Description, Vol. III: Grammatical Categories and the Lexicon*, 2nd edn, Timothy Shopen (ed.), 66–168. Cambridge: CUP.

Thornbury, Scott. 1999. *How to Teach Grammar*. London: Longman.

Thornbury, Scott. 2004. *How to Teach Vocabulary*. Harlow: Pearson Education.

CHAPTER 7

Film dialogue synchronization and statistical dubbese

A corpus-based pilot study of English-Spanish conversational markers

Camino Gutiérrez Lanza
University of León

This paper reports on one of the main problem-triggers in film dialogue synchronization for dubbing: conversational markers (CMs). The synchronized film scripts (TT2s) from the TRACEci corpus of English-Spanish cinema scripts, ready to be delivered by dubbing actors, are compared with their draft translations (TT1s) and with non-translated Spanish data from the *guiones* subcorpus of CORPES XXI. Results confirm that the number of CMs has been reduced in the TT2s in favor of synchronization and that certain CMs are indicators of English-Spanish statistical dubbese (overuse), causing unwanted redundancy. The analysis benefits from corpus data and is intended to help both students and professionals to improve the acceptability of their translations.

Keywords: English-Spanish synchronization, prefabricated orality, statistical dubbese, corpora, conversational markers

1. Introduction

Translation quality in dubbing has traditionally been identified with lip-syncing, that is, the matching of lip movement and dubbed utterances (Fodor 1976) and isochrony, that is, the match between dubbed utterances and the beginning and end of actors' mouth movement (Whitman-Linsen 1992), among other factors such as prefabricated orality, that is, "the writing of *credible* and *realistic* dialogues, according to the oral registers of the target language" (Chaume 2007: 72). Prefabricated orality is a peculiar type of discourse "written to be spoken as if not written" (Gregory & Carroll 1978: 42), creating fake spontaneous conversation written to be delivered orally by fictional characters (Pérez González 2007; Baños Piñero

https://doi.org/10.1075/scl.113.07gut

& Chaume 2009; Bruti 2018). So much so, that the synchronization (Chaume 2004a) or adaptation of the draft translations (TT1s) is mainly done in favor of lip-syncing and isochrony, so that the resulting translations (TT2s) are ready to be delivered by voice talents, fitting the lip and body movement of the actors, especially in close-ups and at utterance level.

The prefabricated orality of fictional language makes use of several language-related features, such as discourse markers (DMs), which are often formally dissimilar across languages (Chaume 2004b; Aijmer & Simon-Vandenbergen 2006; Rabadán & Gutiérrez Lanza, 2023). The use of various translation techniques, for example, word-for-word translation and omission, may result in the overuse or underuse of certain features of prefabricated orality in the translations, compared to film dialogue in non-translated Spanish. This often works in favor of lip-syncing and isochrony, but differs from the way prefabricated orality is built in the target language, causing dubbese, that is, the different use of the target language in translation compared to its use in original texts (Chaume, 2004c; Díaz Cintas 2004; Romero Fresco 2006).

Since, as stated above, DMs have been found to be one of the main problem-triggers in translation, this paper analyses a subcategory of DMs frequently used in prefabricated orality: conversational markers (CMs). The aims are to analyze whether CMs are targeted by the adapter when adjusting the draft translation to the actors' lip movement and to confirm whether their use differs in English-Spanish translations compared to original texts in Spanish. This proposal supports the idea that the avoidance of statistically significant differences in the communication patterns of translated and non-translated target language (Rabadán 2008; Rabadán 2010) would enhance the quality, acceptability and tenor of the dubbed versions (Rabadán & Gutiérrez Lanza 2020).

Section 2 briefly discusses the basics of film dialogue synchronization for dubbing, Section 3 presents CMs as the object of this pilot study, Section 4 describes the data and method, Section 5 provides the results and discussion, and Section 6 submits the conclusions and presents the applicability of the findings.

2. Film dialogue synchronization for dubbing and statistical dubbese

During the dubbing process (Chaume 2012), new dialogue in the target language is added to the audio track of the film. The translator "will usually do a rough translation, that is, a literal translation of the script" (Chaume 2012: 33). Then, the adapter creates "a fresh, workable, convincing, prefabricated oral script that meets all lip-sync requirements, but at the same time gives the impression that it is an original dialogue" (Chaume 2012: 35). During the synchronization process, the target language translation is matched "to the screen actors' body and articulatory movements in a recording made in a dubbing studio" (Chaume 2012: 67).

Together with lip-syncing and isochrony, prefabricated orality greatly contributes to ensuring translation quality, triggering the willing suspension of disbelief on the part of film audiences (Gutiérrez Lanza 2000; Chaume 2007; Zabalbeascoa 2008; Romero Fresco 2009; Chaume 2012). In this respect, "the challenge does not lie so much in trying to imitate spontaneous conversation, but in selecting specific features of this mode of discourse that are widely accepted and recognized as such by the audience" (Baños Piñero & Chaume 2009). These features are named "privileged carriers of orality" by Pavesi (2008). However, the need for isochrony may cause translated prefabricated orality to be affected by dubbese, defined as certain source language features which are transferred to dubbed products and differ from non-translated target language usage (Romero Fresco 2006; Chaume 2007; Pérez González 2007; Romero Fresco 2009; Chaume 2021). As authors like Pavesi (2008) illustrate, dubbese may also involve overusing features of colloquial spontaneous conversation that might not be present in the original text. In this pilot study, statistical dubbese is understood as the statistically significant differences in the use of certain features of translated film dialogue compared to non-translated film dialogue in the target language. They may be the result of interference with the source language or, as supported by Pavesi (2008), of the choices made by translators and adapters.

3. Problem-triggers: Conversational markers

Since discourse markers (DMs) have been found to be often formally dissimilar across languages (Chaume 2004b; Aijmer & Simon-Vandenbergen 2006; Rabadán & Gutiérrez Lanza, 2023), this paper analyzes the use of a subcategory of DMs, CMs, for being characteristic of spontaneous conversation and, therefore, highly likely to be used in film dialogue and prefabricated orality. According to their procedural meaning, Spanish CMs can be classified into the following four categories (Martín Zorraquino & Portolés Lázaro 1999: 4143–4199):

a. Markers of epistemic modality are used in declarative sentences to agree and cooperate with the other speaker. They mainly express reinforcement, agreement, for example, *en efecto, efectivamente, desde luego, por supuesto, naturalmente, claro* and *sin duda*, or the speaker's attitude in relation to the message, for example, *por lo visto*.
b. Markers of deontic modality indicate that the speaker evaluates and accepts or rectifies whatever has been said before, for example, *Bueno, bien* and *vale*.

c. Addressee-oriented markers speak to the listener directly, usually asking for cooperation, for example, *hombre, bueno, vamos, mira/mire, oye/oiga* and *por favor.*
d. Metadiscursive markers signpost the speakers' effort to confirm the reception of the message and to signal the start or the end of a speech turn, for example, *ya, sí, bueno, bien, eh* and *este* (the latter, in non-European Spanish).

Some of the CMs mentioned above have already been studied in the English-Spanish translation of film dialogue (e.g., Chaume 2004b; Romero Fresco 2012). To add to the discussion, this pilot study is based on an English-Spanish parallel corpus of action films which includes the translated and adapted versions and on its comparison with a reference corpus of non-translated Spanish.

4. Data and method

I have compiled the TRACEci parallel corpus of feature film scripts (Gutiérrez Lanza 1999), including the following dialogue lists: the source texts in English (STs: 35,066 words), the draft translations (TT1s: 12,799 words) and the adapted, synchronized translations (TT2s: 14,824 words).[1] They correspond to the action films *The Adventures of Tintin* (Steven Spielberg, 2011) and *Jack Reacher* (Christopher McQuarrie, 2012), released in Spain in 2011 and 2013 respectively. The former is an international coproduction among US, New Zealand, UK, France and Australia, and the latter was produced in the USA.

The TT2s, used by voice talents during the dubbing process, are the result of the adapter's synchronization of the draft translations (TT1s). As shown in Figure 1, both the synchronized and the draft translations have been aligned with their source texts in English (STs) using TAligner 3.0 (Gutiérrez Lanza, Bandín Fuertes, Lobejón Santos & García González 2015; MINECO 2019; Sanz-Villar & Andaluz-Pinedo 2021).

Since I am interested in the study of prefabricated orality, this analysis concentrates not only on the original and translated dialogue, but also on the dubbing symbols, signaled in brackets in the TT2s. Dubbing symbols are relevant because they "help dubbing actors imitate the screen actors' paralinguistic signs" (Chaume 2012: 58) and "refer to where the voices come from" (Chaume 2012: 58–59) (Example (1)). This way, when actors are off screen or at the background, the viewer cannot see their face clearly and does not know exactly when the utterance

1. TT1s and TT2s are authored by professional translator/adapter Quico Rovira-Beleta, who has kindly given us permission to use them for research purposes.

Figure 1. The TRACEci parallel corpus: STs-TT1s-TT2s

starts and finishes, which may allow the translator or adaptor to be more flexible with isochrony.

(1) *EMERSON: [OFF] Vámonos antes [ON] de que se ponga feo.* (Let's go before it gets bad.)

I have not considered other information included in the scripts, such as the notes for translators and adapters, that is, useful explanations of problematic terms or expressions (Example (2)), included in the STs and also signaled in brackets.

(2) HELEN: Oh, well, you're my only defense witness. [defense witness: witness testifying during a trial on behalf of the defense].

The acting directions in the STs (Example (3)) and in the *guiones* subcorpus (Example (4)), that is, valuable indications for actors which cannot be expressed with regular symbols, have also been excluded from the analysis.

(3) REACHER: [smacks lips after sipping coffee] My bus is leaving.

(4) *MODESTO: (Niega con la cabeza, mantiene la mirada). No, por supuesto que no.* ((He shakes his head, holds his gaze). No, of course not.)

Among the examples of CMs mentioned by Martín Zorraquino and Portolés Lázaro (1999: 4143–4199) (see Section 3), those with 5 or more occurrences in the draft translations (TT1s) are selected for further analysis. TT1s are compared to TT2s in order to show whether the selected CMs have been modified or not by the adapter. The quantitative and qualitative analyses of the concordances report on the frequency of use of different synchronization techniques (no change, omission, substitution and addition) and on the most likely reasons for those changes. When there is no change, CMs are used both in the TT1s and in the TT2s in exactly the same place. When they are omitted, they disappear from the TT2s and are not substituted by anything else. Substitution happens when they are changed either by other CMs or by other words or expressions. Finally, addition takes place when CMs that did not exist in the TT1s are used in the TT2s.

In order to find out whether CMs are indicators of dubbese, that is, whether there are statistically significant differences in their use in translated film dialogue compared to non-translated film dialogue in the target language, the TT1s and TT2s from TRACEci are compared with non-translated Spanish data from the equivalent *guiones* (scripts) subcorpus of CORPES XXI (1,501,683 words), the PoS annotated reference corpus of 21st century, European, non-translated Spanish (RAE 2021). Therefore, the *guiones* subcorpus is considered to represent natural, realistic prefabricated orality in the target language. Some examples of concordances from this subcorpus are shown in Figure 2.

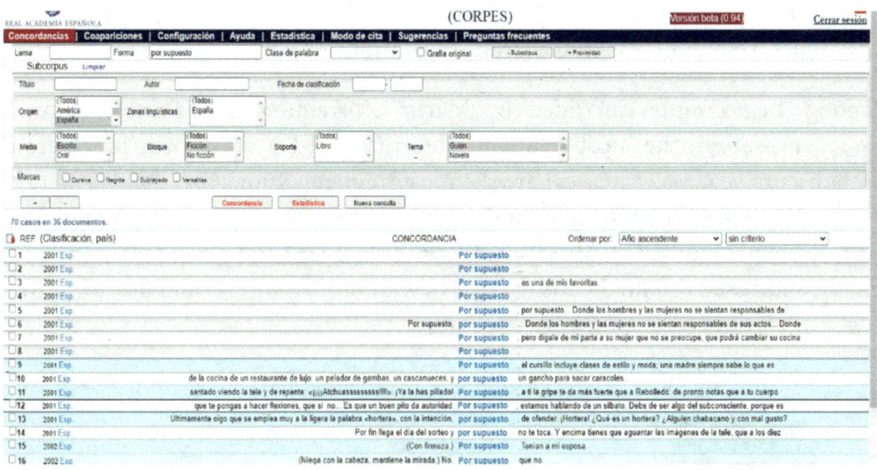

Figure 2. The *guiones* subcorpus of CORPES XXI

The z-test for independent proportions (Schumacker 2015: 223–242) is a useful tool in the search for dubbese, since it reveals whether there are statistically significant differences in the use of CMs in translated (TRACEci: TT1s and TT2s) and non-translated Spanish (CORPES XXI). While performing the test, Z-statistics is computed from the two independent samples, the null hypothesis being that the two population proportions of TRACEci and CORPES XXI are equal. Alternatively, if the difference between the two population proportions is statistically significant, the null hypothesis is rejected, meaning that CMs are affected by dubbese, that is, they are either overused or underused in the translations. Following common practice, the test is run with a 95% confidence interval and a 5% 'alpha level' or estimated error, in order to avoid the probability of incorrectly confirming the null hypothesis when it is false or incorrectly rejecting the null hypothesis when it is true. To be statistically significant, the difference between the two proportions (translated and non-translated cases) has to lie outside the curve ±1.96 for the z-score (either higher than +1.96 or lower than −1.96) and the p-value must be lower than 0.05. A z-score which is higher than +1.96 indicates that the DMs are overused in the translations. On the other hand, a z-score which is lower than −1.96 indicates that the DMs are underused in the translations. Otherwise, when the difference between the two proportions (translated and non-translated cases) does not lie outside the curve ±1.96 for the z-score and the p-value is higher than 0.05, the null hypothesis is not rejected.

5. Results and discussion

5.1 Most frequent CMs in the draft translations (TT1s)

Among the examples provided by Martín Zorraquino and Portolés Lázaro (1999: 4143–4199), the most frequent CMs in the TT1s are shown in Figure 3. Metadiscursive CMs (77 cases) are the most frequent, with *ehm* (42), *bueno* (27) and *ya* (8), followed by deontic modality CMs (34 cases), with *vale* (18) and *bien* (16), epistemic modality CMs (21 cases), with *claro* (14) and *por supuesto* (7) and, finally, addressee-oriented CMs (19 cases), with *mira/mire* (13) and *oye/oiga* (6).

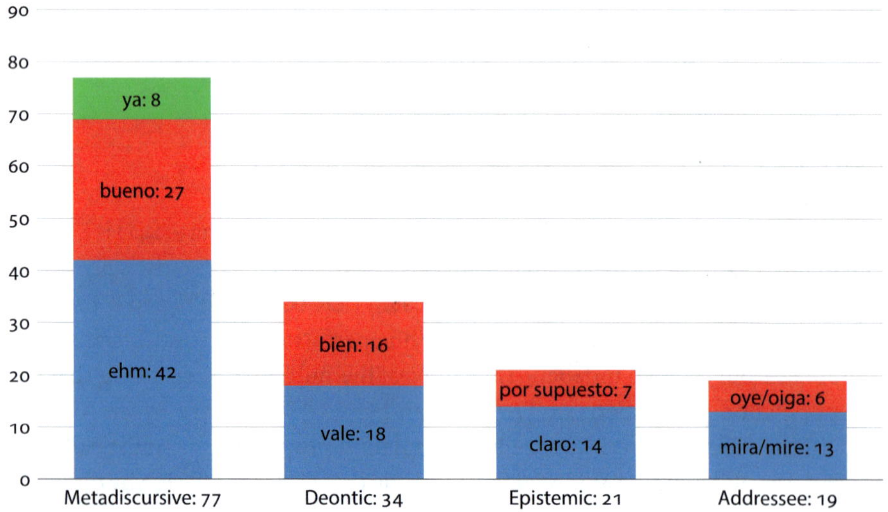

Figure 3. Most frequently used CMs in TT1s

The ST correspondents of these 151 translated CMs are the following:

a. Metadiscursive CMs: *ehm* derives, on the one hand, from markers 'uh', 'eh' and 'um' (83.33%) and, on the other, from incomplete utterances denoting hesitation, such as 'I ..., I'll ...' and 'w-wait' (16.67%), *bueno* is nearly always translated from 'well' (96.30%), while *ya* mostly derives from 'yeah/aye' (62.50%), followed by 'I see' (25%) and 'well' (12.50%).
b. Deontic CMs: *vale* derives from 'okay' (72.22%), '(you) got it' (22.22%) and 'all right' (5.56%), while *bien* comes from 'all right' (50%), 'so', 'now' (6.25% each) and 'well' (3.13%). *Bien* also substitutes the vocative 'Snowy!' (6.25%).
c. Epistemic CMs: *claro* mainly derives from 'of course' (37.71%), followed by 'sure' and 'yes' (14.29% each) and by 'well', 'now' and 'why' (7.14% each), while *por supuesto* mainly derives from attitudinal adverbs such as 'absolutely', 'positively' and 'obviously' (57.14%) as well as from 'of course' (42.86%).
d. Addressee-oriented CMs: *mira/mire* mostly derive from 'look' (69.23%), followed by 'now' (15.38%), 'you know' and 'well' (7.69% each), while *oye/oiga* are translated from 'look' (55.56%), 'you!' and 'hello!' (22.22% each).

5.2 Synchronization techniques (TT1s vs. TT2s)

When comparing the number of cases of the chosen CMs in the draft and in the synchronized translations (TT1s-TT2s), results show that the use of CMs has been reduced, that is, they have been either omitted or substituted, by an average of 39.74% (from 151 in the TT1s to 91 in the TT2s). According to their procedural meaning, this reduction highly affects addressee-oriented markers (from 19 to 6: 68.42%): *mira/mire* (from 13 to 1) and *oye/oiga* (from 6 to 5), followed by metadiscursive markers (from 77 to 47: 38.96%): *ehm* (from 42 to 30), *bueno* (from 27 to 13) and *ya* (from 8 to 5), markers of deontic modality (from 34 to 23: 32.35%): *vale* (from 18 to 8) and *bien* (unchanged, from 16 to 16) and, finally, markers of epistemic modality (from 21 to 15: 28.57%): *claro* (from 14 to 4) and *por supuesto* (from 7 to 3) (Figure 4).

Results confirm that, for the total 151 CMs in the TT1s, the preferred synchronization technique is to leave them unchanged (76: 50.33%), followed by omission (52: 34.44%) and substitution (23: 15.23%). Out of the final 91 CMs in the TT2s, apart from the wide majority of CMs that have been left unchanged (76: 83.52%), 15 of them have been added (16.48%) (Figure 5).

According to the procedural meaning of CMs, the synchronization techniques are used as shown in Figure 6. The procedural meaning of the 151 CMs found in the TT1s is affected by no change, omission, substitution and addition in the following proportions:

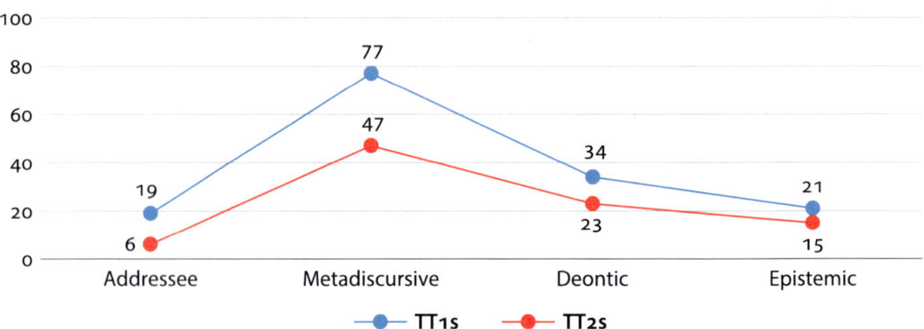

Figure 4. CMs in draft (TT1s) vs. synchronized translations (TT2s)

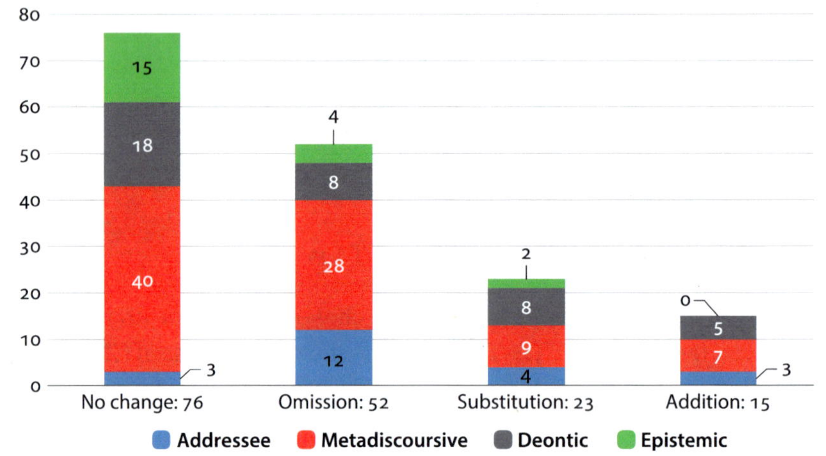

Figure 5. Synchronization techniques: no change, omission, substitution and addition

a. 19 addressee-oriented CMs (*mira/mire* and *oye/oiga*): 63.16% have been omitted, 21.05% have been substituted by other expressions and 15.79% have been left unchanged. Out of the 6 CMs in the TT2s, 50% have been added.
b. 77 metadiscursive CMs (*ehm, bueno* and *ya*): 36.36% have been omitted, 11.69% have been substituted by other expressions and 51.95% have been left unchanged. Out of the 47 CMs in the TT2s, 14.89% have been added.
c. 34 deontic CMs (*vale* and *bien*): 23.53% have been omitted, 23.53% have been substituted by other expressions and 52.94% have been left unchanged. Out of the 23 CMs in the TT2s, 21.74% have been added.
d. 21 epistemic CMs (*claro* and *por supuesto*): 19.05% have been omitted, 9.52% have been substituted by other expressions and 71.43% have been left unchanged. Out of the 21 CMs in the TT2s, none has been added.

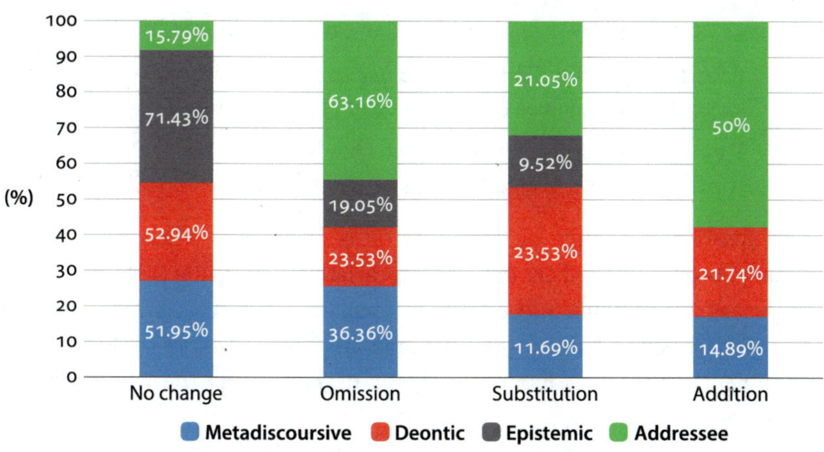

Figure 6. Synchronization techniques and procedural meaning of CMs

The different synchronization techniques are used in the following proportions in relation to the procedural meaning of CMs:

a. No change is found more often with epistemic CMs (71.43%), followed by deontic (52.94%), metadiscursive (51.95%) and addressee-oriented CMs (15.79%). Examples of the absence of change of the different types of CMs are shown in Examples (5) to (8).

(5) **ST:** HELEN: No, **of course** not. I ... [light grunt] (CSST2012JR266)

TT1: *HELEN: No,* ***claro*** *que no.* ***Ehm*** ... (No, **of course** not. **Um** ...) [G]

TT2: *HELEN: No,* ***claro*** *que no.* ***Ehm*** ... (No, **of course** (CSTT12012JR266) not. **Um** ...) [G] (CSTT12012JR266)

(6) **ST:** REACHER: [soft panting – continues under following scenes] **Okay** ... [face obscured] **now** we know who's who. (CSST2012JR415)

TT1: *REACHER: [JADEA]* ***Vale*** ... ***ahora*** *ya sabemos quién es quién.* (**Okay** ... **now** we know who is who.) (CSTT12012JR415)

TT2: *REACHER: [JADEA] [DE]* ***Vale,*** ***Ø*** *ya sabemos quién es quién.* (**Okay** ... **Ø** we know who is who.) (CSTT22012JR415)

(7) **ST:** CHARLIE: [inhales sharply] **Well, we** were **both** pretty wasted.

TT1: *CHARLIE: [RESP.]* ***Bueno, los dos*** *íbamos muy* (CSST2012JR913) *colocados.* (**Well, we** were **both** very stoned.) (CSTT12012JR913)

TT2: *CHARLIE: [G]* ***Bueno, Ø*** *íbamos muy colocados.* (**Well, Ø** were **Ø** very stoned.) (CSTT22012JR913)

(8) **ST:** LINSKY: [grunting] **Um** ... I figured five guys would do it. (CSST2012JR588)

TT1: *LINSKY: [G]* ***Ehm*** *... supuse que con cinco tíos bastaría.* (**Um** ... I figured that with five guys it would be enough.) (CSTT12012JR588)

TT2: *LINSKY:* ***Ehm****, pensé que cinco tíos bastarían.* (**Um** ... I thought five guys would be enough.) (CSTT22012JR588)

The absence of change of translated CMs is justified when isochrony has already been achieved in the draft translation (Example (5)) or when the necessary adjustments affect other elements of utterances, which, for example, are shortened by omitting expendable adverbs (*ahora* in Example (6)) or subjects (*los dos* in Example (7)), or by rephrasing the whole utterance (Example (8)).

b. Omission mostly affects addressee-oriented CMs (63.16%), followed by metadiscursive (36.36%), deontic (23.53%) and epistemic CMs (19.05%). Examples of omission affecting the different types of CMs are shown in Examples (9) to (13).

(9) **ST:** THOMSON: Yes! We also have an arrest warrant, **eh**, issued by both Interpol and the F.B.I. (CSST2011AT1844)

TT1: *HERNÁNDEZ: ¡Sí! Y además tenemos una orden de detención,* ***ehm****, emitida tanto por la Interpol como por el FBI.* (Yes! We also have an arrest warrant, **eh**, issued by both Interpol and the F.B.I.) (CSTT12011AT1844)

TT2: *HERNÁNDEZ: ¡Sí! Y además tenemos una orden de detención* **Ø** *tanto de Interpol como del FBI.* (Yes! We also have an arrest warrant, **Ø** by both Interpol and the F.B.I.) (CSTT22011AT1844)

(10) **ST:** HELEN: **Yeah**, conspiracy to kill five random people? (CSST2012JR873)

TT1: *HELEN:* ***Ya****, ¿una conspiración para matar a cinco personas al azar?* (**Yeah**, conspiracy to kill five random people?) (CSTT12012JR873)

TT2: *HELEN:* **Ø** *¿Una conspiración para matar a cinco personas al azar?* (**Ø** Conspiracy to kill five random people?) (CSTT22012JR873)

(11) **ST:** EMERSON: [off] **Well**, I can tell ......you who he was. (CSST2012JR64)

TT1: *EMERSON:* ***Bueno****, puedo decirle quién era.* (**Well**, I can tell ......you who he was.) (CSTT12012JR64)

TT2: *EMERSON: [OFF]* **Ø** *Puedo decirle [ON] quién era.* (**Ø** I can tell ......you who he was.) (CSTT22012JR64)

(12) **ST:** MALE PATRON #5: [face obscured] [low] **Okay**, who wants it?
TT1: *CLIENTE BAR 4: [BAJO]* ***Vale***, *¿quién lo quiere?* (CSST2012JR345)
(**Okay**, who wants it?) (CSTT12012JR345)
TT2: *CLIENTE BAR 4: [OFF] Ø ¿Quién lo quiere?* (Ø Who wants it?)
(CSTT22012JR345)

(13) **ST:** EMERSON: [overlapping] [to Rodin] **Look**, let me handle it.
TT1: *EMERSON: [P]* ***Mire***, *deje que me ocupe yo.* (**Look**, (CSST2012JR999)
let me handle it.) (CSTT12012JR999)
TT2: *EMERSON: [P] Ø Déjeme a mí.* (Ø Leave it to me.)
(CSTT22012JR999)

Omission either seems to work in favor of isochrony (Examples (9) and (10)) or is used when the actor's face is either off screen or obscured (Examples (11) and (12)) because, since the actors' mouth cannot be seen by viewers, the adaptor can be more flexible with the beginning and end of utterances. It is also used when utterances overlap (Example (13)).

c. Substitution is more frequent with deontic CMs (23.53%), followed by addressee-oriented CMs (21.05%), metadiscursive CMs, (11.69%) and epistemic CMs (9.52%). Examples of substitution affecting the different types of CMs are shown in Examples (14) to (16).

(14) **ST:** LINSKY: [incredulous chuckle] **Look,** [...] (CSST2012JR623)
TT1: *LINSKY: [RÍE]* ***Oye***, *[...]* (**Hey,** [...]) (CSTT12012JR623)
TT2: *LINSKY: [G]* ***No*** *... [...]* (**No** ... [...]) (CSTT22012JR623)

(15) **ST:** CAPTAIN HADDOCK: [overlapping] **Look.** Did you ever see a more beautiful sight? (CSST2011AT1155)
TT1: *CAPITÁN HADDOCK:* ***Mira.*** *¿Alguna vez has visto algo más hermoso?* (**Look.** Have you ever seen anything more beautiful?
TT2: *CAPITÁN HADDOCK:* ***Fíjate.*** *¿Dime, has visto* (CSTT12011AT1155)
alguna vez algo tan hermoso? (**Look at this**, have you ever seen anything so beautiful? (CSTT22011AT1155)

(16) **ST:** GARY: **Okay.** I'm calling the police. (CSST2012JR671)
TT1: *GARY:* ***Vale.*** *Voy a llamar a la policía.* (**Okay.** I'm calling the police.)
TT2: *GARY:* ***Muy bien.*** *Voy a llamar a la policía.* (**All** (CSTT12012JR671)
right. I'm calling the police.) (CSTT22012JR671)

The substitution of CMs for other words or expressions sometimes results in a change of meaning (Example (14) shows that the vocative meaning of 'look' and *oye* has been substituted by the negation expressed by *no*). Other times, substitution adds extra emphasis (in Example (15), *mira* meaning 'look' has been substituted by the emphatic *fíjate* meaning 'look at this') or results in the reinforcement of the procedural meaning of the CM (in Example (16) the more neutral *vale* meaning 'Okay' has been substituted by the more reassuring *muy bien* meaning 'all right').

d. Finally, addition is more frequent in the case of addressee-oriented CMs (50%), followed by deontic (21.74%) and metadiscursive CMs (14.89%) and it is completely absent from epistemic CMs. Examples of addition affecting the different types of CMs are shown in Examples (17) to (19).

(17) **ST:** HELEN: Ø Excuse me? (CSST2012JR557)

TT1: *HELEN: Ø ¿Perdona?* (Ø Excuse me?) (CSTT12012JR557)

TT2: *HELEN:* ***Ehm,*** *¿cómo?* (**Em**, what?) (CSTT22012JR557)

(18) **ST:** MALE PATRON #8: [off] [overlapping] [very low] Ø You got it taken care of? (CSST2012JR355)

TT1: *CLIENTE BAR 7: [P] [MUY BAJO] Ø ¿Te has ocupado de eso?* (Ø You got it taken care of?) (CSTT12012JR355)

TT2: *CLIENTES BAR:* ***Oye,*** *¿te has ocupado de lo que te pedí?* (**Hey**, did you take care of what I asked for?) (CSTT22012JR355)

(19) **ST:** BAR PATRONS: [low and indistinct chatter – continues intermittently under following scenes and dialogue] Ø (CSST2012JR1140)

TT1: *CLIENTES BAR: [AMBIENTE GRAL.] Ø* (CSTT12012JR1140)

TT2: *CLIENTES BAR: [DE FONDO] [AMBIENTE GRAL.] [¿ME?] [ALGUNOS AD LIBS] [2H.]* ***Vale,*** *pero ahora ya ha pasado ...* (**Okay**, but now it's over ...) (CSTT22012JR1140)

Addition makes the procedural meaning of CMs explicit in favor of isochrony or message understanding. The dynamics of dialogue exchange favors the addition of hesitations (*ehm* in Example (17)) or the addition of CMs addressing the listener (*oye*, meaning 'hey' in Example (18)). It also seems to be practiced often when indistinct or background chatter, absent from the ST and TT1 but likely to be heard in this context in Spanish, is added to TT2 *ad libitum (ad lib)*, that is, to the adapter's will (Example (19)).

The examples commented above illustrate that CMs seem to have become useful synchronizing tools in the hands of the adapter. The overall reduction of CMs seems to point to isochrony and agile dialogue interchange as being more relevant than the procedural meaning of CMs, confirming that "losing discourse markers in the process of translating does not seriously affect the target text in terms of semantic meaning" (Chaume 2004b: 854). This may be possible either because "the audience accepts deficiencies in cohesion and coherence in audiovisual translations as part of their inherent characteristics" (Chaume 2004b: 854) or because the procedural meaning of CMs may at times be redundant, being inferred from images (Chaume 2004b), neighbouring utterances and/or the prosodic features of dubbed language.

5.3 In search for statistical dubbese

As described in the previous section, during the synchronization process the use of CMs has been reduced from 151 to 91, that is, by 39.74%. The number of cases of each CM in TRACEci and CORPES XXI is shown in Table 1.

Table 1. Frequencies of CMs across corpora

CMs	TRACEci TT1s 12,799 w.		TRACEci TT2s 14,824 w.		CORPES XXI *guiones* 1,501,683 w.	
	Raw	Per 10,000 w.	Raw	Per 10,000 w.	Raw	Per 10,000 w.
mira/mire	13	10.16	1	0.67	268	1.78
oye/oiga	6	4.69	5	3.37	277	1.84
ehm	42	32.82	30	20.24	31*	0.21
bueno	27	21.10	17	11.47	514	3.42
ya	8	6.25	5	3.37	295	1.96
vale	18	14.06	8	5.40	435	2.90
bien	16	12.50	16	10.80	78	0.52
claro	14	10.94	4	2.70	644	4.29
por supuesto	7	5.47	3	2.02	70	0.47

* Instead of *ehm* ..., with only 1 case, non-translated Spanish prefers *eh* ..., with 30 cases.

The z-test for independent proportions reveals whether there are statistically significant differences in the use of CMs in translated and non-translated Spanish. The TT1s and the TT2s are compared with the *guiones* subcorpus of CORPES XXI, with the results shown in Table 2.

Noticeably, results show that all CMs have been overused in the TT1s. This may be the case because, being "a literal translation of the script" (Chaume 2012: 33), draft translations tend to stick to source language norms using target language equivalents, instead of imitating the use of non-translated target language (see translated CMs and their ST correspondents in Section 5.1.). In spite of the drastic reduction of metadiscoursive *ehm* (from 42 to 30) and *bueno* (from

Table 2. CMs: verification of dubbese

CM	z	p	TT1s	z	p	TT2s
mira/ mire	6.925	0	O*	−1.01	0.3125	NR**
oye/oiga	2.343	0.0191	O	1.358	0.1745	NR
ehm	52.913	0	O	38.266	0	O
bueno	10.536	0	O	5.21	0	O
ya	3.414	0.0006	O	1.213	0.225	NR
vale	7.275	0	O	1.772	0.0763	NR
bien	17.133	0	O	15.811	0	O
claro	3.595	0.0003	O	−0.932	0.3512	NR
por supuesto	7.905	0	O	2.72	0.0065	O

* 'O' stands for 'overused', which means there is a statistically significant difference in the use of CMs in translated and non-translated Spanish, being more frequent in translated Spanish.
** 'NR' stands for 'not rejected', which means that the null hypothesis, that is, that there is no statistically significant difference between the two population proportions of TRACEci and CORPES XXI, has been confirmed.

27 to 17) and epistemic *por supuesto* (from 7 to 3), they still have been overused in the TT2s, together with deontic *bien* (unchanged, with 16 cases), which also proves the existence of statistical dubbese in the synchronized translations. In this respect, especially visible in the z-value is the massive overuse of metadiscoursive *ehm* and deontic *bien* both in the TT1s and in the TT2s, the latter being commonly used in formal situations. Romero Fresco (2012) has also found that *bien* is common in English-Spanish film script translation and argues that it sounds unnatural and creates a considerable distance among characters. CM overuse may be due to the fact that audiovisual translation, heavily controlled by synchronization, "overwhelmingly abide[s] by the constraints of micro-, intra-turn equivalence, making local decisions that are not necessarily informed by the overall picture of what is going on outside the turn at hand" (Pérez González 2007: 10).

On the other hand, the reduction in the number of addressee-oriented *mira/mire, oye/oiga*, metadiscoursive *ya*, deontic *vale* and epistemic *claro* has confirmed the null hypothesis, causing them to be used similarly both in translated and non-translated Spanish. Therefore, it may be argued that losing CMs in the synchronization process tends to improve the quality of the translations, avoiding overuse and bringing the language of dubbing closer to non-translated target language.

6. Conclusions

Synchrony is one of the aspects considered essential for good quality dubbing, especially in close-ups (Chaume 2007; Chaume 2012). However, when the actors' face is either off screen or obscured, the need for lip-syncing and isochrony is less relevant.

This pilot study has proved that CMs function as useful syncing tools during the synchronization process. Synchrony and agile dialogue interchange seem to be more important than the procedural meaning of CMs, most likely inferred from neighbouring utterances, images and/or the prosodic features of dubbed language. However, prefabricated orality is often sacrificed in favor of isochrony, resulting in statistical dubbese, that is, statistically significant differences between translated and non-translated dialogue in the target language.

Results confirm that all CMs have been overused in the draft translations. Although the use of translated CMs has been reduced by 39.74% during synchronization, *ehm, bueno, bien* and *por supuesto* have also been overused in the TT2s in respect to non-translated Spanish, proving the existence of dubbese. However, synchronization has eliminated the overuse of *mira/mire, oye/oiga, ya* and *claro*, which seems to work in favor of natural, realistic prefabricated orality, thus reducing redundancy and improving the quality of dubbing.

This paper is part of a more ambitious ongoing research exploring dialogue synchronization and statistical dubbese. Results may benefit the dubbing industry, being useful both for translation training and in the development of applications for professional audiovisual translators. In this respect, academic research may help to raise trainees' and professionals' awareness of the fact that there is a general trend towards the overuse of CMs in the rough translations and also of the fact that CMs can be used as synchronizing tools to bridge the gap between translated and non-translated uses in the target language. In the near future, the corpus of translated cinema scripts will be enlarged in order to test the results of this pilot study and to replicate the study, as has already been done with problem-triggers *can/could* and subject pronouns (Gutiérrez Lanza & Rabadán, 2023).

References

Aijmer, Karin & Simon-Vandenbergen, Anne-Marie. 2006. *Pragmatic Markers in Contrast.* Leiden: Brill.

Baños Piñero, Rocío & Chaume, Frederic. 2009. Prefabricated orality: A challenge in audiovisual translation. In The Translation of Dialects in Multimedia, Michela Giorgio Marrano, Giovanni Nadiani & Chris Rundle (eds). Special issue of *InTRAlinea*. <https://www.intralinea.org/specials/article/1714> (29 May 2023).

Bruti, Silvia. 2018. Spoken discourse and conversational interaction in audiovisual translation. In *The Routledge Handbook of Audiovisual Translation* [Routledge Handbooks in Translation and Interpreting Studies Series 4], Luis Pérez González (ed.), 192–208. London: Routledge.

Chaume, Frederic. 2004a. Synchronization in dubbing: A translational approach. In *Topics in Audiovisual Translation* [Benjamins Translation Library Series 56], Pilar Orero (ed.), 35–52. Amsterdam: John Benjamins.

Chaume, Frederic. 2004b. Discourse markers in audiovisual translating. *Meta: Journal des Traducteurs / Meta: Translators' Journal* 49(4): 843–855.

Chaume, Frederic. 2004c. *Cine y traducción*. Madrid: Cátedra.

Chaume, Frederic. 2007. Quality standards in dubbing: A proposal. *TradTerm* 13: 71–89.

Chaume, Frederic. 2012. *Audiovisual Translation: Dubbing*. Manchester: St. Jerome.

Chaume Frederic. 2021. Dubbing. In *The Palgrave Handbook of Audiovisual Translation and Media Accessibility* [Palgrave Studies in Translating and Interpreting Series 25], Łukasz Bogucki & Mikołaj Deckert (eds), 103–132. London: Palgrave Macmillan.

Díaz Cintas, Jorge. 2004. In search of a theoretical framework for the study of audiovisual translation. In *Topics in Audiovisual Translation* [Benjamins Translation Library Series 56], Pilar Orero (ed.), 21–34. Amsterdam: John Benjamins.

Fodor, István. 1976. *Film Dubbing*. Hamburg: Buske.

Gregory, Michael & Carroll, Susanne. 1978. *Language and Situation. Language Varieties in their Social Contexts*. London: Routledge.

Gutiérrez Lanza, Camino. 1999. *TRACEci. Corpus of English-Spanish Cinema Scripts* (version 2, TRACEci XML ed.). <https://trace.unileon.es/es/fondos-trace/catalogos/textos-audiovisuales-cine-y-tv/> (7 February 2022).

Gutiérrez Lanza, Camino. 2000. *Traducción y censura de textos cinematográficos en la España de Franco: Doblaje y subtitulado inglés-español (1951–1975)*. León: Universidad de León.

Gutiérrez Lanza, Camino, Bandín Fuertes, Elena, Lobejón Santos, Sergio & García González, José Enrique. 2015. Desarrollo de software de etiquetado y alineación textual: TRACE Corpus Tagger/Aligner 1.0©. Paper presented at II Congreso Internacional de Humanidades Digitales Hispánicas: Innovación, globalización e impacto, UNED, Madrid, October 2015.

Gutiérrez Lanza, Camino & Rabadán, Rosa. (2023). Corpus-based contrast in audiovisual customization: A pilot study on *can/could* and subject pronouns in Spanish dubbing. In *Contrastive Corpus Linguistics: Crossing Boundaries* [Corpus and Discourse Series], Anna Čermáková, Hilde Hasselgård, Markéta Malá & Denisa Šebestová (eds). London: Bloomsbury.

Martín Zorraquino, María Antonia & Portolés Lázaro, José. 1999. Los marcadores del discurso. In *Gramática descriptiva de la lengua española*, Vol. 3, Ignacio Bosque & Violeta Demonte (eds), 4051–4213. Madrid: Espasa Calpe.

MINECO (Ministerio de Economía y Competitividad). 2019. TAligner 3.0. *CorpusNet*, <http://corpusnet.unileon.es/herramientas-tecnicas> (7 February 2022).

Pavesi, Maria. 2008. Spoken language in film dubbing: Target language norms, interference and translational routines. In *Between Text and Image. Updating Research in Screen Translation* [Benjamins Translation Library Series 78], Delia Chiaro, Christine Heiss & Chiara Bucaria (eds), 79–99. Amsterdam: John Benjamins.

Pérez González, Luis. 2007. Appraising dubbed conversation. Systemic functional insights into the construal of naturalness in translated film dialogue. *The Translator* 13(1): 1–38.

Rabadán, Rosa. 2008. Refining the idea of 'applied extension'. In *Beyond Descriptive Translation Studies* [Benjamins Translation Library Series 75], Anthony Pym, Miriam Shlesinger & Daniel Simeoni (eds), 103–117. Amsterdam: John Benjamins.

Rabadán, Rosa. 2010. Applied Translation Studies. In *Handbook of Translation Studies*, Vol. 1 [Handbook of Translation Studies Series 1], Yves Gambier & Luc van Doorslaer (eds), 7–11. Amsterdam: John Benjamins.

Rabadán, Rosa & Gutiérrez Lanza, Camino. 2020. Developing awareness of interference errors in translation: An English-Spanish pilot study in popular science and audiovisual transcripts. *Lingue e Linguaggi* 40: 137–168.

Rabadán, Rosa & Gutiérrez Lanza, Camino. 2023. Interference, explicitation, implicitation and normalization in third code Spanish: Evidence from discourse markers. *Across Languages and Cultures* 24(1): 1–24.

RAE (Real Academia Española). 2021. CORPES XXI. Corpus del Español del Siglo XXI (version 0,94, CORPES XXI XML ed.). <https://www.rae.es/banco-de-datos/corpes-xxi> (7 February 2022).

Romero Fresco, Pablo. 2006. The Spanish dubbese: A case of (un)idiomatic Friends. *The Journal of Specialised Translation* 6: 134–151. <https://www.jostrans.org/issue06/art_romero_fresco.pdf>

Romero Fresco, Pablo. 2009. Naturalness in the Spanish dubbing language: A case of not-so-close Friends. *Meta: Journal des Traducteurs / Meta: Translators' Journal* 54(1): 49–72.

Romero Fresco, Pablo. 2012. Dubbing dialogues … naturally: A pragmatic approach to the translation of transition markers in dubbing. *MonTI. Monografías de Traducción e Interpretación* 4: 181–205.

Sanz-Villar, Zuriñe & Andaluz-Pinedo, Olaia. 2021. TAligner 3.0. A tool to create parallel and multilingual corpora. In *Corpora in Translation and Contrastive Research in the Digital Age. Recent Advances and Explorations* [Benjamins Translation Library Series 158], Julia Lavid-López, Carmen Maíz-Arévalo & Juan Rafael Zamorano-Mansilla (eds), 125–146. Amsterdam: John Benjamins.

Schumacker, Randall E. 2015. *Learning statistics using R.* Los Angeles CA: Sage.

Whitman-Linsen, Candace. 1992. *Through the Dubbing Glass: The synchronization of American motion pictures into German, French, and Spanish.* Frankfurt: Peter Lang.

Zabalbeascoa, Patrick. 2008. La credibilidad de los diálogos traducidos para audiovisuales. In *La oralidad fingida: descripción y traducción. Teatro, cómic y medios audiovisuales,* Jenny Brumme (ed.), 157–175. Madrid/ Frankfurt: Iberoamericana/Vervuert.

CHAPTER 8

Opera audio description in the spoken-written language continuum

Irene Hermosa-Ramírez
Autonomous University of Barcelona

Corpus linguistics research on audio description (AD) – the verbal rendering of visual information generally targeted at people with visual impairment – has focused on film and museums. The present corpus gathers opera AD scripts from the Liceu opera house (Bacelona) and Teatro Real (Madrid), and sorts them into four subcorpora, two devoted to AD throughout the performance and two comprising audio introductions (AI). I set to interrogate where opera AD falls in the spoken-written language continuum. The results suggest that all subcorpora are of a high lexical density, and in terms of lexical variation, the standardised type-token ratio remains below 50%. The mean sentence and word length, and the Flesch-Szigriszt readability results lead us to place the AIs closer to written language than ADs.

Keywords: audio description, opera, corpus linguistics, spoken-written language, readability

1. Introduction

The language used in the different audiovisual translation modalities – subtitling (Levshina 2017; Arias-Badia 2020), dubbing (Matamala 2008; Baños 2013; Pavesi 2013) and voice-over (Sepielak 2016) – and media accessibility services – subtitling for the Deaf and hard of hearing (Jiménez Hurtado & Martínez 2018), AD (Salway 2007; Arma 2011; Jiménez Hurtado & Soler Gallego 2013; Reviers 2017; Matamala 2018; Perego 2019) – has steadily attracted the interest of academics in the field. Corpus linguistics has often been the methodology of choice for such studies, and the present chapter follows suit, interrogating where opera AD fits in the spoken-written language continuum.

https://doi.org/10.1075/scl.113.08her

The question of spoken vs. written language in audiovisual translation has been particularly relevant in the subtitling and dubbing spheres, especially considering the notion of "fictive orality". In dubbing, the dialogue is to retain a sense of naturalness and spontaneity in spite of both the original script and the dubbed version being "written to be spoken" (Romero-Fresco 2009). In subtitling, a certain degree of credibility is also the goal, although subtitles tend to be more neutral than the original dialogue, for instance when it comes to grammar rules (Díaz-Cintas 2003). Curiously, the dual written-to-be-spoken nature of AD and its linguistic implications have been mostly overlooked. An exception is Arma (2011), who situates the language of AD in the middle of the language continuum between spoken-spoken texts (spontaneous conversations) and written-written texts (planned and formal texts): "Considered as a process, it tends to be closer to spoken language. However, from a product perspective, it appears to be closer to written language" (p. 279). The spoken-written nature of opera AD in particular has thus far not been researched.

Unlike other AD modalities, opera AD is always accompanied by an audio introduction (AI)[1] and audio subtitles: a synthesised verbal rendering of the projected surtitles. For this study, I investigate AD scripts in Catalan and in Spanish, delivered at the Liceu opera house in Barcelona and the Teatro Real in Madrid, respectively. The aim of this chapter is to interrogate whether AIs, on the one hand, and ADs, on the other hand, present linguistic features typical of written, spoken language or both. Linguistic differences are expected to arise. As opera AI is a self-contained text, it includes some functions unique to it, such as a foreshadowing function, which introduces visual information on the production to compensate for the time constraints in the AD itself (Reviers, Roofthooft & Remael 2021: 86). Opera AI – unlike AD – does not have to be synchronised with other overlapping semiotic signs. Additionally, the corpus of opera AI and AD is compared with the existing data on film and museum AD.

The chapter is structured as follows. First, the existing literature on AD applying corpus linguistics is presented, followed by the study's theoretical framework including some of the most common measurements applied to assess spoken and written language. Third, the methodology of this paper is introduced, with an emphasis in the sampling strategy and the applied measures. Fourth, the results are discussed, and the conclusions close the chapter.

1. As outlined by Romero-Fresco and Fryer (2013: 289), AIs are introductory texts in prose lasting from five to fifteen minutes that provide "relevant information from the printed program, including running time, cast and production credits, as well as detailed descriptions of the set, costumes, and characters". They are mostly delivered in the context of the scenic arts.

2. The language of audio description through the lens of corpus linguistics

Since the outset of AD research over twenty years ago, several authors have set to define the idiosyncratic linguistic features of AD in different languages and modalities, for instance, Salway (2007) and Arma (2011) for filmic AD in English, Reviers (2017) in Dutch, Jiménez Hurtado and Soler Gallego (2013) and Matamala (2018) in Spanish, and Soler Gallego (2018) and Perego (2019) for museum AD in English.

A number of similarities have been found across languages and modalities, some of them deriving from AD standards and guidelines. Among them are the prevalence of the third person and present tense, and a preference for simpler sentences (AENOR 2005; Rai, Greening & Petré 2010; Remael, Reviers & Vercauteren 2015). Other linguistic idiosyncrasies across film AD corpora can be found in the overlapping most frequent lemmas, which often are nouns and verbs related to objects, body parts, characters, scenes, and actions around movement and looking (Salway 2007; Reviers 2017; Matamala 2018).

The present opera AD corpus study hopes to contribute to defining the language of AD and its nuances among its different modalities, with an emphasis in spoken-written language and readability. Comparisons with the above cited corpora are drawn in the results section.

3. The spoken-written continuum

For the purposes of this paper, spoken and written language are addressed from a linguistic perspective. That is, phenomena such as proxemics and psycholinguistics will not be addressed. From the linguistic perspective, Biber (1988: 5) defines "typically written" language as "structurally elaborated, complex, formal, and abstract, while spoken language is concrete, context-dependent, and structurally simple". Among other "written" characteristics, Casagrande and Cortini (2008: 147) cite a higher prevalence of nouns, less propositions, and a higher lexical density, while in spoken language "nouns tend to become verbs and the number of propositions increases with coordination and collocation connections". In Spanish, one of the two languages of the present corpus, Biber, Davies, Jones and Tracy-Ventura (2006: 13) undertake a multi-dimensional analysis of a large corpus including different levels of register (from conversational to academic prose) and find that written registers have a higher type-token ratio, long words, derived nouns and postmodifying adjectives, among other features. Precisely, these are some of the measures applied to the opera AD corpus.

The present study takes an interest in the spoken-written nature of AD for three reasons: (1) to contribute to the general characterisation of the language of opera AD; (2) because it can be a defining characteristic for certain AD modalities as opposed to others (and even within the opera AD/AI subcorpora); and (3) to contribute to the on-going conversation in the field of media accessibility regarding the application of easy-to-understand principles to access services such as subtitles, AD, etc. (Bernabé Caro & Orero 2019; Arias-Badia & Matamala 2020), as several measures of spoken language overlap with those found in texts with an "easier" readability index.

4. Methodology

For this study I adopt the corpus linguistics methodology to assess a number of lexical and syntactical similarities and discrepancies between opera AI and opera AD, as well as to define where such texts can be placed in the spoken-written language continuum. In this section, I describe the compiled corpus and the measures applied to its analysis.

4.1 Sample of scripts

A common concern when undertaking a corpus linguistics study is the question of representativeness. Undoubtedly, this is a shortcoming typical of audiovisual translation and media accessibility corpora, where text availability is sometimes limited. Because opera AD scripts are limited to two theatres and the trajectory of this modality is shorter than others such as film, I cannot claim that the chosen sample has been randomly selected, a requirement for a corpus to be representative according to Oakes (1998: 9–10). Instead, the focus is placed on qualitative representativeness (van Doorslaer 1995), sampling scripts considering contextual criteria such as (1) the full diachronic trajectory of AD in the two main opera houses in Spain, the Liceu opera house and the Teatro Real; (2) the inclusion of all of the different audio describers that have provided their services in both theatres; (3) overlapping plays described at the venues; (4) the inclusion of different composers, and (5) scenic production styles (i.e. traditional vs. avant-garde). Table 1 summarises the corpus sample developed according to the above-mentioned criteria.

Overall, the corpus is comprised of 13 scripts in Spanish and 15 scripts in Catalan. With the purposes of distinguishing the AI from the AD sections, the corpus is divided into four subcorpora: two devoted to AIs (in Spanish and Catalan) and likewise two devoted to ADs. I will refer to them as AI_ES, comprising 8,535 words,

Table 1. Sample of the opera AD corpus

Teatro Real AD scripts			Liceu AD scripts		
Play	**Number of words**	**Year of production**	**Play**	**Number of words**	**Year of production**
Aida	AI: 768 AD: 2,929	2018	*Aida*	AI: 1,637 AD: 5,039	2007
			Aida	AI: 806 AD: 3,506	2020
Carmen	AI: 501 AD: 4,028	2017	*Carmen*	AI: 1,415 AD: 4,099	2010
Der fliegende Holländer	AI: 569 AD: 3,165	2017	*Der fliegende Holländer*	AI: 1,008 AD: 3,957	2017
Il trovatore	AI: 633 AD: 3,243	2019	*Il trovatore*	AI: 940 AD: 3,670	2017
La bohème	AI: 955 AD: 3,161	2017	*La bohème*	AI: 764 AD: 2,590	2016
Die Zauberflöte	AI: 1,262 AD: 5,780	2016	*Die Zauberflöte*	AI: 859 AD: 5,682	2016
L'elisir d'amore	AI: 483 AD: 3,337	2019	*L'elisir d'amore*	AI: 5,756 AD: 8,042	2018
Turandot	AI: 722 AD: 3,149		*Turandot*	AI: - AD: 2,965	2009
Lucia di Lammermoor	AI: 451 AD: 3,262	2018	*La fille du régiment*	AI: 1,843 AD: 6,796	2010
Lucio Silla	AI: 587 AD: 4,018	2017	*Rusalka*	AI: 1,021 AD: 4,610	2013
Madama Butterfly	AI: 743 AD: 4,088	2017	*Salomé*	AI: 1,396 AD: 2,288	2009
Billy Budd	AI: 675 AD: 4,118	2017	*La Cenerentola*	AI: 1,525 AD: 3,632	2008
La clemenza di Tito	AI: 186 AD: 3,054	2016	*Quartett*	AI: 884 AD: 3,224	2017
	Words total: AI: 8,535 AD: 47,332		*Doña Francisquita*	AI: 1,437 AD: 2,052	2010
				Words total: AI: 21,291 AD: 62,152	

AI_CAT with 2,129,[2] AD_ES with 47,332, and AD_CAT with 62,152 words. It is found that the high variation between comparative texts was not connected to the length of the opera described. There was no correlation between play length and AI length in the AI_ES subcorpus ($r_s(14) = -.17, p > 0.05$) and neither in the AI_CAT subcorpus ($r_s(14) = .14, p > 0.05$). Indeed, there was only a statistically significant correlation between the opera length and the word count of Liceu's AD subcorpus ($r_s(14) = .57, p < 0.05$). AI length and AD length did not correlate either at the Liceu ($r_s(14) = .44, p > 0.05$) nor at Teatro Real ($r_s(14) = .14, p > 0.05$). The principal software applications applied to analyse the data were Sketch Engine and WordSmith Tools, as well as INFLESZ for computing of readability of the scripts.

4.2 Measures

For this study, five formal parameters of analysis were chosen: lexical density, lexical variation, mean word length, mean sentence length and the Flesch-Szigriszt readability index. The first four are common parameters for analysing prototypical written-spoken characteristics, and I added the Flesch-Szigriszt index to cross-reference written-spoken features with readability, inspired by the up-and-coming hybrid access services that incorporate easy-to-understand language to access services such as subtitles and AD (Arias-Badia & Matamala 2020).

Lexical density is calculated dividing the number of lexical words in a corpus by the total number of words. It is generally accepted that a higher lexical density is a distinguishing feature between written and spoken language (Stubbs 1996: 172), and that the higher the lexical density the higher the information load. For illustration:

1. According to Ure (1971), most spontaneous oral texts remain below 40% in terms of lexical density.
2. Biber, Johansson, Leech, Conrad and Finegan (1999: 61–62) found that the spontaneous oral register in English scored a lexical density of 41%, as opposed to journalistic texts that amounted to 63%.
3. In Catalan, Castellà (2002: 256–257) contrasted the lexical density of informal conversations (34%), master lectures (41%) and academic prose (45%).

Next, the division of unique words (types) by the total running words (tokens) or type-token ratio (TTR) in a corpus is a typical measure of *lexical variation*. For

---

2. The significant difference in size between the two AI subcorpora is linked to the Liceu's AIs including more details regarding the play's historical context and plot. Furthermore, there is a great variability within the length of the different AIs at the Liceu (SD = 1266.90, as opposed to Teatro Real's SD of 266.00). This notable internal variability is likely due to the five different describers' personal styles.

the purposes of this study, spontaneous oral corpora tend to have a lower TTR when compared to planned written corpora (van Gijsel, Speelman & Geeraerts 2005). In other words, vocabulary richness is typical of written corpora, while lexical repetition is representative of oral text. However, the TTR measure entails an inherent problem in that it is very sensitive to text length, as the TTR decreases as a text or collection of texts gets longer. An option to overcome this shortcoming is to report the standardised TTR (STTR), which is calculated by dividing the texts into standard-size segments (1,000 words), then calculating the TTR for each segment and taking the mean value (Brezina 2018: 58). Previous corpus studies on AD have utilised TTR (Arma 2011; Perego 2019) and STTR (Reviers 2017; Soler Gallego 2018) to report lexical variation, which is problematic for the purposes of comparison. I therefore resort to reporting both.

Mean word length and *mean sentence length* – as well as mean syllable length – are generally considered to be parameters of readability in corpora. That is, they assess the difficulty of a given collection of texts. Mean sentence length is used to measure text complexity, while mean word length is an indicator of lexical complexity. Written text is generally considered to have higher mean word length (Stromqvist, Johansson, Kritz, Ragnarsdottir, Aisenman & Ravid 2002). For general reference, Kalimeri, Constantoudis, Papadimitriou, Karamanos, Diakonos and Papageorgiou (2015: 108) find that the mean word length of Romance languages falls to around 5 characters, as per the authors' study on the Europarl parallel corpus.

Mean sentence length has also been used as a parameter to compare written and spoken language, although Biber (1986: 385–386) points out that the results of such analyses have sometimes been contradictory. Halliday (1979), for instance, attributes longer sentences with low lexical density to spoken language, while written language is characterised by simple sentences with high lexical density. On the contrary, Blankenship (1962) found that sentence length was almost the same in speech and writing, and O'Donnell (1974) found mean sentence length to be higher in writing. For the purposes of this study, it is worth computing this contested measure together with the rest of the defined measures to define opera AI and AD language more accurately. For general reference, Gispert and Mariño (2006: 65) assessed that the mean sentence length in general newspapers was 19.86 in Catalan and 19.05 in Spanish.

Last, out of several existing readability indexes available (from the SMOG to the Gunning fog index), the *Flesch-Szigriszt readability index* was selected because it has been validated for Spanish (Barrio Cantalejo 2007).[3] The Flesch-Szigriszt index formula is calculated as follows, bearing in mind that "P" refers to the number of

3. It was also deemed appropriate for Catalan, because of the similarities in terms of morphology and syntax in both languages.

words in the text, "S" to the number of syllables in the text and "F" to the number of sentences:

$$\text{FLESCH-SZIGRISZT Index} = 206.835 - (62.3 * S/P) - P/F$$

This formula yields five possible levels of reading difficulty: "very easy" (>80), "fairly easy" (65–80), "normal" (55–65), "fairly difficult" (40–55), and "very difficult" (<40). For reference (Barrio Cantalejo 2007:292), "very easy" texts are suitable for children with a primary education and an example could be a comic book, "fairly easy" texts are also in the primary education range, with some examples being tabloids and bestsellers. "Normal" texts fall within the range of secondary education, with examples being the general and sports press, while "fairly difficult" texts belong to science popularisation and specialised media. "Difficult" texts are scientific papers. To assess the readability of opera AD scripts, the data was computed automatically through the free software INFLESZ for the Spanish subcorpora and semi-automatically for the Catalan subcorpora, with the aid of the online Softcatalà syllable counter and WordSmith Tools.

5. Results

5.1 Lexical density

Lexical density in the opera AD subcorpora amounts to 60.20% in AI_ES, 57.31% in AI_CAT, 53.79% in AD_ES, and 57.33 in AD_CAT. That is, both AI and AD resemble written text, as they fall above the 40% limit proposed by Ure (1971). A possible explanation for this is the inherent need of both modalities to condense a lot of information in a short span of time. According to the existing standards and recommendations for AD (AENOR 2005; Rai et al. 2010; Remael et al. 2015), descriptions have to be succinct yet evocative, which in this case translates to a higher lexical density.

Other AD modalities share similar results, though relatively lower than both the Liceu and the Teatro Real AI subcorpora, as observed in Matamala (2018:192–193), where AD for a short film scores 52.73% for the student corpus and 54.47% for professionals. Reviers (2017:76–77) finds similar results in her corpus of film AD in Dutch (46.51%), and so does Perego's (2019:339) corpus of museum AD, with a mean lexical density of 52.53%. All in all, opera AI reaches the highest lexical density of all modalities researched thus far, and opera AD falls just above the typical results in film and museum AD.

5.2 Lexical variation

Biber (1986: 405) remarked that professional letters, official documents and academic prose tend to have a higher TTR, and he attributed it to the need for conveying the maximum amount of content in the minimum number of words. This is precisely to be expected in AD, but Perego (2019: 339) points out that (as shown by the TTR) museum AD is limited in lexical variation and average in terms of text difficulty, likely due to a desire not to overload the listener and the didactic nature of AD, which in Perego's case alludes to the use of art-related terms. The results, accompanied by the TTR and STTR of other AD corpora are illustrated in Table 2.

Table 2. TTR and STTR in AD corpora

	Opera AD				Film AD		Museum AD	
	AI_ES	AI_CAT	AD_ES	AD_CAT	Arma (2011)	Reviers (2017)	Soler Gallego (2018)	Perego (2019)
TTR	34.06	25.10	15.21	14.75	26 (EN) 31.5 (IT)	-	-	51.07 (EN)
STTR	44.30	46.78	35.62	40.18	-	38 (NL)	42.50 (EN)	-

As I highlighted in the methodology section, the TTR is skewed by the size of the subcorpora: Opera ADs are lengthier than AIs. As per the STTR, AI scripts do demonstrate a higher lexical variation (SD = 4.89), most notably in the case of the AIs from the Liceu. In my corpus, a higher lexical variation in AI can be linked with a higher lexical density. Opera AD "throughout" the performance falls closer to other AD modalities in terms of lexical variation: Both film AD (Reviers 2017) and museum AD (Soler Gallego 2018) appear near 40%. For further comparison, Durán, Malvern, Richards and Chipere (2004) found that academic writing ranges from 80–105%, while general spoken language has a lexical variation of 40–70%. In this regard, opera AI and even more so AD would fall closer to spoken language.

5.3 Mean sentence length

Regarding mean sentence length, a radical difference is noticed between the opera AI and AD subcorpora, regardless of the theatre/language, as illustrated in Table 3. Before delving into the results, it is worth recalling that the average sentence length in general newspaper texts in Catalan and Spanish was just under 20 words (Gispert & Mariño 2006).

Table 3. Mean sentence length in AD corpora

	Opera AD subcorpora				Film AD		Museum AD
	AI_ES	AI_CAT	AD_ES	AD_CAT	Reviers (2017)	Matamala (2018)	Perego (2019)
Mean sentence length	24.00	24.46	7.64	12.49	14.27	8.4	19.32

AI subcorpora yield a higher mean sentence length, and a one-way ANOVA test contrasting AI scripts and AD scripts demonstrates that the difference is significant: $F(1, 53) = 100.35$, $p < .0001$. Moreover, film AD (Reviers 2017; Matamala 2018) appears to be closer to the AD subcorpora, while museum AD (Perego 2019) resembles the AI results. This could be explained by the textual differences in opera and film AD vs. opera AI and museum AD: The latter are both unconstrained pieces of process, unaffected by any existing soundtrack.

It should also be noted that mean sentence length is not a definitive measure when it comes to assessing written and spoken language, as different authors have found contradicting results in this regard (Biber 1986). In any case, a higher mean sentence length is added to the already established trends of higher lexical density and variation in AI.

5.4 Mean word length

Both mean word length and number of "long words" can account for the difficulty of a text or collection of texts. Table 4 gathers the mean word length in the subcorpora, accompanied by previous results in other AD modalities that report this measure. For additional reference, McNamee and Mayfield (2004) found that the mean word in Spanish had 4.90 characters.

Table 4. Mean word length in AD corpora

	Opera AD subcorpora				Film AD	Museum AD
	AI_ES	AI_CAT	AD_ES	AD_CAT	Reviers (2017)	Perego (2019)
Mean word length	4.83	4.58	4.21	4.20	4.69	4.39

In order to assess the mean word length disparities among the AI and AD subcorpora, another ANOVA test is computed. The difference between the opera subcorpora is statistically significant: $F(1, 53) = 89.77$, $p < .0001$, and, in this regard, I may claim that the AIs are closer to written language. However, a *post-hoc* Tukey's HSD test demonstrates that there are also significant differences between the AIs of the Liceu and those of the Teatro Real ($p<.0001$). Some caution is therefore called for in the assertion of one such claim.

5.5 Flesch-Szigriszt readability index

After computing the Flesch-Szigriszt readability index for every AI and AD script, it is found that AIs range from a "fairly easy" to a "normal" readability index (mean = 64.73 = "normal" readability; SD = 5.16), while ADs are mostly "very easy", with some "fairly easy" exemptions (mean = 84.88 = "very easy" readability; SD = 5.34). The AI subcorpora showcase a higher complexity in terms of readability, as has been the trend in the two previous measures. The "easier" readability of ADs could be explained by an effort to limit the intrinsic load (complexity of the message) (Fryer 2016: 30), considering the extrinsic load (the complexity of the medium by which the message is communicated) of opera AD, as well as a need to reduce the mean sentence length due to the time and synchronisation constrains that are not comparably present in AI.

Curiously, Reviers' (2017) corpus of film ADs in Dutch places the scripts in the highest level of difficulty, yet any comparison should be considered with caution, as this study applied a different readability index: Flesch Reading Ease (Flesch, 1948).

6. Conclusions

The present study suggests that both opera AI and AD share features with (planned) written language, particularly when it comes to lexical density, but also some with (spontaneous) spoken language, as is the case in lexical variation. Taken the results of mean sentence length and mean word length, AI does fall closer to written language if I am to place both access modalities in the spoken-written language continuum. Furthermore, AI showcases greater complexity in terms of readability: It not only comprises a higher mean sentence and word length, but it often fits into the "normal" readability, as opposed to the "very easy" AD texts.

If I assess the application of these results in practice, I can infer that AIs are "targeted" versions of the programme or leaflet, not only because of their written characteristics but because they could be of interest for a wider population. As such, they are potential candidates for personalisation: from AIs for the general audience to easy-to-understand AIs. These versions could be yet another opportunity for experimentation and collaboration between academia and the industry.

Bearing the presented results in mind, the principal shortcoming in this study lies in the limited number of measures considered. According to Biber (1986), the preferred way to assess spoken and written characteristics is to undertake a multi-dimensional analysis that accounts for a large number of co-occurring factors so as to avoid contradicting findings, as seen in the case of sentence length. I hope to develop one such analysis in the future, ideally with a larger corpus that is closer to the quantitative "representative" ideal.

Among other future research avenues, I would like to advocate for the expansion of AD studies deploying the corpus linguistics methodology, particularly if they involve the added input of the audio describers. Furthermore, although it is true that media accessibility has shifted from maker- and product-centred approaches to user-centred approaches (Greco 2018), the results of corpus studies can indeed be utilised as a basis to design reception and preference studies. In this regard, it may be possible assess with users whether they are satisfied with the current opera AD and AI readability and manipulate the AI and AD placement in the spoken-written language continuum to create stimuli to be tested in experimental settings.

Funding

This chapter is drawn from a PhD thesis undertaken by the author at the Autonomous University of Barcelona. This research is part of the RAD project (Researching Audio Description: Translation, Delivery and New Scenarios), reference code PGC2018-096566-B-I00 (MCIU/AEI/FEDER, UE). The author is a member of the Transmedia Catalonia research group (2021SGR00077) and has been awarded a PhD grant from the Catalan Government (2019FI_B 00327).

References

AENOR. 2005. *Norma UNE 153020. Audiodescripción para personas con discapacidad visual. Requisitos para la audiodescripción y elaboración de audioguías* (Audio description for visually impaired people. Guidelines for audio description procedures and for the preparation of audio guides). Madrid: AENOR.

Arias-Badia, Blanca & Matamala, Anna. 2020. Audio description meets Easy-to-Read and Plain Language: Results from a questionnaire and a focus group in Catalonia. *Zeitschrift für Katalanistik* 33: 251–270.

doi Arias-Badia, Blanca. 2020. *Subtitling Television Series: A Corpus-Driven Study of Police Procedurals*. Berlin: Peter Lang.

Arma, Saveria. 2011. The Language of Filmic Audio Description: A Corpus-Based Analysis of Adjectives. PhD dissertation, Università de-gli Studi di Napoli Federico II.

doi Baños, Rocio. 2013. 'That is so cool': Investigating the translation of adverbial intensifiers in English-Spanish dubbing through a parallel corpus of sitcoms. *Perspectives* 21(4): 526–542.

Barrio Cantalejo, Inés M. 2007. Legibilidad y salud. Los métodos de medición de la legibilidad y su aplicación al diseño de folletos educativos sobre salud. PhD dissertation, Universidad Autónoma de Madrid.

doi Bernabé Caro, Rocío & Orero, Pilar. 2019. Easy to read as multimode accessibility service. *Hermeneus* 21: 53–74.

doi Biber, Douglas, Davies, Mark, Jones, James K. & Tracy-Ventura, Nicole. 2006. Spoken and written register variation in Spanish: A multi-dimensional analysis. *Corpora* 1: 1–37.

Biber, Douglas, Johansson, Stig, Leech, Geoffrey, Conrad, Susan & Finegan, Edward. 1999. *Longman Grammar of Spoken and Written English*. London: Longman. Also published as Biber, Douglas, Johansson, Stig, Leech, Geoffrey, Conrad, Susan & Finegan, Edward. 2021. *Grammar of Spoken and Written English*. Amsterdam: John Benjamins.

doi Biber, Douglas. 1986. Spoken and written textual dimensions in English: Resolving the contradictory findings. *Language* 62: 384–414.

doi Biber, Douglas. 1988. *Variation across Speech and Writing*. Cambridge: CUP.

doi Blankenship, Jane. 1962. A linguistic analysis of oral and written style. *Quarterly Journal of Speech* 48: 419–422.

doi Brezina, Vaclav. 2018. *Statistics in Corpus Linguistics: A Practical Guide*. Cambridge: CUP.

doi Casagrande, Maria & Cortini, Paolo. 2008. Spoken and written dream communication: Differences and methodological aspects. *Consciousness and Cognition* 17(1): 145–158.

Castellà, Josep M. 2002. La complexitatlLingüística en el discurs oral i escrit: Densitat lèxica, composició original i connexió textual. PhD dissertation, Universitat Pompeu Fabra.

Díaz-Cintas, Jorge. 2003. *Teoría y práctica de la subtitulación Inglés-Español*. Barcelona: Ariel.

doi van Doorslaer, Luc. 1995. Quantitative and qualitative aspects of corpus selection in Translation Studies. *Target* 7(2): 245–260.

doi Durán, Pilar, Malvern, David, Richards, Brian & Chipere, Ngoni. 2004. Developmental trends in lexical diversity. *Applied Linguistics* 25(2): 220–242.

doi Flesch, Rudolph. 1948. A new readability yardstick. *Journal of Applied Psychology* 32: 221–233.

doi Fryer, Louise. 2016. *An Introduction to Audio Description: A Practical Guide*. London: Routledge.

Gispert, Adrià & Mariño, José B. 2006. Catalan-English statistical machine translation without parallel corpus: Bridging through Spanish. In *Proceedings of the 5th International Conference on Language Resources and Evaluation*, 65–68. <https://aclanthology.org/www.mt-archive.info/LREC-2006-Gispert.pdf> 29 May 2023.

van Gijsel, Sofie, Speelman, Dirk & Geeraerts, Dirk. 2005. A variationist, corpus linguistics analysis of lexical richness. *Proceedings from the Corpus Linguistics Conference Series* 1(1): 1–16.

doi Greco, Gian Maria. 2018. The nature of accessibility studies. *Journal of Audiovisual Translation* 1(1): 205–232.

Halliday, Michael A. K. 1979. Differences between spoken and written language: Some implications for literacy teaching. Communication through Reading: Proceedings of the 4th Australian Reading Conference, Brisbane, 25–27 August 1978, Glenda Page, John Elkins & Barrie O'Connor (eds), 37–52. Adelaide: Australian Reading Association.

Jiménez Hurtado, Catalina & Martínez, Silvia. 2018. Concept selection and translation strategy: Subtitling for the Deaf based on corpus analysis. *Linguistica Antverpiensia, New Series – Themes in Translation Studies* 14: 114–139.

Jiménez Hurtado, Catalina & Soler Gallego, Silvia. 2013. Multimodality, translation and accessibility: A corpus-based study of audio description. *Perspectives* 21(4): 577–594.

Kalimeri, Maria, Constantoudis, Vassilios, Papadimitriou, Constantinos, Karamanos, Konstantinos, Diakonos, Fotis K. & Papageorgiou, Harris. 2015. Word-length entropies and correlations of natural language written texts. *Journal of Quantitative Linguistics* 22(2): 101–118.

Levshina, Natalia. 2017. Online film subtitles as a corpus: An n-gram approach. *Corpora* 12(3): 311–338.

Matamala, Anna. 2008. La oralidad en la ficción televisiva: Análisis de las interjecciones de un corpus de comedias de situación originales y dobladas. In *La oralidad fingida: Descripción y traducción. Teatro, cómic y medios audiovisuales*, Jenny Brumme (ed.), 81–94. Frankfurt/Madrid: Vervuert/Iberoamericana.

Matamala, Anna. 2018. One short film, different audio descriptions: Analysing the language of audio descriptions created by students and professionals. *Onomázein* 41: 185–207.

McNamee, Paul & Mayfield, James. 2004. Character ngram tokenization for European language text retrieval. *Information Retrieval* 7: 73–97.

O'Donnell, Roy C. 1974. Syntactic differences between speech and writing. *American Speech* 49: 102–110.

Oakes, Michael P. 1998. *Statistics for Corpus Linguistics*. Edinburgh: EUP.

Pavesi, Maria. 2013. 'This' and 'that' in the language of film dubbing: A corpus-based analysis. *Meta* 58(1): 103–133.

Perego, Elisa. 2019. Into the language of museum audio descriptions: A corpus-based study. *Perspectives* 27(3): 333–349.

Rai, Sonali, Greening, Joan & Petré, Leen. 2010. *A Comparative Study of Audio Description Guidelines Prevalent in Different Countries*. London: RNIB.

Remael, Aline, Reviers, Nina & Vercauteren, Gert (eds). 2015. *Pictures Painted in Words: ADLAB Audio Description Guidelines*. Trieste: EUT.

Reviers, Nina, Roofthooft, Hanne & Remael, Aline. 2021. Translating multisemiotic texts: The case of audio introductions for the performing arts. *The Journal of Specialised Translation* 35: 69–95.

Reviers, Nina. 2017. Audio-description in Dutch: A Corpus-based Study into the Linguistic Features of a New, Multimodal Text Type. PhD dissertation, University of Antwerp.

Romero-Fresco, Pablo & Fryer, Louise. 2013. Could audio-described films benefit from audio introductions? An audience response study. *Journal of Visual Impairment and Blindness* 107(4): 287–295.

Romero-Fresco, Pablo. 2009. Naturalness in the Spanish dubbing language: A case of not-so-close *Friends*. *Meta* 54(1): 49–72.

Salway, Andrew. 2007. A corpus-based analysis of audio description. In *Media for All: Subtitling for the Deaf, Audio Description, and Sign Language*, Jorge Díaz-Cintas, Pilar Orero & Aline Remael (eds), 151–174. Amsterdam: Rodopi.

Sepielak, Katarzyna. (2016). Voice-Over in Multilingual Fiction Movies in Poland. Translation and Synchronization Techniques, Content Comprehension and Language Identification. PhD dissertation, Universitat Autònoma de Barcelona.

Soler Gallego, Silvia. 2018. Audio descriptive guides in art museums: A corpus-based semantic analysis. *Translation and Interpreting Studies* 13(2): 230–249.

Stromqvist, Sven, Johansson, Victoria, Kritz, Sarah, Ragnarsdottir, Hrafnhildur, Aisenman, Ravid & Ravid, Dorit. 2002. Toward a cross-linguistic comparison of lexical quanta in speech and writing. *Written Language and Literacy* 5(1): 45–68.

Stubbs, Michael. 1996. *Text and Corpus Analysis. Computer-assisted Studies of Language and Culture*. Oxford: Blackwell.

Ure, Jean. 1971. Lexical density and register differentiation. In *Applications of Linguistics*, George E. Perren & John L.M. Trim (eds), 443–452. London: CUP.

CHAPTER 9

Using a multilingual parallel corpus for Journalistic Translation Research

The (re)construction of national images in global news*

Biwei Li
Southwestern University of Finance and Economics

By introducing the New York Times Multilingual Parallel Corpus (NYTMPC), this contribution illustrates how multilingual parallel corpora can be designed, constructed, and used for Journalistic Translation Research (JTR). Also, by drawing on a theoretical framework interconnecting imagology and journalistic translation, I conduct a pilot study to demonstrate the exploitation of the NYTMPC for studying national image construction in news translation. The results indicate that stereotyped images of China in English news are reconstructed differently in their Chinese and Spanish translations, and the translational factors that underlie this process are uncovered more clearly with the aid of multilingual parallel corpora.

Keywords: parallel corpus, multilingual, journalistic translation, national image, China

1. Introduction

Although imagological studies have traditionally been rooted in Comparative Literature and thus mostly concentrated on literary works (Leerssen 2016: 14; Barkhoff & Leerssen 2021: 3), interconnections between journalistic translation and imagology are indicated by recent studies (e.g. van Doorslaer 2012; Caimotto 2016; Filmer 2016; Valdeón 2016; van Doorslaer 2021). While the interdisciplinarity of Journalistic Translation Research or JTR is calling for more combined methodological frameworks (Valdeón 2020: 8–10), the use of parallel corpora (bilingual or multilingual) in corpus-based studies of journalistic translation is

* At the time of writing, the author was working on his PhD at the University of Oviedo, Spain.

https://doi.org/10.1075/scl.113.09li

still far from abundant due to the scarcity of identifiable source texts in news translation (Caimotto & Gaspari 2018). In this context, the New York Times Multilingual Parallel Corpus (NYTMPC) was built as part of our PhD project on global news translation in multilingual contexts.

This contribution aims to demonstrate how multilingual parallel corpora can be designed and exploited for JTR and illustrate this point with a case study on the (re)construction of China's images in multilingual news translation. Firstly, the theoretical framework for studying national images in journalistic translation will be presented, followed by some methodological considerations on corpus-based studies of journalistic translation and the use of multilingual parallel corpora. Then the structure and building process of the NYTMPC will be explained before I enter into the pilot study analyzing news headlines and section labels, based on which the body text of the news items will be explored for future research.

2. Approaching national images in journalistic translation

Imagology, in short, is the study of national and cultural images, stereotypes, or ethnotypes (Leerssen 2016; van Doorslaer 2021: 205). Nowadays, studying national images in news media is particularly important for imagology, especially with "the decline of print fiction as the premier narrative medium" (Leerssen 2016: 13) and the omnipresence of journalistic discourse in our modern media world (van Doorslaer 2021: 206). In this sense, journalistic sources can be as relevant as literary ones for imagology, since the constant repetition of national and cultural images in the media can have similar effects to those of literary canonization (van Doorslaer 2021: 206). National images are codified in texts (Beller 2007: 3) as a product of discursive construction. On the one hand, they are embedded in "imaginated discourses", namely a specific set of characterizations and attributes (Leerssen 2007: 27–28) and "imageme", the deep structures of discursively established national attributes (Leerssen 2000: 279, 2016: 29). On the other, unlike studying national identity construction, imagology is essentially comparative and prioritizes cross-national relations over national identities (Leerssen 2007: 29). It is in these two fundamental properties that the values of translation studies lie for imagology, especially in multilingual contexts where national images are constructed and reconstructed across different languages and cultures.

Kuran-Burçoğlu (2000: 145) proposes that the impact of "the image of the other" on the translation process can be analyzed in three stages: prior to and during the translation process, and during the reception process of the target text. In the first stage, the influence of image is reflected in the choice of the text to translate, which is illustrated in the case study by van Doorslaer (2012) on image construction of neighboring countries in TV news media of Flanders, Belgium. The author concludes that the projection of national and cultural images through translation is closely linked to the choice of news topics. In the second stage, images can influence the decision-making processes of translation, which is reflected in the product, that is, the target text. In this regard, previous studies demonstrate that links between translation and image construction can be examined by drawing on discourse-based frameworks such as narrative-frame (Valdeón 2008; Feinauer 2016), Critical Discourse Analysis or CDA (Valdeón 2007; Kim 2017), and systemic functional theories (Valdeón 2009; Li & Pan 2021). These works reveal that national images can be mediated and reconstructed in news translation by means of linguistic, discursive, and narrative devices. Also, it is worth noting that corpus-based approaches are widely applied in some latest studies to investigate national image construction in translation (e.g. Kim 2017; Anagrande 2020; Li & Pan 2021; Turzynski-Azimi 2021), which will be further discussed. In the third stage, image impacts the reception of the target text in the interaction with the perceptions of the target readers or audiences.

This contribution will mainly focus on the first and the second stages by addressing: (1) media choices regarding what to translate and what not to translate in order to construct national images, and (2) how national images are transferred into different languages and cultures as the result of multilingual news production. By building and making use of a parallel corpus composed of the multilingual news items published by *The New York Times*, the study aims to answer the following research questions:

RQ1. What are the most frequent topics associated with the coverage of China and what images of China can be evoked by these topics?
RQ2. How can images of China be reconstructed in different languages when they are transferred into Chinese and Spanish?

3. Multilingual parallel corpora: Methodological considerations

A multilingual corpus involves more than one language, but the term *multilingual* can refer to different corpus structures. For example, Baker (1995: 232) defines multilingual corpora as "sets of two or more monolingual corpora in different languages" designed and built up under similar criteria, and McEnery and Xiao (2007: 131) proposed that the term can be used either in a broad sense, which refers to corpora involving more than one language, or in a narrowed sense, which means the involvement of at least three languages. In this contribution, the narrowed sense of multilingual, that is, containing at least three languages, is adopted.

Multilingual corpora can be parallel or comparable, and these two types are usually differentiated by how their subcorpora correspond with each other. More specifically, as McEnery and Xiao (2007: 132) put it, a corpus is considered parallel when it "contains source texts and translations in parallel", and comparable if the "subcorpora are comparable by applying the same sampling frame", in accordance with the criteria validated by Teubert (1996: 245) and Hunston (2002: 15).

As mentioned in the previous section, translation scholars are resorting to corpus-related methodologies to study image construction in journalistic translation. In her monograph on using multilingual comparable corpora for studying audio-visual news translation, Aragrande (2020) investigated the media representation of national identities in reporting the eastern Ukrainian conflict around 2015 with a combined framework of CDA, narrative theory, and corpus linguistics. The use of comparable corpora for image construction is also illustrated by Kim (2017) in a comparative study of the discursive construction of China's images in Newsweek and its Korean translation. Both studies employed collocation and concordance as efficacious tools to obtain an overview of the discursive reconstruction of national images reflected in translation patterns involving topic selection and news labeling. Nonetheless, the lack of parallel concordance has undoubtedly hindered the authors from delving into the "actual translational correspondences" (Zanettin 2011: 19) to elucidate the interaction between image construction and translation. Having recourse to bilingual parallel corpora, Li and Pan (2021) found that a more negative representation of China is realized by shifting epithets in the English translation of Chinese political discourse, and Turzynski-Azimi (2021) discovered that micro-level translation procedures of culture-specific items in Japanese tourism texts can have macro-level impact on Japan's image as a tourist destination. Since parallel corpora enable comparisons from lexical to syntactic and discursive level (Kenning 2010: 492), imagological concepts such as "imaginated discourse" and "imageme" can be operationalized, identified, and cross-linguistically compared at different levels.

Multilingual parallel corpora are, to our knowledge, scarcely utilized for studying image construction in journalistic translation, even if translation scholars have already pointed out its numerous advantages. Firstly, multilingual corpora can be used to uncover both unique features and characteristics shared by different languages (Johansson 2003: 137). Secondly, by including as many translated versions of the same source text as possible, it can overcome the shortcomings of one-to-one parallel corpora (Malmkjær 1998: 6; McEnery & Xiao 2007: 135). Thirdly, the multilingualism of news production has become inevitable in our globalized world (Aragrande 2020), which implies the necessity of comparisons between two or more languages to investigate journalistic translation (Caimotto & Gaspari 2018: 211). Finally, multilingual approaches can be especially suitable for studying image construction in multicultural contexts since "patterns of national characterization will stand out most clearly when studied supranationally as a multinational phenomenon" (Leerssen 2007: 29). In light of these considerations, now I move to explain how multilingual parallel corpora can be built and used to study national image construction in news translation.

4. The New York Times multilingual parallel corpus

4.1 Corpus structure

The New York Times Multilingual Parallel Corpus (NYTMPC) contains more than one million running words in 753 news texts in three languages (English, Chinese and Spanish) aligned at the paragraph level (see Figure 1), which enables the parallel concordance retrieved from the corpus to display richer textual and contextual information. Composed of a source subcorpus in English and two target subcorpora in Chinese and Spanish, the structure of the NYTMPC (see Table 1) corresponds to the star model described by Johansson (2003: 140–141), which can be particularly helpful for uncovering general features of translation and comparing translation patterns between specific language pairs.[1]

Table 1. Structure information of the NYTMPC

	Source subcorpus	Target subcorpus 1	Target subcorpus 2	Total
Data source	The New York Times	纽约时报中文网	The New York Times En Español	/
Title	NYT	NYTC	NYTS	/
Language	English	Chinese	Spanish	/
Timespan	Jan. 2016 – Dec. 2021	Jan. 2016 – Dec. 2021	Jan. 2016 – Dec. 2021	/
Texts	251	251	251	753
Encoding	UTF-16 LE (.txt)	UTF-16 LE (.txt)	UTF-16 LE (.txt)	/
Numbering	s-1, s-2, …, s-202	t1-1, t1-2, …, t1-202	t2-1, t2-2, …, t2-202	/
Words	351,191	310,369	341,864	1,003,424

1. An alternative Chinese subcorpus was created for word segmentation with SegmentAnt. This alternative subcorpus is completely identical to the Chinese subcorpus in the NYTMPC in terms of content and structure, except the sentences being segmented into Chinese words for computational analysis.

1. <date>2017-04-12</date>	1. <date>2017-04-13</date>	1. <date>2017-04-12</date>
2. <sec>Asia Pacific</sec>	2. <sec>亚太</sec>	2. <sec>Asia</sec>
3. <hln>Xi and Trump Discuss Rising Tensions With North Korea</hln>	3. <hln>朝鲜半岛局势严峻，特朗普与习近平再次 通话</hln>	3. <hln>Aumentan las tensiones en la penÃnsula coreana tras la advertencia de Trump</hln>
4. <lead>null</lead>	4. <lead>null</lead>	4. <lead>null</lead>
5. China's leader, Xi Jinping, and President Trump spoke by phone on Wednesday about the escalating tensions with North Korea as a prominent Chinese state-run newspaper warned the North that it faced a cutoff of vital oil supplies if it dared test a nuclear weapon.	5. 中国领导人习近平与美国总统特朗普周三就朝鲜紧张局势升级问题通了电话，同时，中国一家主要官方报纸警告说，如果朝鲜敢再次测试核武器的话，该国将面临其重要的石油供应被切断的可能。	5. El presidente chino Xi Jinping y el presidente Donald Trump discutieron la escalada de tensiones en la península coreana por teléfono este 12 de abril, en momentos en que un medio estatal chino alertó a Corea del Norte que podría enfrentarse a un bloqueo en la venta de crudo si se atreve a probar un arma nuclear.
6. The phone call, reported by China's state broadcaster, CCTV, came hours after Mr. Trump cautioned Beijing in a Twitter message and a television interview that it needed to help Washington rein in North Korea, a Chinese ally. During the call, which was initiated by Mr. Trump, Mr. Xi said that the matter should be solved through peaceful means, the state news agency Xinhua reported.	6. 中国官方电视台网中央电视台报道了两位领导人的通话，通话发生的几小时前，特朗普曾发推文、并在一次电视采访中告诫北京，中国需要帮助华盛顿控制中国的盟友朝鲜。据官方通讯社新华社报道，这次通话是特朗普发起的，习近平在电话中表示，应该以和平方式解决朝鲜问题。	6. La llamada se dio horas después de que Trump alertara a Pekín en un mensaje de Twitter y una entrevista televisiva que necesitaba ayudar a Washington a refrenar a Pyongyang. Durante la llamada, según la agencia estatal china Xinhua, el presidente Xi destacó que el asunto debía resolverse por medios pacíficos.
7. Tensions escalated further on Wednesday as reports said the Japanese Navy would join the United States Navy strike group led by the aircraft carrier Carl Vinson in its mission off the Korean coast. Those joint exercises will take place as the American ships pass through waters close to Japan, Reuters said.	7. 紧张气氛周三进一步升级，有报道称，日本海军将加入到由卡尔文森号航空母舰带领的美国海军打击编队中来，一起在朝鲜半岛附近水域执行任务。路透社说，联合演习将在美国舰队从日本海域经过时进行。	7. Las tensiones han ido en aumento desde que la marina estadounidense movi|lizó el portaaviones Carl Vinson el 8 de abril pasado a la costa coreana: Japón anunció el miércoles que se sumará a los ejercicios militares cuando la nave pase por aguas japonesas, según Reuters.
8. The Carl Vinson and several other warships are heading toward the Korean Peninsula in a show of force intended to deter the North from testing a sixth nuclear weapon or launching missiles.	8. 卡尔文森号及其他几艘军舰正在驶向朝鲜半岛，以展示力量，目的是阻止朝鲜进行第六次核武器试验或发射导弹。	8. El Carl Vinson y otras embarcaciones se dirigen hacia la península coreana en una muestra de fuerza para desincentivar a Pyongyang de lanzar misiles o llevar a cabo una sexta prueba de armas nucleares.
9. North Korea celebrates the 105th anniversary of the birth of Kim Il-sung, the nationÂ's founder, on Saturday. Its current leader, Kim Jong-un, his	9. 朝鲜将于本周六庆祝开国领袖金日成诞辰105周年。预计金日成的孙子、现任领导人金正恩将利用这个机会上演一次核武器试验，或进行导弹测试，以对美国和朝鲜的主要资助者中国表	9. Este 15 de abril Corea del Norte celebra el 105 aniversario del natalicio de Kim Il-sung, el fundador de la nación y abuelo del actual líder, Kim Jong-un. Se espera que este aproveche la

Figure 1. Example of aligned parallel text in the NYTMPC

4.2 Data source, text selection and corpus building

The New York Times (NYT), a traditional quality newspaper of the United States (US), launched two news websites targeted at Chinese and Spanish readerships, namely《纽约时报》中文网 (The New York Times Chinese Edition, hereafter NYTC) and The New York Times *en Español* (The New York Times in Spanish, hereafter NYTS) in 2012 and 2016, respectively. In NYTC, about 80% of the news articles in Chinese are translated from English undergoing an editorial process in which the adjustment of textual length and the reformulation of news headlines are permitted (Zhang & Liu 2014:3–4). In a parallel way, NYTS publishes global news mostly produced in the US and translated from English into Spanish by a Mexican company before going through certain editing filters (López 2017). As Figure 2 shows, in most cases the three websites share a similar clear layout, where hyperlinks to the translated versions, when available, are always attached to the English contents, so is the access to the original version from NYTC or NYTS.

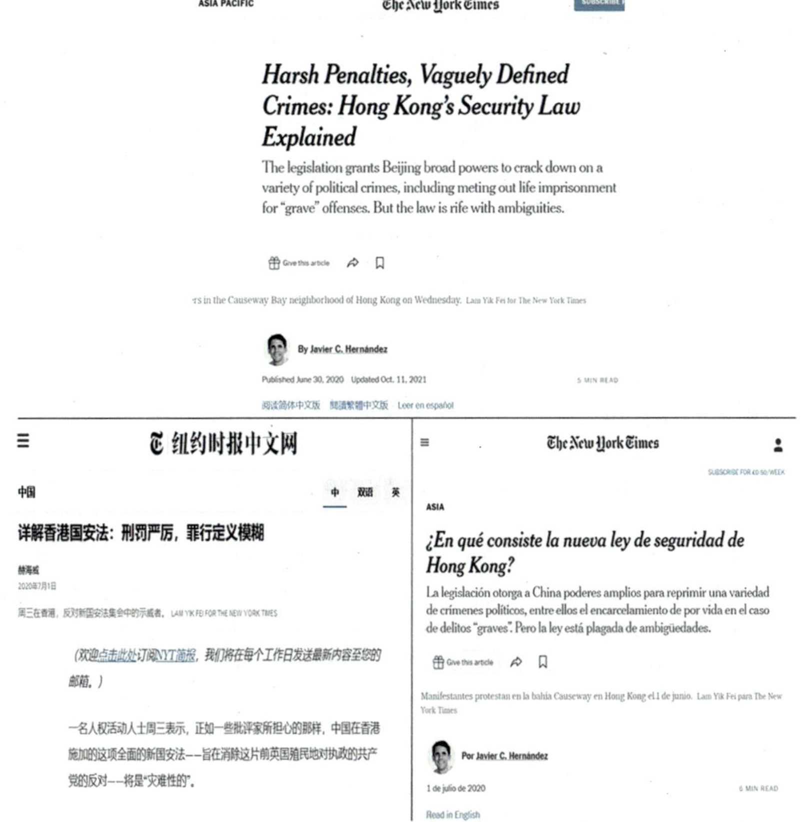

Figure 2. Layout of NYT (upper center), NYTC (lower left) and NYTS (lower right)

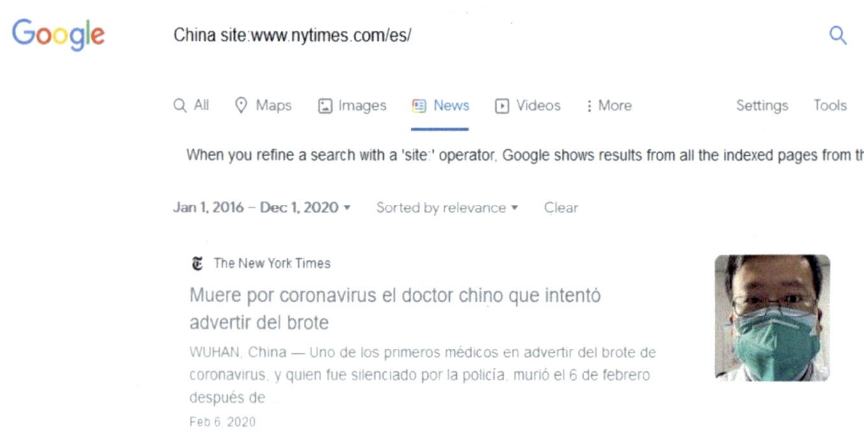

Figure 3. Searching for China-related news items in NYTS with Google News tools

The text selection process started from collecting Spanish news items covering China-related events in NYTS. The reason for doing so lies in the significant connection between the topics that news media may choose to translate and the languages involved in the translation process (van Doorslaer 2009), that is to say, NYT may translate more China-related news into Chinese than into Spanish, and as a result, if the Spanish version of a China-related news item is found, it should be much easier to find its Chinese counterpart and trace back to the source text than vice versa. In this respect, Google News search engine lends itself ideally to the method as it allows the configuration of keywords, website address, and timespan for news search (see Figure 3). By this means, all the Spanish news articles with the keyword "China" published on NYTS from January 2016 to December 2021 are tracked down. After a thorough examination of the search results, 251 news articles in Spanish were identified and collected along with their Chinese counterparts and original versions in English. Subsequently, the collected texts were organized, aligned, and annotated by means of automated tools aided by manual correction. [2]

The NYTMPC is compiled for studying the translation of news discourse in multilingual contexts. Considering the crucial role news section, headline and lead play in the organization of the thematic and schematic structures of news discourse (van Dijk 1988: 40, 53) and their important connections with news production strategies like selection and summarization (van Dijk 1988: 115–117), these

2. Software employed in the text preparation procedures includes the following computer programs: PowerGREP 4 (for text cleaning), ABBYY Aligner 2.0 (for text aligning) and SegmentAnt (for Chinese text segmentation).

news elements are paid special attention to during the corpus building process. To facilitate their retrieval, a tagset is elaborated for the manual annotation of news headlines, leads (or subheadlines) and paratextual information such as publication date and news section. In addition to this, translation shifts involving textual transformations at sentential and paragraph levels including omissions, additions, and permutations identified in the target subcorpora are also manually annotated (see Appendix 1), since, on the one hand, such transformations are among the most frequent strategies for source text processing in news production (van Dijk 1988: 117). On the other hand, translation shifts involving those transformations are often driven by translators' ideological motivations or the ideological positioning of news media. As a result, they can effectively reconstruct the narratives about certain nations (Baker 2006: 71–77) and reframe the perception of the world through translation (Valdeón 2005, 2007, 2008). In this way, the NYTMPC not only enables us to approach news discourse within suitable analytical frameworks, but also to focus on the transferring of news discourse in multilingual contexts by comparisons between different language pairs.

5. Reconstructing national images in multilingual news

In mainland China, public access to the websites of NYT and NYTC has been blocked since a few years ago, probably due to the coverage of politically sensitive issues about the country. However, users from mainland China still constitute the majority of NYTC's readership, followed by those from Taiwan and other regions where Chinese is spoken, according to the executive editor of NYTC (Zhang & Liu 2014: 3–4).

In 2016, NYTS was founded with the aim, in the words of Budasoff (2016), editor in charge, to present local events with global characteristics to Spanish-speaking readers by producing and translating news stories from around the world. In parallel with the increasing amount of coverage of China in NYT during the recent decades (Peng 2004: 63), both NYTC and NYTS have been publishing a considerable number of news covering a variety of China-related topics, most of which are translated from English, as will be shown later in this contribution.

Considering the huge differences that may exist between the two target languages, questions can be raised regarding the news content NYT selects to translate in multilingual contexts and, as a result, to construct and/or reconstruct the images of China in different social, political, and cultural contexts.

5.1 Reconstructing images of China by labeling news

Most of the online news items of NYT, NYTC, and NYTS carry a section label that precedes the headline. As one of the most visually salient elements in the webpage layout, the labels can not only represent the sections or subsections the news items are categorized into but also function as "superheadline" (van Dijk 1988: 53; Frandsen 1992: 148) to summarize the topic or participate in thematic organization.

The news labels tagged in the NYTMPC are retrieved with CUCParaConc.[3] A quantitative analysis shows that China-related news items are most frequently labeled with Asia Pacific, Business, Technology, etc. by NYT (see Table 2), linking China with topics such as international relations, global trading, and science and technology. This association is more or less maintained by NYTC through similar labels including '商业与经济' (business and economy), '科技' (technology), etc., and by NYTS through 'Negocios' (business), 'Tecnología' (technology), etc. Despite the similarity, the discrepancies between NYTC and NYTS also can be observed. The label 'Energy&Environment', for instance, is partially kept by NYTS as 'Medioambiente' (environment) yet totally discarded by NYTC. By invoking different topics, these labels can activate some images of a contemporary China related with international politics, global economy, science and technology, environmental issues, etc. Interestingly, NYTC tends to preserve the labels invoking positive perceptions of China (e.g. economic opportunities, high-tech) and avoid those reminiscent of more negative images (e.g. pollution, coronavirus), and NYTS, by contrast, seems to be less concerned in this respect.

Connections between image construction and target language can be more conspicuous when more sensitive topics are involved, as is the case in covering the COVID-19 pandemic. Since the initial outbreaks in 2020, the denomination of the novel coronavirus has been subject to huge controversy in international media due to serious consequences including racist violence caused by naming the virus with "China" or "Wuhan", where the disease was firstly observed (Bowker 2020: 2; Khalfan, Batool & Shehzad 2020: 195). The sensitive aspects of the connection between China and the topic of coronavirus can explain why none of the labels from the source text is COVID-19-related, even in news items factually covering the epidemic situation in China. This strategy is clearly endorsed by NYTC, which does not use any COVID-19-related labels either, while it is arguably given less importance by NYTS, in which the label 'Coronavirus' (coronavirus) appears.

3. CUCParaConc is a software for parallel concordance retrieving similar to ParaConc but more compatible for the Chinese language. Guo (2021) illustrates its usefulness in studying image-building in Chinese-English interpretation.

Table 2. Section labels of NYT, NYTC and NYTS

NYT	**Num.**	**%**
Asia Pacific	91	36.3%
Business	43	17.1%
Technology	22	8.8%
Opinion	12	4.8%
Health	10	4.0%
Europe	9	3.6%
Science; U.S.	8	3.2%
Politics; World	7	2.8%
Americas; Economy	6	2.4%
Energy&Environment	4	1.6%
Other labels	18	7.2%
No labels	1	0.4%
Total	251	100%
NYTC	**Num.**	**%**
中国 (China)	82	32.7%
商业与经济 (business and economy)	47	18.7%
国际 (international)	32	12.7%
科技 (technology)	19	7.6%
美国 (U. S.); 亚太 (Asia Pacific)	17	6.8%
观点与评论 (opinion and commentary)	13	5.2%
科学 (science)	10	4.0%
健康 (health)	9	3.6%
风尚 (fashion)	2	0.8%
教育(education); 体育(sports); 文化(culture)	1	0.4%
Other labels	0	0.0%
No labels	0	0.0%
Total	251	100.0%
NYTS	**Num.**	**%**
Asia (Asia)	66	26.3%
Negocios (business)	32	12.7%
Internacional (international)	18	7.2%

Table 2. *(continued)*

Mundo (world)	17	6.8%
Opinión (opinion)	13	5.2%
Tecnología (technology)	12	4.8%
Ciencia (science)	9	3.6%
Estados Unidos (the United States)	8	3.2%
Coronavirus (coronavirus)	7	2.8%
China (China); *Economía* (economy); *Medioambiente* (environment); *Salud* (health)	4	1.6%
Other labels	53	21.1%
No labels	31	12.4%
Total	251	100.0%

National or cultural images can be reinforced through journalistic translation, because "[s]ome topics are more pointedly associated with one country than with another" (van Doorslaer 2012: 1057). The analysis of news labels in the NYTMPC suggests that China is frequently associated with international politics, economy, and technology. The latter, despite being an important news topic, was not one of the most covered topics in global news about China around 2008 (Willnat & Luo 2011: 264). The increased presence of technology may stem from changing perceptions of China, which was stereotyped as "the land of cheap goods" and now also "of high-tech products" (Schweiger 2007: 130). When transferred into different languages, these images of China can be maintained or avoided by being associated with or dissociated from topics invoking more positive or negative perceptions through the selection (or de-selection) process in labeling the news.

5.2 Depicting China in news headlines

A news headline functions as an initial summary to formulate the main themes and indicate the preferred overall meanings of the text (van Dijk 1988: 40, 53; Fairclough 1995: 29). Various studies in journalistic translation demonstrate that news headlines can be subject to different types of alterations in the translation process (Valdeón 2007; 2008; Kontos & Sidiropoulou 2012; Zhang 2013), and the diversity of changes observed in translated headlines is expected to be meaningful and consistent with cross-culturally varying patterns (Sidiropoulou 1995: 286). Based on these assumptions, this section aims to uncover how national images embedded in news discourse are reconstructed through the translation of headlines.

NYT Wordlist.lst | NYTC Wordlist.lst | NYTS Wordlist.lst

File Edit View Compute Settings Windows Help

N	Word	Freq.	%	Word	Freq.	%	Word	Freq.	%
1	China	131	5.04	中国	131	5.96	de	179	6.26
2	s	79	3.04	的	106	4.82	China	120	4.20
3	to	66	2.54	美国	30	1.37	la	98	3.43
4	the	63	2.43	在	25	1.14	en	90	3.15
5	a	57	2.19	#	21	0.96	el	71	2.48
6	in	55	2.12	如何	19	0.86	a	65	2.27
7	and	36	1.39	新冠	18	0.82	los	56	1.96
8	of	35	1.35	和	17	0.77	que	43	1.50
9	U	38	1.46	特朗普	17	0.77	y	42	1.47
10	Is	26	1.00	疫情	17	0.77	una	40	1.40
11	#	24	0.92	全球	16	0.73	El	36	1.26
12	Hong	24	0.92	是	13	0.59	las	35	1.22
13	A	23	0.89	疫苗	13	0.59	para	35	1.22
14	How	23	0.89	病毒	13	0.59	La	33	1.15
15	Trump	22	0.85	了	12	0.55	un	27	0.94
16	The	21	0.81	吗	12	0.55	del	26	0.91
17	Coronavirus	19	0.73	香港	12	0.55	por	26	0.91
18	for	18	0.69	与	11	0.50	su	23	0.80
19	Are	16	0.62	你	11	0.50	se	20	0.70
20	In	16	0.62	经济	11	0.50	Trump	20	0.70
21	World	16	0.62	被	11	0.50	Estados	26	0.91
22	With	15	0.58	引发	10	0.46	Hong	18	0.63
23	It	14	0.54	新	9	0.41	con	17	0.59
24	New	14	0.54	一个	8	0.36	es	17	0.59
25	From	12	0.46	到	8	0.36	no	17	0.59
26	Its	12	0.46	后	8	0.36	al	16	0.56
27	What	12	0.46	年	8	0.36	coronavirus	16	0.56
28	He	11	0.42	我们	8	0.36	Los	14	0.49
29	an	10	0.39	为何	7	0.32	#	13	0.45
30	on	10	0.39	习近平	7	0.32	sus	13	0.45
31	by	8	0.31	了解	7	0.32	mundo	12	0.42
32	Global	8	0.31	人	7	0.32	En	10	0.35
33	Up	8	0.31	什么	7	0.32	más	10	0.35
34	About	7	0.27	有	7	0.32	pero	10	0.35
35	as	7	0.27	问题	7	0.32	Una	10	0.35
36	Beijing	7	0.27	世界	6	0.27	entre	9	0.31
37	Can	7	0.27	为	6	0.27			

frequency alphabetical statistics

1,163 entries Row 188 | 1,200 entries Row 220 | 1,174 entries Row 434

Figure 4. Wordlists of NYT, NYTC and NYTC generated with WordSmith7

753 headlines in the three languages were tagged and respectively retrieved from the NYTMPC and processed with the Wordlist tool of WordSmith7 to generate high-frequency wordlists (Figure 4), from which the terms invoking relevant news topics were selected for imagological analysis. The selected words and their frequencies were collated on the basis of the contextual information provided by the parallel concordance retrieved with CUCParaConc. Subsequently, they were categorized into seven thematical groups representing the topics most frequently addressed by the headlines, as shown in Appendix 2. The results suggest

that the main topics are, to some extent, consistent between the three languages. However, the variation of some lexical units in each category and the difference in frequencies among the versions are also imagologically relevant and hence cannot be overlooked. Firstly, the English headlines bring up some traditional or novel images of China related with state and territories (e.g. Taiwan-台湾-Taiwán), heads of government (e.g. Mao-毛泽东-Mao), COVID-19 (e.g. vaccine-疫苗-vacuna), technology corporations (e.g. Huawei-华为-Huawei), and political ideology (e.g. communist-共产党-comunista), which are consistently conveyed through the Chinese and Spanish translation equivalents. Secondly, the varying quantity of the instances identified under each category indicates that greater emphasis can be placed on certain topics in one language than in another. For example, COVID-19-related subjects have relatively higher exposure in Chinese headlines, and the "politics" category is obviously preferred by NYTS representing 10.7% of the Spanish keywords, which is remarkably higher than the proportions of this category in English (6.9%) and Chinese (4.6%).

It is worth noting that the "U.S." category has a strong presence in terms of frequency. Like in many traditional news media of U.S., the China-U.S. relationship is one of the major topics covered by NYT (Peng 2004; Wang 1998; Yan 1998). By looking into the cooccurrence of lexical units from the "U.S." and "China" categories in news headlines, we can see how and to what extent images of U.S. and China are interlinked with each other. As Table 3 indicates, nouns referring to U.S. or its presence often cooccur with references to China or the Chinese president in the source headlines. The patterns are basically followed by NYTC and NYTS, but the former has a higher frequency and the latter shows smaller quantity and variety.

Table 3. Cooccurrence patterns of "U.S." and "China" categories in headlines

	Cooccurrence patterns	Freq.	Total
NYT	U.S.<==>China, Chinese	11	27
	America(n)<==>China, Chinese	5	
	Trump<==>China, Chinese, Xi	10	
	Biden<==>China	1	
NYTC	美国<==>中国, 中, 北京	17	34
	美<==>中, 中国	8	
	特朗普<==>中国, 习近平	7	
	拜登<==>中国, 中	2	
NYTS	Estados Unidos, EE. UU.<==>China, chino	7	18
	estadounidense<==>chino	1	
	Trump<==>China	10	

To understand what causes such differences, it is necessary to delve into the parallel text. The following excerpts can exemplify how U.S.-China relations are reconstructed in the headlines:

(1) *NYT*: Future vaccines depend on test subjects in short supply: monkeys
NYTC: 新冠疫苗研发背后的中美"战略猴子储备"竞赛
(*Gloss*: The China-U.S. race of "strategic monkey reserve" behind the development of the COVID-19 vaccine)
NYTS: El futuro de las vacunas depende de algo que escasea: los monos de laboratorio
(*Gloss*: The future of vaccines depends on something that is in short supply: laboratory monkeys)

(2) *NYT*: As Huawei loses Google, the U.S.-China tech cold war gets its iron curtain
NYTC: 华为禁令拉下中美科技冷战的数字铁幕
(*Gloss*: Huawei ban draws down the digital iron curtain of technology cold war between China and U.S.)
NYTS: Muro digital: las implicaciones de las sanciones estadounidenses a Huawei
(*Gloss*:Digital wall: the implications of US sanctions on Huawei)

(3) *NYT*: The Huawei executive's arrest is igniting fear. The U.S. should take notice.
NYTC: 孟晚舟案会让中国科技精英疏远美国吗?
(*Gloss*: Will the Meng Wanzhou case alienate Chinese technology elites from U.S.?)
NYTS: Los efectos negativos del arresto de una ejecutiva de Huawei
(*Gloss*: The negative effects of the arrest of a Huawei executive)

(4) *NYT*: Biden to face long list of foreign challenges, with China No. 1
NYTC: 拜登接手外交事务"烂摊子",美中关系为头号挑战
(*Gloss*: Biden takes over "the mess" in foreign affairs. U.S.-China relations are the number one challenge)
NYTS: Joe Biden: los desafíos y prioridades de su política exterior
(*Gloss*: Joe Biden: the challenges and priorities of his foreign policy)

Excerpts (1) and (2) respectively illustrate that an image of U.S.-China rivalry can be activated or avoided by adding or omitting mentions of both countries. In Excerpt (3), reference to China is added by NYTC to hint at the unpleasantness in bilateral relations, while NYTS evades mentioning either country. Similarly, Excerpt (4) is another example of how the discourse of U.S.-China relationship is brought forward by NYTC and ignored by NYTS.

In fact, the U.S.-China rivalry has been a recurrent theme used by U.S. media to depict China as a geopolitical threat (Liss 2003: 301–303). This threatening image of China may have roots in the American resistance to Chinese immigration in the 1840s and became dominant in American imaginations in the twentieth century after the founding of the People's Republic of China (Turner 2014: 51–57, 95–102). Leerssen (2000: 271, 2016: 14, 17, 22) justifiably states that national characterization takes shape in the constant confrontation between the Self and the Other by creating auto-images vis-à-vis hetero-images. In reinforcing images of rivalry between U.S. and China, it is in effect the stereotypical image of China as a threatening power to U.S. that is being perpetuated. The results demonstrate that NYTC tends to depict China as more threatening to U.S. by foregrounding hostile relations between the two countries, and NYTS is inclined to avoid the imagery of U.S.-China relations.

6. Conclusion

To conclude the contribution, I would like to give some tentative answers to the research questions. Regarding RQ1, the qualitative and quantitative analyses based on the NYTMPC manifest that a vast array of topics, from international politics to fashion, are associated with news coverage of China. As some topics are more frequently touched upon than others, certain images of China, especially those connected with the U.S., COVID-19, politics, economy, and technology, can be consequently activated. As for RQ2, when the news items are transferred into different languages, some aspects of these images of China are consistently present, yet others are reconstructed to varying degrees. The analysis of parallel text reveals that image reconstruction can be realized by selecting and de-selecting news labels and reformulating news headlines. The case of reconstructing the U.S.-China rivalry image specifically shows that China is depicted differently in Chinese and Spanish, since a more threatening image of China is presented by the Chinese headlines.

The results of the pilot study showcase that the methodological synergies between imagology and journalistic translation studies and their "added value" for each other (van Doorslaer 2021: 206–211) can be better exploited with the aid of multilingual parallel corpora. For future research, the "story proper" of the news items (Bell & Garret 1998) can be thoroughly explored for more insights into the cross-linguistic and -cultural patterns of image reconstruction (Leerssen

2007). Also, guided by the findings of the current study, the exploitation of the annotated parallel text will better demonstrate the potential of the NYTMPC for studying journalistic translation in multilingual contexts.

References

Aragrande, Gaia. 2020. *Fascinating Transitions in Multilingual Newscasts: A Corpus-based Investigation of Translation in the News.* Cham: Palgrave Macmillan.

Baker, Mona. 1995. Corpora in translation studies: An overview and some suggestions for future research. *Target. International Journal of Translation Studies* 7(2): 223–243.

Baker, Mona. 2006. *Translation and Conflict: A Narrative Account.* London: Routledge.

Barkhoff, Jürgen & Leerssen, Joep. 2021. *National Stereotyping and Identity Politics in Times of European Crises.* Leiden: Brill.

Bell, A., & Garrett, P. D. 1998. *Approaches to Media Discourse.* Oxford: Wiley-Blackwell.

Beller, Manfredi. 2007. Perception, image, imagology. In Beller & Leerssen (eds), 3–16.

Beller, Manfredi & Leerssen, Joep (eds). 2007. *Imagology. The Cultural Construction and Literary Representation of National Characters: A Critical Survey.* Amsterdam: Rodopi.

Bowker, Lynne. 2020. French-language COVID-19 terminology: International or localized? *The Journal of Internationalization and Localization* 7(1–2): 1–27.

Budasoff, Eliezer. 2016. Eliezer Budasoff, editor de "The New York Times" en español: "En esta campaña se ha visto más que nunca el intento de conquistar al público hispano". *11 Minutos.* 22 November 2016. <https://www.hispaniccouncil.org/eliezer-budasoff-editor-de-the-new-york-times-en-espanol-en-esta-campana-se-ha-visto-mas-que-nunca-el-intento-de-conquistar-al-publico-hispano> (6 September 2021).

Caimotto, M. Cristina. 2016. Images of turmoil. Italy portrayed in Britain and re-mirrored in Italy. In van Doorslaer, Flynn & Leerssen (eds), 239–256.

Caimotto, M. Cristina & Gaspari, Federico. 2018. Corpus-based study of news translation: Challenges and possibilities. *Across Languages and Cultures* 19(2): 205–220.

van Dijk, Teun A. 1988. *News as Discourse.* Hillsdale NJ: Lawrence Erlbaum Associates.

van Doorslaer, Luc. 2009. How language and (non-) translation impact on media newsrooms: The case of newspapers in Belgium. *Perspectives: Studies in Translatology* 17(2): 83–92.

van Doorslaer, Luc. 2012. Translating, narrating and constructing images in journalism with a test case on representation in Flemish TV news. *Meta: Journal des Traducteurs/Meta: Translators' Journal* 57(4): 1046–1059.

van Doorslaer, Luc. 2021. Stereotyping by default in media transfer. In *National Stereotyping and Identity Politics in Times of European Crises*, Jürgen Barkhoff & Joep Leerssen (eds), 205–220. Leiden: Brill.

van Doorslaer, Luc, Flynn, Peter & Leerssen, Joep (eds). 2016. *Interconnecting Translation Studies and Imagology* [Benjamins Translation Library 119]. Amsterdam: John Benjamins.

Fairclough, Norman. 1995. *Media Discourse.* London: Hodder Arnold.

Feinauer, Ilse. 2016. Are South African print newspaper narratives reframed for Internet news portals or not? *Stellenbosch Papers in Linguistics Plus* 49: 167–197.

Filmer, Denise. 2016. Images of Italy? The words Berlusconi never (officially) said. In van Doorslaer, Flynn & Leerssen (eds), 257–276.

Frandsen, Finn. 1992. News discourse: The paratextual structure of news texts. In *Nordic Research on Text and Discourse*, Ann-Charlotte Lindeberg, Nils Erik Enkvist & Kay Wikberg (eds), 147–157. Turku: Åbo Academy Press.

doi Hunston, Susan. 2002. *Corpora in Applied Linguistics*. Cambridge: CUP.

Johansson, Stig. 2003. Reflections on corpora and their uses in cross-linguistic research. In *Corpora in Translator Education*, Federico Zanettin, Silvia Bernardini & Dominic Stewart (eds), 135–144. Manchester: St. Jerome.

doi Kenning, Marie-Madeleine. 2010. What are parallel and comparable corpora and how can we use them? In *The Routledge Handbook of Corpus Linguistics*, Anne O'Keeffe & McCarthy Michael (eds), 487–500. London: Routledge.

doi Khalfan, Maryah, Batool, Huma & Shehzad, Wasima. 2020. COVID-19 neologisms and their social use: An analysis from the perspective of linguistic relativism. *Linguistics and Literature Review* 6(2): 117–129.

doi Kim, Kyung, H. 2017. Newsweek discourses on China and their Korean translations: A corpus-based approach. *Discourse, Context & Media* 15: 34–44.

doi Kontos, Petros & Sidiropoulou, Maria. 2012. Socio-political narratives in translated English-Greek news headlines. *Intercultural Pragmatics* 9(2): 195–224.

doi Kuran-Burçoğlu, N. 2000. At the crossroads of translation studies and imagology. In *Translation in Context: Selected Contributions from the EST Congress, Granada, 1998* [Benjamins Translation Library 39], Andrew Chesterman, Natividad Gallardo San Salvador & Yves Gambier (eds), 144–150. Amsterdam: John Benjamins.

doi Leerssen, Joep. 2000. The rhetoric of national character: A programmatic survey. *Poetics today* 21(2): 267–292.

Leerssen, Joep. 2007. Imagology: History and method. In Beller & Leerssen (eds), 17–32.

Leerssen, Joep. 2016. Imagology: On using ethnicity to make sense of the world. *Iberic@l, Revue d'Études Ibériques et Ibéro-américaines* 10: 13–31.

doi Li, Tao & Pan, Feng. 2021. Reshaping China's image: A corpus-based analysis of the English translation of Chinese political discourse. *Perspectives: Studies in Translatology* 29(3): 354–370.

doi Liss, Alexander. 2003. Images of China in the American print media: A survey from 2000 to 2002. *Journal of Contemporary China* 12(35): 299–318.

López, Elías. 2017. Diez preguntas sobre The New York Times en Español. *The New York Times en Español*, 4 October 2017. <https://www.nytimes.com/es/2017/10/04/espanol/america-latina/diez-preguntas-esenciales-sobre-the-new-york-times-en-espanol.html> (5 September 2021).

doi Malmkjaer, Kirsten. 1998. Love thy neighbour: Will parallel corpora endear linguists to translators? *Meta: Journal des Traducteurs/Meta: Translators' Journal* 43(4): 539.

doi McEnery, Tony & Xiao, Zhonghua. 2007. Parallel and comparable corpora: The state of play. In *Corpus-based Perspectives in Linguistics* [Usage-Based Linguistic Informatics 6] Yuji Kawaguchi, Toshihiro Takagaki, Nobuo Tomimori & Yoichiro Tsuruga (eds), 131–146. Amsterdam: John Benjamins.

Peng, Zengjun. 2004. Representation of China: An across time analysis of coverage in the New York Times and Los Angeles Times. *Asian Journal of Communication* 14(1): 53–67.

Schweiger, Irmy. 2007. China. In Beller & Leerssen (eds), 126–130.

Sidiropoulou, Maria. 1995. Headlining in translation: English vs. Greek press. *Target. International Journal of Translation Studies* 7(2): 285–304.

Teubert, W. 1996. Comparable or parallel corpora? *International Journal of Lexicography* 9(3): 238–264.

Turner, Oliver. 2014. *American Images of China: Identity, Power, Policy*. London: Routledge.

Turzynski-Azimi, Angela. 2021. Constructing the image of Japan as a tourist destination: Translation procedures for culture-specific items. *Perspectives* 29(3): 407–425.

Valdeón, Roberto A. 2005. The "translated" Spanish service of the BBC. *Across Languages and Cultures* 6(2): 195–220.

Valdeón, Roberto A. 2007. Ideological independence or negative mediation: BBC Mundo and CNN en Español's (translated) reporting of Madrid's terrorist attacks. In *Translating and Interpreting Conflict*, Myriam Salama-Carr (ed), 97–118. Amsterdam: Rodopi.

Valdeón, Roberto A. 2008. Anomalous news translation: Selective appropriation of themes and texts in the internet. *Babel* 54 (4): 299–326.

Valdeón, Roberto A. 2009. Euronews in translation: Constructing a European perspective for/of the world. *FORUM. Revue Internationale d'Interprétation et de Traduction/International Journal of Interpretation and Translation* 7(1): 123–153.

Valdeón, Roberto A. 2016. The construction of national images through news translation. In van Doorslaer, Flynn & Leerssen (eds), 219–237.

Valdeón, Roberto A. 2020. Journalistic translation research goes global: Theoretical and methodological considerations five years on. *Perspectives: Studies in Translatology* 28(3): 325–338.

Wang, Mei-ling. 1998. Creating a virtual enemy: U.S.-China relations in print. In *Image, Perception, and the Making of US-China Relations*, Hongshan Li & Zhaohui Hong (eds), 73–100. Lanham MD: University Press of America.

Willnat, Lars & Luo, Yunjuan. 2011. Watching the dragon: Global television news about China. *Chinese Journal of Communication* 4(3): 255–273.

Yan, Wenjie. 1998. A structural analysis of the changing image of China in the New York Times from 1949 through 1988. *Quality and Quantity* 32(1): 47–62.

Zanettin, Federico. 2011. Translation and corpus design. *SYNAPS – A Journal of Professional Communication* 26: 14–23.

Zhang, Meifang. 2013. Stance and mediation in transediting news headlines as paratexts. *Perspectives: Studies in Translatology* 21(3): 396–411.

Zhang, Zhian & Liu, Hongcen. 2014. Providing readers with diverse perspectives and curious facts: An interview with Cao Haili, executive editor-in-chief of the New York Times Chinese website (为读者提供多元的视角和稀缺的事实: 专访纽约时报中文网执行总编辑曹海丽). *Journalism and Mass Communication Monthly* 20: 2–8.

Appendix 1. Tagset information for the NYTMPC

	Source subcorpus	Target subcorpus 1	Target subcorpus 2	Description
Date	<date></date>	<date></date>	<date></date>	Date format: year-month-day
Section	<sec></sec>	<sec></sec>	<sec></sec>	No section labels: <sec>null </sec>
Headline	<hln></hln>	<hln></hln>	<hln></hln>	/
Lead (Subhead)	<lead></lead>	<lead></lead>	<lead></lead>	No leads or subheads: <lead>null </lead>
Omission	/	<omi_c1></omi>	<omi_s1></omi>	Omitting a whole paragraph
		<omi_c2></omi>	<omi_s2></omi>	Omitting sentence(s) within a paragraph
Addition	/	<add_c1></add>	<add_s1></add>	Adding a whole paragraph
		<add_c2></add>	<add_s2></add>	Adding sentence(s) to a paragraph
Permutation	/	<pmt_c1></pmt>	<pmt_s1></pmt>	Using a segment as an individual paragraph
		<pmt_c2></pmt>	<pmt_s2></pmt>	Merging two or more paragraphs into one
		<pmt_c3></pmt>	<pmt_s3></pmt>	Moving a whole paragraph
		<pmt_c4></pmt>	<pmt_s4></pmt>	Moving a segment from one paragraph to another

Appendix 2. Thematic categories and lexical units in headlines

	China	COVID-19	U.S.	International affairs	Technology	Economy	Politics
NYT	China[113], Chinese[18],	coronavirus[19],	Trump[22],	world[16], global[8],	Huawei[5], tech[4],	economic[7], trade[5],	leader[5], war[5],
	Hong Kong[12],	vaccine(s)[11], pandemic[5],	U.S.[15],	Asia(n)[6], Russia[3],	Apple[4], Facebook[3],	economy[5],	president[3], communist(s)[3],
	Beijing[7], Xi[7], Mao[4],	COVID[4], mask(s)[4],	America[5],	Tokyo[2],	iPhone[2], Silicon	company(ies)[3],	officials[2], party[2], power[2],
	Taiwan[3], Tiananmen[2],	virus[3], epidemic[2],	American(s)[3],	North Korea[2],	Valley[2], Twitter[2],	tourism[2], trademarks[2],	communism[1], diplomacy[1],
	Xinjiang[2], Wuhan[1]	outbreak[2], quarantine[2]	Biden[3]	Kim Jong-un[2],	App(s)[2], A.I.[2],	business[1], capitalize[1],	diplomatic[1], diplomats[1],
				Olympic[1]	supercomputers[2],	commerce[1], markets[1]	policy[1]
					Alibaba[1], Google[1]		
#(%)	**169 (42.90%)**	**52 (13.20%)**	**48 (12.20%)**	**41 (10.40%)**	**29 (7.40%)**	**28 (7.10%)**	**27 (6.90%)**
NYTC	中国[121], 中[12],	新冠[18], 疫苗[13],	美国[24],	全球[16], 各国[4],	华为[4], 互联网[3],	经济[11], 贸易战[5],	政府[6], 政策[4], 外交官[2],
	香港[12], 习近平[7],	病毒[13], 感染[3],	特朗普[17],	世界[6], 日本[2],	人工智能[3], 苹果[3],	贸易[3], 企业[3],	战略[2], 战争[2], 政治[2],
	武汉[6], 北京[4],	疫情[17], 口罩[3],	美[7],	俄罗斯/俄[4],	Facebook[2], iPhone[2],	公司[2], 市场[1]	权力[2], 共产党[2],
	台湾[4], 新疆[3]	封城[2], 病例[2],	拜登[3]	金正恩[3], 亚洲[2],	技术[2], 推特[2],		共产主义[1]

Appendix 2. *(continued)*

	China	COVID-19	U.S.	International affairs	Technology	Economy	Politics
毛泽东[3], 维吾尔[2], 天安门[1]	防疫[2]		全球化[2], 多国[2], 冬奥会[1]	硅谷[2], 科技[2], 网络[2], 超级计算机[2], 阿里[1]			
#(%)	**175 (42.0%)**	**73 (17.5%)**	**51 (12.2%)**	**44 (10.6%)**	**30 (7.2%)**	**25 (6.0%)**	**19 (4.6%)**
NYTS	China[107], chino/a(s)[15], Hong Kong[9], Pekín[5], Mao[4], Taiwán[3], Wuhan[3], Xi[3], Sinkiang[2], Tiananmén[2]	coronavirus[20], vacuna(s)[11], pandemia[5], virus[5], COVID[4], cuarentena(s)[2] epidemia[2], cubrebocas[1], mascarilla(s)[2]	Trump[20], Estados Unidos[9], Biden[3], EE. UU. [3], estadounidense[3] Norteamérica[1]	mundo[13], global[9] Asia[3], Tokio[2], asiáticas[2], Kim Jong-un[2], Rusia[2], olímpica[1], norcoreano[1]	Huawei[5], tecnología[3], tecnológico/a(s)[2], Apple[3], Facebook[3], Internet[2], supercomputadora[2], Twitter/tuits[2], iPhone[1], web[1], Alibaba[1]	economía[4], económico[4], comercial[4], comercio[4], empresa(s)[3], marcas[2], mercados[2]	política[5], comunista(s)[5], diplomático/a(s)[5], guerra[5], líder[4], partido[4], gobierno(s)[4], políticos[2], presidente[2], diplomacia[2], comunismo[1]
#(%)	**153 (42.0%)**	**53 (14.6%)**	**39 (10.7%)**	**35 (9.6%)**	**24 (6.6%)**	**21 (5.8%)**	**39 (10.7%)**

CHAPTER 10

Domain-adapting and evaluating machine translation for institutional German in South Tyrol

Antonio Giovanni Contarino & Flavia De Camillis
University of Bologna | Eurac Research, Institute for Applied linguistics

Building on a prior small-scale study on machine translation adaptation in the same language pair and domain (De Camillis 2021), this chapter reports on a (i) domain-adaptation, (ii) quality assessment, and (iii) automatic legal terminology evaluation experiment for legal South Tyrolean German. After collecting, sentence-aligning, and cleaning the LEXB parallel corpus, we used this bilingual resource to domain-adapt a ModernMT engine. Performance improvements were measured in terms of automatic quality metrics. The machine-translation of South Tyrolean legal terms was evaluated using an *ad hoc* automatic terminology evaluation tool. We observed a significant boost in performance and term accuracy in the output of the ModernMT adapted engine, but the improvement in legal terminology translation was deemed unsatisfactory.

Keywords: machine translation adaptation, legal terminology, institutional language, machine translation evaluation

1. Introduction

This chapter reports on a machine translation (MT) adaptation and evaluation experiment carried out on institutional South Tyrolean German, the first to use a domain-adapted Neural Machine Translation (NMT) system. This variety of German can be considered a low-resource domain as it is used only in the public institutions of South Tyrol, a small Italian autonomous province. In Section 2, we explain why South Tyrolean German differs from other varieties of German, namely for its legal and administrative terminology and phraseology. We also describe how South Tyrolean German legal terminology is standardised and harmonised. Minor experiments on MT for South Tyrolean institutional German carried out previously are presented in Section 3. To date, the only

https://doi.org/10.1075/scl.113.10con

publicly accessible repository of local bilingual texts is the legislative database LexBrowser.[1] As explained in Section 4, its texts were retrieved, sentence-aligned, and cleaned to build the LEXB corpus for domain-adaptation purposes. Next, we present the MT domain-adaptation and testing phase carried out using ModernMT (MMT), as well as the taxonomy behind a terminology evaluation tool we developed in order to identify correct and wrong South Tyrolean terms. Section 5 presents our main results, which rely both on automatic scores and manual analyses, and we conclude the article with a summary of the achievements and drawbacks of our experiment, as well as pointers for future research.

2. German in South Tyrol

South Tyrol is a small autonomous province in Italy, where Italian and German are co-official languages since 1972, the year in which the promulgation of its new Statute of Autonomy brought radical change to the German local minority. From 1948 to 1972, German-speaking people had had only the possibility – but formally not yet the right – to interact with public authorities in German, while the new Statute stated their right to do so (DPR 670/1972, art. 100). On a practical level, local authorities and public offices underwent a major reorganisation. In order for them to be able to communicate in German, civil servants capable of speaking this language were hired, and laws and documents began to be translated.

Between the 1970s and the 1980s, several decrees were promulgated to better define local language policies. One out of many fundamental policies concerned a Terminology Commission. Made up of 6 legal German- and Italian-speaking experts, the commission "was entrusted with the task of standardising a full set of German language terms that could faithfully reflect the Italian legal language" (Chiocchetti, Ralli & Stanizzi 2017: 257). The standardised terminology was vital to the legislative, the judiciary and the administration to fulfil their duties in both Italian and German. To this day, official documents, including laws and acts, must be published in both official languages and must contain standardised terminology. The judiciary must grant the right to German-speaking people to have a fair trial in their own language.

There is a specific reason why legal and administrative terminology could not simply be borrowed from the German, Swiss, or Austrian legal systems. Legal terminology is system-bound, that is, "it is intimately linked to the legal system it belongs to" (Chiocchetti 2019a: 177). As legal terminology is deeply rooted in a cultural, social, and economic environment, many legal concepts of the Italian system could not be expressed with foreign terms only (Chiocchetti et al. 2017: 257).

1. <http://lexbrowser.provinz.bz.it/> (last consulted in July 2022).

The Terminology Commission carried out its work from 1991 until 2012. This consisted in checking, approving and publishing bilingual term couples from several law subdomains. An essential part of this procedure was devoted to micro-comparison, that is, a contrastive research of legal terms among German-speaking and Italian legal systems. Their work highly contributed to reducing terminological variation as well as regionalisation for South Tyrolean German and consisted of around 15,000 to 20,000 standardised terms (Chiocchetti 2019b: 10–11; Chiocchetti et al. 2017: 260). Despite the fact that the Terminology Commission nowadays no longer carries out terminological standardisation, as the law constantly evolves German legal and administrative terminology in South Tyrol must be harmonised. For this reason, the Institute for Applied Linguistics of Eurac Research (that stands for European Academy) and the Office for Language Issues of the Province of Bolzano pursue the mission and disseminate their joint work via bistro,[2] an information system providing standardised and harmonised terminology for free (Ralli & Andreatta 2018). Unlike standardised terminology, the use of harmonised terminology is not legally binding, but recommended by the Office for Language Issues.[3] To date, bistro contains 13,700 bilingual entries (December 2021).

Apart from bistro, there are two other important local language resources: LexBrowser, a database that contains provincial legislation, resolutions, and decisions of the Constitutional Court and the Regional Administrative Court in Italian, German and, partly, Ladin (the second local minority language), as well as a reduced amount of national laws and constitutional legislation translated into German. Another database, the Official Regional Gazette (Bollettino Ufficiale),[4] contains regional legislation in Italian and German. Local authorities, such as the Provincial Administration, have internal translation departments, but do not share their working translation memories with the public. The majority of the documents published by local authorities are not collected in any repository. According to van der Wees (2017), the fact that a possibly large number of bilingual resources for South Tyrolean is yet to be gathered for research purposes makes this variety a low-resource domain. She identified three main elements constituting a domain: provenance, topic and genre. Our domain consists of South Tyrolean (provenance) legal and administrative (topic) texts, such as laws and decrees (genre). A similar definition was given by Koehn and Knowles (2017) (see also Saunders 2021). In Section 4, we will present the first attempt carried out so far to feed an MT-system with local bilingual resources.

2. <http://bistro.eurac.edu/> (last consulted in February 2022).

3. In South Tyrol, harmonised terminology indicates terminology elaborated through the joint work of Eurac Research and the Office for Language Issues of the Province of Bolzano to pursue consistent use and diffusion of legal and administrative terms in the local institutions.

4. <http://old.regione.taa.it/burtaa/it/default.aspx> (last consulted in February 2022).

3. Previous experiments on MT and legal German

A first MT experiment on South Tyrolean German was carried out by Heiss and Soffritti (2018), who tested the performance of DeepL[5] translation from Italian into German on several text typologies shortly after its release in late 2017. DeepL's performance seemed highly promising from the very beginning. In particular, the test they carried out on a decree of the Province of Bolzano (South Tyrol) revealed flawless syntax and morphology, good enough to offer German-speaking readers a general understanding of the text. In contrast, South Tyrolean legal and administrative terminology was mostly wrongly translated, leading to a very modest BLEU score of 23.69 points (Heiss & Soffritti 2018: 3).

Despite it being of little use for South Tyrolean institutions at that time, DeepL performed surprisingly well on the translation of a legal text, a notoriously very complex domain for human translators, as stated by Wiesmann (2019: 121). This scholar, too, studied the performance of MT from Italian into German on legal texts from the legislative area, legal practice and legal theory. She carried out a diachronic test using both DeepL and MateCat[6] (a system integrating a combination of Google Translate, Microsoft Translator and DeepL) over a period of four months. The test revealed poor results as far as comprehensibility/meaningfulness and correspondence between source and target text are concerned, with law and legal essays performing better than texts from legal practice (e.g., contracts). The scholar ascribes this result to the higher presence of particularly complex text features in texts of legal practice, which pose a serious obstacle for MT-systems. Overall, DeepL outperformed the MT systems integrated in MateCat (Wiesmann 2019: 132–35).

Finally, De Camillis (2021: 291–300) achieved very similar results to those of Heiss and Sofritti. She translated two decrees of the Province of Bolzano from German into Italian and vice versa with ModernMT (MMT) (Bertoldi, Caroselli & Federico 2018)[7] and eTranslation.[8] She fed MMT two translation memories (TM) of 22,500 segments overall, but the results diverged highly from one language direction to the other. The highest BLEU score was achieved by MMT trained with the TMs (41.34) (DE > IT), while the decree translated into German obtained only 15.60 points. However, a qualitative manual analysis revealed sufficiently good syntax and the general preservation of the original meaning. Instead, legal terminology represented a major drawback, which probably influenced the BLEU

5. <https://www.deepl.com/translator> (last consulted in February 2022).

6. <https://www.matecat.com/> (last consulted in February 2022).

7. <https://www.modernmt.com/> (last consulted in February 2022).

8. <https://ec.europa.eu/cefdigital/wiki/display/CEFDIGITAL/eTranslation> (last consulted in February 2022).

score. Harking back to Wiesmann (2019: 133), this result could be affected by the translation of only one legal text type, namely legislation, as much as the results of Heiss and Soffritti (2018). Other legal texts from South Tyrol may achieve different results, so further research in this area would be very much welcome.

4. Methodology

4.1 Corpus building

The resource compiled to carry out MT adaptation in our experiment is LEXB, a parallel corpus of 4,987 bilingual normative texts published in the LexBrowser collection and of 20 Italian national laws and codes (Civil Code, Criminal Code, etc.) translated into German by the provincial Office for Language Issues.

LexBrowser is a publicly accessible online database of South Tyrolean legislation. Texts or single articles can be retrieved by keywords, drafting year, article, number or text type. All documents, however, can only be consulted monolingually: a link to the translated versions exists, but it is not possible to display the original and the translated texts side by side.

To build the LEXB corpus, all bitexts available on the LexBrowser database were collected and extracted by means of web scraping techniques.[9] After undergoing a first stage of pre-processing and text filtering operations, bitexts were aligned using LF Aligner,[10] a tool for automatic sentence alignment based on hunalign (Varga et al. 2007). The features of the collected legal texts made it possible to obtain a very high quality of automatic alignment. Firstly, South Tyrolean bilingual legal-administrative texts must have the same typographical layout in both language versions (Presidential Decree 574/1988, art. 4). Moreover, institutional translators are bound to preserve the same number of sentences when translating Italian laws into German (Chiocchetti et al. 2013: 265) resulting in a "mirroring effect" between source and target documents (Woelk 2000: 216). As a consequence, segmentation discrepancies, reformulations, and sentence inversions between source and target were very infrequent, which therefore reduced the number of potential issues in automatic alignment. Automatic segmentation and alignment accuracy were further improved by integrating a list of legal abbreviations into LF Aligner's sentence splitter and a set of Italian-German legal terms from the bistro terminology database into hunalign's bilingual dictionary.

9. The scrapers for parallel URL collection and text extraction used to create the LEXB corpus are available at <https://github.com/antcont/LEXB> (last consulted in February 2022).

10. <https://sourceforge.net/projects/aligner/> (last consulted in February 2022).

Finally, the corpus was cleaned at the sentence level and filtered in order to remove noisy sentence pairs using an in-house corpus cleaning and filtering toolkit written in Python. Sentence cleaning operations included removing legal-specific textual elements occurring at the beginning and the end of segments (e.g., alpha-numerical list markers, superscript numbers, etc.) and automatically correcting mis-hyphenated words. Corpus filtering operations entailed removing sentences that could harm the performance of the MT system. Sentence pairs discarded include:

1. Duplicate and near-duplicate sentence pairs.
2. Sentence pairs with identical or highly similar source and target.
3. Sentence pairs with source and/or target sentence above or below given length thresholds (2 words < sentence length < 80 words).
4. Sentence pairs with same source and different target sentences.
5. Sentence pairs with a high ratio of non-alphabetical (numbers and symbols) to alphabetical characters.
6. Sentence pairs with a length ratio between source and target exceeding a given threshold.[11]

The corpus filtering stage reduced the initial corpus size by approximately 38%. The size of the LEXB corpus after cleaning and filtering operations adds up to 174,468 translation units and 9,479,569 tokens.

The collected data represents only a small amount of the textual capital stored by local administration. A data collection campaign in public offices might prove useful to expand the overall data amount.

4.2 MT adaptation and testing

The MT system chosen for the experiments was MMT, since its adaptive algorithm significantly boosts the accuracy of translated terminology. Moreover, with regards to time and computational resources, adapting MMT was deemed less expensive than training a new model from scratch. Finally, MMT allows users to carry out MT adaptation in the Italian-German language pair, which is not offered by other commercial adaptive MT systems.

MMT's adaptation approach performs an on-the-fly fine-tuning of the model at inference time. More specifically, it retrieves a set of bilingual sentences in which the source is similar to the sentence to be translated, it fine-tunes the model

11. Sentence pairs were discarded if a sentence exceeded the length of the respective translation by more than 50%. In order to avoid discarding short valid sentence pairs, an arbitrary value of 15 was added to the character count of each sentence's length.

using these bilingual sentences, it translates the given sentence, and it resets the adapted model to the original parameters (Farajian et al. 2018).

The MMT model enhanced with the collected parallel corpus was tested on a test set of 2,000 sentences. While setting up the datasets for the experimental stage, careful attention was paid in order to avoid possible overlaps of identical or near-identical sentences between the adaptation set and the test set. Improvement in terms of performance after adaptation was measured using the BLEU (Papineni et al. 2002) and chrF3 (Popović 2015) evaluation metrics. Despite its known limitations (Callison-Burch, Osborne & Kohen 2006), we chose BLEU as it is still the *de facto* standard quality metric in MT research and industry. To corroborate BLEU scores, we also provide chrF3 scores, since character-based metrics have shown a higher correlation to human judgements than word-based approaches. Following the guidelines of Marie, Fujita & Rubino (2021), BLEU and chrF3 scores were computed using a standardised toolkit, SacreBLEU (Post 2018), and improvements were tested for statistical significance by means of a paired bootstrap resampling test (Koehn 2004).

4.3 Automatic terminology evaluation

Evaluation of terminology accuracy is gaining importance in machine translation research. Along with the introduction of evaluation metrics that take terminology into account – like TREU (Dougal & Lonsdale, 2020) and TERm (Alam et al. 2021) – several methodologies for the automatic evaluation of terminology accuracy in machine translation have recently been proposed, including THR (Farajian et al. 2018) and TermEval (Haque, Hasanuzzaman & Way 2019). However, such evaluation frameworks have not been deemed adequate to evaluate the accuracy of legal terminology in the South Tyrolean context, since they are, respectively, either limited to classifying terms between correct and wrong terms binarily or take into account the terms' morphological and syntactical features only.

Legal terminology in South Tyrolean German features a number of peculiarities that differentiate it from legal terminologies pertaining to other German-speaking legal systems, as described in Section 2. Moreover, terminological variation is, to a certain extent, still a common phenomenon, resulting in the co-existence of several terms designating the same concept. Some of these terms may have been officially 'standardised' by the Terminology Commission or 'recommended' for use in South Tyrol (i.e., harmonised), whereas other concurrent terms could be outdated or in use despite the standardisation of another term.

We, therefore, adopted a novel terminology evaluation framework that assesses the term accuracy rate in machine translated sentences. It also automatically categorises German legal terms into a fine-grained *ad hoc* taxonomy according to the term's 'status' and 'adequacy to the legal system' (Contarino 2021: 65–77). Automatic term classification is based on the bistro terminology database, which contains accurate metadata at the term level, including information about the term status (standardised, recommended, obsolete), and the legal system(s) to which a term pertains (South Tyrol, Germany, Austria, Switzerland, etc.). At the finest level of granularity, the taxonomy contains five categories for 'wrong' terms and three categories for 'correct' terms (see Figure 1). At the end of the evaluation, two statistics are generated: overall 'term accuracy', defined as the rate of correct terms out of all evaluated terms yielded by the MT system, and counts for each category of the evaluation taxonomy.[12]

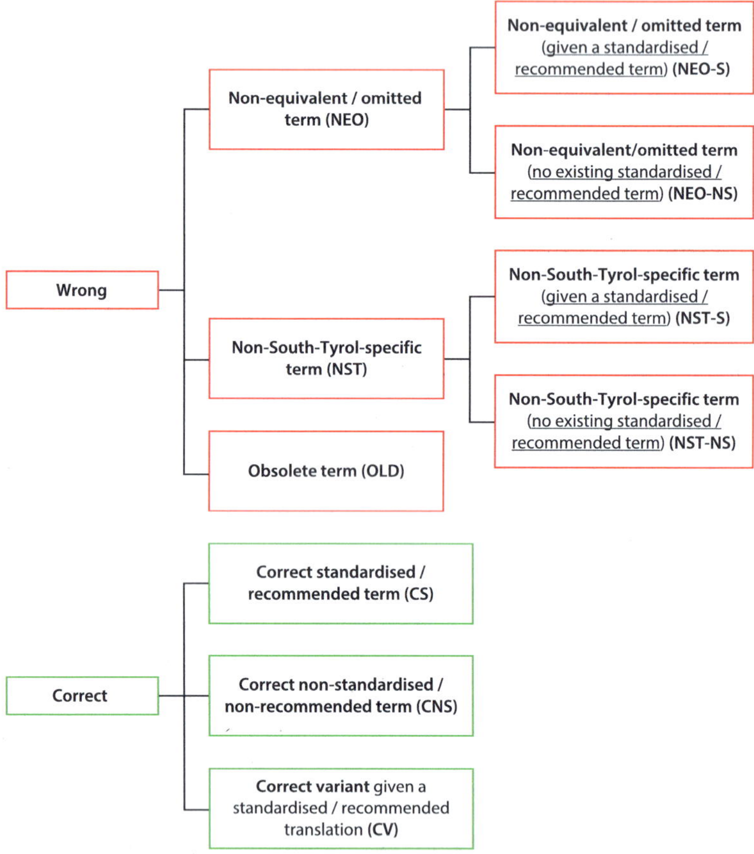

Figure 1. Overview of the taxonomy for the evaluation of South Tyrolean legal terminology (Contarino 2021: 68)

12. A more detailed overview of the evaluation framework can be found in Contarino (2021: 65–77).

5. Results

To evaluate overall quality improvement of the domain-adapted MMT model, evaluation metric scores computed for the adapted system were compared with scores obtained by the MMT generic baseline system and by two state-of-the-art generic MT systems, Google Translate and DeepL, as shown in Table 1.

Table 1. Evaluation scores of generic MT systems vs. the MMT domain-adapted system

	BLEU	chrF3	hLEPOR
Google Translate	**27.61**	0.529	0.637
DeepL	26.93	**0.536**	**0.648**
MMT (baseline)	25.73	0.517	0.626
MMT (adapted)	**34.73**	**0.569**	**0.664**

DeepL came up as the best performing system on our test set among the generic systems in terms of chrF3 and hLEPOR scores. Results uncovered a particularly promising performance improvement achieved by the MMT domain-adapted system, which consistently outperformed the MMT baseline system by +9 BLEU, +0.052 chrF3 and +0.048 hLEPOR points (see Table 1). Quality improvement scores are statistically significant ($p < 0.001$) according to a paired bootstrap resampling test.

As for legal terminology translation, results of the automatic term evaluation showed a substantial, although not particularly striking, improvement over the score and category counts obtained by the MMT baseline system (see Table 2 and Figure 2).

Table 2. Automatic terminology evaluation results achieved by the MMT baseline system and the MMT domain-adapted system

	Categories	MMT baseline	MMT adapted	% difference
correct	CS	891	986	+ 10.66%
	CNS	1,644	1,664	+ 1.21%
	CV	95	96	+ 0.95%
	total	2,630	2,746	+ 4.41%
wrong	NEO	856	744	– 13.08%
	⌊ NEO-S	539	446	– 17.25%
	⌊ NEO-NS	317	298	– 5.99%

Table 2. *(continued)*

Categories	MMT baseline	MMT adapted	% difference
NST	17	13	− 23.52%
╚ NST-S	11	8	− 27.27%
╚ NST-NS	6	5	− 16.6%
OLD	0	0	
total	873	757	− 14.43%
evaluated terms	3,503	3,503	
term accuracy	75.07%	78.39%	+ 3.31%

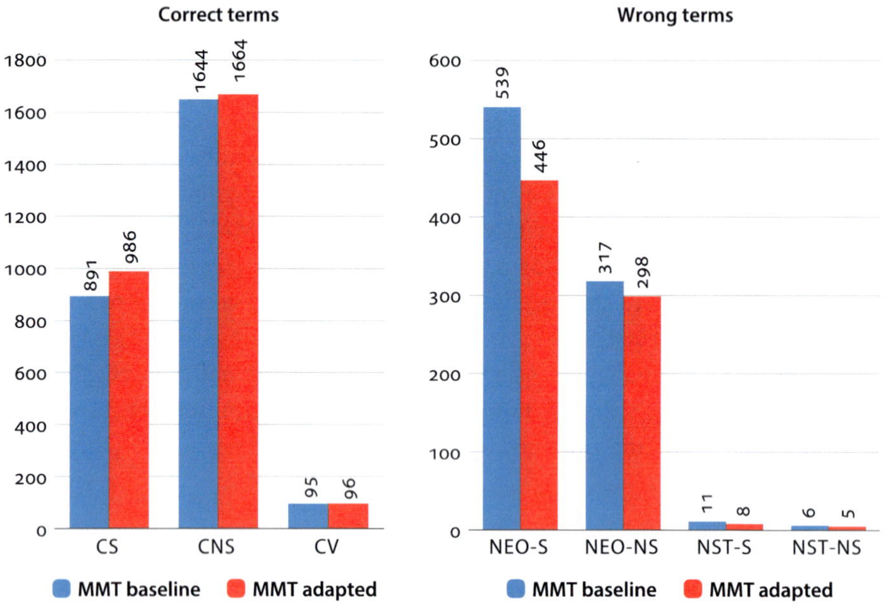

Figure 2. Categories and numbers of correct and wrong terms yielded the MMT baseline and the MMT adapted systems

After leveraging the LEXB corpus as in-domain adaptation data, the MMT system correctly translated 2,746 terms out of the 3,503 evaluated terms (+116 correct terms over the MMT baseline system), achieving 78.39% in legal term accuracy. Overall improvement in terms of total correct and wrong terms is statistically significant according to a McNemar test ($\chi^2 = 25.389$, df=1, p-value<0.001). The most relevant improvements are observed with regards to the number of correct standardised/recommended terms translated correctly (CS) and the number of non-equivalence/omission errors (NEO). More specifically, among the 539 NEO-S term errors yielded by the MMT baseline system, the MMT domain-adapted system managed to translate correctly (CS) 190 terms that are standardised, and therefore legally binding, in South Tyrol. Examples are shown in Table 3.

Table 3. Example of a NEO-S error in the MMT baseline system improved to a term of category CS after domain-adaptation. 'hyp' indicates the output of the baseline system, 'hyp2' the output of the adapted system

	Sentence	C/W	Category
src	*All' articolo 4 / bis del* ***decreto del Presidente della Repubblica*** *28 marzo 1975, n. 474, sono apportate le seguenti modifiche :*		
hyp	*Artikel 4 / bis des Präsidialerlasses Nr. 474 vom 28. März 1975 wird wie folgt geändert :*	W	NEO-S
hyp2	*In Artikel 4 / b des Dekrets des Präsidenten der Republik vom 28. März 1975, Nr. 474, werden folgende Änderungen vorgenommen :*	C	CS

In the examples from Table 3, the Italian term *decreto del Presidente della Repubblica* was translated incorrectly by the MMT baseline system, whereas the domain-adapted MMT system managed to translate it with the correct standardised term *Dekret des Präsidenten der Republik.*

Several terms (19) categorised as NEO-S in the baseline system were translated correctly after domain-adaptation, but using a valid terminological variant attested in the bistro database (CV) in place of the term standardised or recommended for South Tyrol. As can be seen in Table 4, the Italian term *sussidio* (subsidy) was translated by the baseline system using the hypernym *Subvention* (NEO-S), whereas the domain-adapted system yielded the attested variant *Zuschuss* in place of the standardised term *Beihilfe.* Apart from NEO-S, further term categories in the baseline system that improved to the CS category after domain-adaptation include the NST-S and CV categories (see Table 5).

Table 4. Instance of a NEO-S error in the MMT baseline system improved to a term of category CV after domain-adaptation

	Sentence	C/W	Category
src	*L' ammontare del* ***sussidio*** *concesso alle associazioni riconosciute non può superare il 60 per cento della spesa ammessa.*		
hyp	*Die den anerkannten Vereinigungen gewährte Subvention darf 60% der zuschussfähigen Ausgaben nicht überschreiten.*	W	NEO-S
hyp2	*Der den anerkannten Vereinigungen gewährte Zuschuss darf 60% der zuschussfähigen Ausgaben nicht überschreiten.*	C	CV

Table 5. Instance of CV term in the MMT baseline system improved to a term of category CS after domain-adaptation. Although being considered a correct variant, CV terms are deviations from the standardised term (CS). In this example, domain-adaptation allowed the system to yield the most appropriate, standardised term (CS)

	Sentence	C/W	Category
src	*Nel* ***contratto collettivo*** *8 marzo 2006 l'articolo 8 è così sostituito :*		
hyp	*Im Tarifvertrag vom 8. März 2006 erhält Artikel 8 folgende Fassung :*	W	CV
hyp2	*Im Kollektivvertrag vom 8. März 2006 erhält Artikel 8 folgende Fassung :*	C	CS

The overall number of terms improved between the baseline and the domain-adapted MMT system is 340, including 'wrong' to 'correct' improvements as well as improvements within the 'correct' and 'wrong' macro-categories. As opposed to the observed improvements, however, 336 terms categorised as non-equivalent/omitted terms (NEO-S) in the MMT baseline system were yielded as NEO-S even after domain adaptation, whereas 100 standardised terms translated correctly by the baseline system (CS) were mistranslated or omitted (NEO-S) by the adapted system.

Manual analysis of the evaluated sentences showed that improvement of legal term translation is not always systematically consistent over different sentences, with several terms occurring multiple times in the test set and not being translated consistently by the MMT domain-adapted system. The term *Giunta provinciale* (provincial council), for instance, occurred 59 times in the test set and was translated by the MMT adapted system with the correct term *Landesregierung* only 16 times. The remaining instances were translated with the non-equivalent terms *Landesrat, Provinzialrat* and *Provinzrat.* Furthermore, the manual analysis also revealed some weaknesses of the automatic terminology evaluation tool. The algorithm erroneously identified terms as correct if they occurred as part of compound terms designating different concepts. For example, *Vollzeit* (full-time), a short form for *Vollzeitarbeit* (full-time job), is identified in the term *Vollzeitlehrplan* (full-time syllabus), so the algorithm erroneously considers the two compound terms as pertaining to the same concept. A similar problem was observed for the term *Tausch* (exchange), identified by the algorithm within the term *Austausch* (replacement), which was erroneously identified as a compound and split by the compound splitter into *Aus* and *Tausch* during the term identification stage.

6. Conclusions

The results of our study are particularly relevant to understand the potential of exploiting adaptive NMT to translate legal-administrative texts in the context of South Tyrol. The significant improvements in the system's performance in terms of automatic metrics show that adapting an MMT model by leveraging a corpus of in-domain data can be useful to profitably translate legal-administrative texts, at least the types used in our experiments. The observed leap in performance is particularly promising considering the complexity of legal-administrative language, the relatively limited size of in-domain data and the reduced similarity between adaptation set and training set.

Moreover, quality improvement related to MT adaptation is also mirrored in terminology translation. MMT's instance-based adaptation yielded a significant improvement in the translation of legal-administrative terminology. Term accuracy improved by 3% between the baseline and the domain-adapted MMT system, with the latter yielding 116 more correct terms – out of the 3,503 evaluated – than the generic system. In particular, most of the improved terms are standardised and recommended legal terms, which are highly crucial since they are legally binding or have been officially harmonised for use in South Tyrol.

On the other hand, terminology improvements observed are not exceptionally striking. Term accuracy did not reach high rates and critical problems, including terminology inconsistency, could still be observed in the MT output. The reason behind such term inconsistency may be related to the adaptation approach adopted by the MMT system. Since model adaptation is carried out on the fly by retrieving a set of sentences in which the source is similar to the sentence to be translated, if few or no similar sentences are available in the pool of parallel data, domain-adaptation may not be fully achieved at the sentence level and single legal terms may not be translated properly. This can be a drawback when the size of the available in-domain data is relatively small. Term inconsistency may be mildened by exploring further approaches, including direct terminology integration.

Despite achieving a statistically significant increase in term accuracy, instance-based adaptation with relatively limited pool of parallel data may therefore not be deemed the ideal approach to achieve a systematic enhancement in South Tyrolean legal terminology translation in the considered language pair and domain. Nonetheless, further research is necessary to confirm or reject these results, as much as to continue developing the terminological evaluation tool in order to enhance its precision and recall. Aside from furthering research in the fields of MT adaptation and automatic terminology evaluation in the present language pair and domain, our work also paves the way towards the creation of translation aids for civil servants working in South Tyrol, thus ensuring they receive proper linguistic support. It is for this reason that both LEXB and the automatic terminology evaluation tool are shared with the scientific community.[13]

References

Alam, Md Mahfuz ibn, Anastasopoulos, Antonios, Besacier, Laurent, Cross, James, Gallé, Matthias, Koehn, Philipp & Nikoulina, Vassilina. 2021. On the evaluation of machine translation for terminology consistency. *ArXiv:2106.11891* [Cs]. http://arxiv.org/abs/2106.11891

Beller, Manfredi & Leerssen, Joep (Eds). Imagology: The Cultural Construction and Literary Representation of National Characters, *Studia Imagologica Vol. 13*, Amsterdam & New York: Rodopi, 2007

Bertoldi, Nicola, Caroselli, Davide & Federico, Marcello. 2018. The ModernMT project. In *Proceedings of the 21st Annual Conference of the European Association for Machine Translation*, Juan Antonio Pérez-Ortiz, Felipe Sánchez-Martínez, Miquel Esplà-Gomis, Maja Popović et al. (eds), 345. Alicante: European Association for Machine Translation. <http://eamt2018.dlsi.ua.es/proceedings-eamt2018.pdf> (30 May 2023).

Callison-Burch, Chris, Osborne, Miles & Koehn, Philipp. 2006. Re-evaluating the role of Bleu in machine translation research. In *Proceedings of the 11th Conference of the European Chapter of the Association for Computational Linguistics*, Diana McCarthy & Shuly Wintner (eds), 249–256 Trento: Association for Computational Linguistics.

Chiocchetti, Elena, Kranebitter, Klara, Ralli, Natascia & Stanizzi, Isabella. 2013. Deutsch ist nicht gleich Deutsch. Eine terminologische Analyse zu den Besonderheiten der deutschen Rechtssprache in Südtirol. In *Diatopische Variation in der deutschen Rechtssprache*, Marina Marzia Brambilla, Joachim Gerdes, & Chiara Messina (eds), 253–285. Berlin: Frank & Timme. <https://cris.unibo.it/handle/11585/412840#.XaQ1_UYzbIU> (30 May 2023).

Chiocchetti, Elena. 2019a. Legal comparison in terminology work: Developing the South Tyrolean German legal language. In *Diszciplínák találkozása: Nyelvi közvetítés a XXI. században*, Szilvia Szoták (ed.), 175–185. Budapest: OFFI.

doi Chiocchetti, Elena. 2019b. Terminology work in South Tyrol: New approaches, new termbase, new contents. *Terminologija* 26: 6–23.

Chiocchetti, Elena, Ralli, Natascia & Stanizzi, Isabella. 2017. From DIY translations to official standardisation and back again? 50 years of experience with Italian and German legal terminology work in South Tyrol. In *Terms and Terminology in the European Context*, Paola Faini (ed.), 254–270. Newcastle upon Tyne: Cambridge Scholars.

13. <https://github.com/antcont/LEXB> and <https://github.com/antcont/LexTermEval> (last consulted in February 2022).

Contarino, Antonio Giovanni. 2021. *Neural Machine Translation Adaptation and Automatic Terminology Evaluation: A Case Study on Italian and South Tyrolean German Legal Texts.* Master's dissertation, University of Bologna. <https://amslaurea.unibo.it/24989> (30 May 2023).

De Camillis, Flavia. 2021. *La traduzione non professionale nelle istituzioni pubbliche dei Territori di lingua minoritaria: Il caso di studio dell'amministrazione della Provincia Autonoma di Bolzano.* PhD dissertation, University of Bologna. <http://amsdottorato.unibo.it/9695> (30 May 2023).

Dougal, Duane K. & Lonsdale, Deryle. 2020. Improving NMT quality using terminology injection. In *Proceedings of the 12th Language Resources and Evaluation Conference*, 4820–4827. Marseille: European Language Resources Association. <https://aclanthology.org/2020.lrec-1.593> (30 May 2023).

DPR 670/1972. Decreto del Presidente della Repubblica 31 agosto 1972, n. 670 "Approvazione del testo unico delle leggi costituzionali concernenti lo statuto speciale per il Trentino – Alto Adige". <https://www.consiglio.provincia.tn.it/doc/clex_31437.pdf?zid=42f432f8-2b55-4f72-8c53-b2bcdef81c57> (30 May 2023).

Farajian, M. Amin, Bertoldi, Nicola, Negri, Matteo, Turchi, Marco & Federico, Marcello. 2018. Evaluation of terminology translation in instance-based neural MT adaptation. In *Proceedings of the 21st Annual Conference of the European Association for Machine Translation*, Juan Antonio Pérez-Ortiz, Felipe Sánchez-Martínez, Miquel Esplà-Gomis, Maja Popović et al. (eds), 149–158. Alicante: European Association for Machine Translation. <http://eamt2018.dlsi.ua.es/proceedings-eamt2018.pdf> (30 May 2023).

Haque, Rejwanul, Hassanuzzman, Mohammed & Way, Andy. 2019. Terminology Translation in Low-Resource Scenarios. *Information* 10 (9), 273, 1–28.

Heiss, Christine & Soffritti, Marcello. 2018. DeepL traduttore e didattica della traduzione dall'italiano in tedesco. In Translation And Interpreting for Language Learners (TAIL). Special issue of *inTRAlinea*, 1–11. <https://www.intralinea.org/print/article_specials/2294> (30 May 2023).

Koehn, Philipp. 2004. Statistical significance tests for machine translation evaluation. In *Proceedings of the 2004 Conference on Empirical Methods in Natural Language Processing*, Dekang Lin & Dekai Wu (eds), 388–395. Barcelona: Association for Computational Linguistics. <https://aclanthology.org/W04-3250> (30 May 2023).

Koehn, Philipp & Knowles, Rebecca. 2017. Six challenges for neural machine translation. In *Proceedings of the First Workshop on Neural Machine Translation*, Thang Luong, Alexandra Birch, Graham Neubig & Andrew Finch (eds), 28–39. Vancouver: Association for Computational Linguistics. <https://aclanthology.org/W17-3204.pdf> (30 May 2023).

Marie, Benjamin, Fujita, Atsushi & Rubino, Raphael. 2021. Scientific credibility of machine translation research: A meta-evaluation of 769 papers. In *Proceedings of the 59th Annual Meeting of the Association for Computational Linguistics and the 11th International Joint Conference on Natural Language Processing, Vol. 1: Long Papers*, 7297–7306. Stroudsburg PA: Association for Computational Linguistics. (30 May 2023)

Papineni, Kishore, Roukos, Salim, Ward, Todd & Zhu, Wei-Jing. 2002. Bleu: A method for automatic evaluation of machine translation. In *Proceedings of the 40th Annual Meeting of the Association for Computational Linguistics*, Pierre Isabelle, Eugene Charniak & Dekang Lin (eds), 311–318. Stroudsburg PA: Association for Computational Linguistics.

Popović, Maja. 2015. ChrF: Character n-gram F-score for automatic MT evaluation. In *Proceedings of the Tenth Workshop on Statistical Machine Translation*, Ondřej Bojar, Rajan Chatterjee, Christian Federmann, Barry Haddow et al. (eds), 392–395. Lisbon: Association for Computational Linguistics.

Post, Matt. 2018. A call for clarity in reporting BLEU scores. In *Proceedings of the Third Conference on Machine Translation: Research Papers*, Ondřej Bojar, Rajen Chatterjee, Christian Federmann, Mark Fishel et al. (eds), 186–191. Brussels: Association for Computational Linguistics

Ralli, Natascia & Andreatta, Norbert. 2018. bistro – ein Tool für mehrsprachige Rechtsterminologie. *trans-kom* 11(1):7–44. <http://www.trans-kom.eu/bd11nr01/trans-kom_11_01_02_Ralli_Andreatta_Bistro.20180712.pdf> (30 May 2023)

Saunders, Danielle. 2021. Domain adaptation and multi-domain adaptation for neural machine translation: A survey. *CoRR abs/2104.06951*. <https://arxiv.org/abs/2104.06951> (30 May 2023).

van der Wees, Marlies. 2017. *What's in a Domain?: Towards Fine-grained Adaptation for Machine Translation*. PhD dissertation, University of Amsterdam. <https://pure.uva.nl/ws/files/19726462/Thesis.pdf> (30 May 2023).

Varga, Daniel, Halacsy, Peter, Kornai, Andras, Nagy, Viktor, Nemeth, Laszlo & Tron, Viktor. 2007. Parallel corpora for medium density languages. In *Recent Advances in Natural Language Processing IV: Selected papers from RANLP 2005* [Current Issues in Linguistic Theory 292], Nicolas Nicolov, Kalina Bontcheva, Galia Angelova & Ruslan Mitkov (eds), 247–258. Amsterdam: John Benjamins.

Wiesmann, Eva. 2019. Machine translation in the field of law: A study of the translation of Italian legal texts into German. *Comparative Legilinguistics* 37:117–53.

Woelk, Jens. 2000. Von 'Advokat' bis 'Zentraldirektion der Autonomien'. Die Südtiroler Rechtssprache aus Sicht eines 'bundesdeutschen' Juristen. In *Linguistica giuridica italiana e tedesca*, Daniela Veronesi (ed.), 209–222. Padova: Unipress.

CHAPTER 11

Word alignment in the Russian-Chinese parallel corpus

Anastasia Politova[1], Olga Bonetskaya[2], Dmitry Dolgov[3], Maria Frolova[3] & Anna Pyrkova[2]
[1] Soochow University | [2] HSE University | [3] Independent researcher

The Russian-Chinese parallel corpus (RuZhCorp) was created in 2016 by sinologists and computational linguists. So far, it has accumulated 1 074 texts and over 4.6 million words that are aligned on a sentence level. To produce word alignment for the entire corpus, we used deep neural networks trained both on the whole RuZhCorp and on a manually aligned at a word level gold dataset. Using the principles presented in previous publications, we compiled the first word-to-word alignment guideline for the Russian-Chinese language pair, which makes the manual alignment process less ambiguous and more consistent. The joint fine-tuning of the LaBSE deep learning model on RuZhCorp and the gold dataset achieved the best AER of 18.9%.

Keywords: word alignment, gold dataset, linguistic guideline, deep learning, language model

1. Introduction

Word alignment of parallel corpora is defined as finding word-to-word[1] relationships between bitexts already aligned on a sentence level (Brown et al. 1990). A fundamental task in both natural language processing (NLP) and linguistics, word alignment not only serves as a basis for further research or information extraction in multilanguage search systems (Davis & Dunning 1995; Nie et al. 1999; Chen & Nie 2000) but can also be considered a final product for end

1. By "word-to-word" relations, we also mean the relations on the level of lexical units, where lexical units may be represented by single words or groups of words. This approach allows to align verb phrases and idiomatic expressions as single slots with one-to-many or many-to-many relations.

https://doi.org/10.1075/scl.113.11pol

users: instead of regular dictionaries or machine translation tools, people may use context-aware dictionaries that show how a given word has been translated by real human translators in different contexts.[2] Word-aligned corpora are beneficial for bilingual lexical or grammar usage extraction (Kuhn 2004) and assist linguists and professionals working with language data (translators, foreign language teachers, etc.) in theoretical and language data search (Östling 2016; Wälchli & Cysouw 2012; Mayer & Cysouw 2012; Cysouw & Wälchli 2007).

In NLP, word alignment is intricately related to machine translation (MT). Historically, automatic word alignment per se has mainly been done using statistical methods. The expectation-maximization algorithm was first proposed by Dempster et al. (1977) and implemented for word alignment under the name of IBM models by Brown et al. (1993). Och and Ney (2003) created a tool called GIZA++ that remains a standard benchmark until now. Later, several MT-related approaches were proposed. Bahdanau et al. (2015) used a DNN (deep neural network) to learn to align and translate jointly. Stengel-Eskin et al. (2019) used supervised learning to extract alignments from the attention module of a Transformer DNN. Several papers using BERT pre-trained models were published in recent years (Dou & Neibig 2021; Nagata, Chousa & Nishino 2020; Li et al. 2019). Some authors conversely used alignment data to either improve or explain machine translation (Chen et al. 2016; Tamer & Ney 2017; Stahlberg, Saunders & Byrne 2018). All the mentioned models are mainly trained on English plus one other language.

However, the results of existing aligners still need to be evaluated and further developed for other language pairs. Previous research reveals that most models show better AER (Alignment Error Rate) when trained on a manually annotated gold dataset. So far, there are several manually annotated gold datasets: Myanmar-English (Han & Thida 2019), Hindi-English (Yadav & Gupta 2010), Dutch-English (Macken 2010), Chinese-Korean (Li, Kim & Lee 2008), six pairs of 4 cognate languages (Graça et al. 2008), Czech-English (Kruijff-Korbayová, Chvátalová & Postolache 2006), English-Spanish (Lambert 2005), and English-French (Och & Ney 2003). However, no gold dataset is available for Russian-Chinese word alignment. Therefore, the current study expands the language pairs list, presents the first word-alignment manual for Russian-Chinese, and provides a deep learning language model trained on the Russian-Chinese parallel corpus (RuZhCorp, <https://linghub.ru/rnc_parallel_chinese/search>).

This collaborative paper written by linguists and data scientists presents our results for RuZhCorp word alignment with a neural network model. Section 2

2. Several decades earlier word-aligned corpora were used for automatic dictionary and concordance lists compilation (Sahlgren & Karlgren 2005).

describes how the gold dataset of Russian-Chinese sentence pairs was created and elaborates on the developed rules for Russian-Chinese alignment. This should be helpful for further improvements of word alignment models for this pair of languages and any other. Section 3 presents results obtained at different stages of model training and compares them to the results for other comparable pairs of non-similar languages. The final section concludes with our results and discusses the significance and future perspectives of our work.

2. Corpus

2.1 Building the gold dataset

2.1.1 *Types of alignment*

A gold dataset is a set of sentences manually aligned by linguists according to pre-established guidelines that make the alignment process as unambiguous as possible. Following the experience of Graça et al. (2008) and Och and Ney (2000), who both differentiated between Sure and Possible alignments, we similarly distinguished between S(ure) and P(ossible) alignments. However, in comparison to the previous works, our demarcations of S and P are slightly different. Och and Ney used S-alignment for unambiguous alignments and P(ossible) for those that might or might not exist. Besides, "the P relation is used especially to align words within idiomatic expressions, free translations, and missing function words" (Och & Ney 2000). For Graça et al., S-alignments represent a translation that is possible in every context, and "P-alignments when translation [is] possible in certain contexts or in the presence of functional words might be absent in one of the languages of a language pair" (Graça et al. 2008). We define S-alignments as a sure/direct/unarguable word translation. S-alignments are also used to align the established idiomatic expressions that are marked as many-to-many sure correspondences. P-alignment is for a translation that is possible in a certain context or is a euphemistic translation of a word. In other words, our alignment is paradigmatic and not syntagmatic, that is words/expressions are aligned based on meaning or usage differences and not on the grammatical structure (see Section 2.2 and Figure 3).

2.1.2 *Alignment tool*

Manual word alignment requires a tool where the source and target sentences are presented intuitively and compactly. Graça et al. (2008) used a special software called Alignment Tool. We used Google Sheets to display source and target sentences in the same way as they were shown in the Alignment Tool: source and target sentences arranged in column and row headers of a spreadsheet with each word put in a different cell. One sheet or tab represents one sentence pair only. In order to minimize the manual work and provide annotators with a draft, the body of the table was prepopulated with the results of a word-to-word alignment performed by an unsupervised learning model, where "X" represents the matches made by the system. Figure 1 shows our raw input. Such a simple tool is more accessible and allows the work to be done simultaneously by several linguists working remotely. Additionally, Google Sheets easily shows what modifications have been made recently.

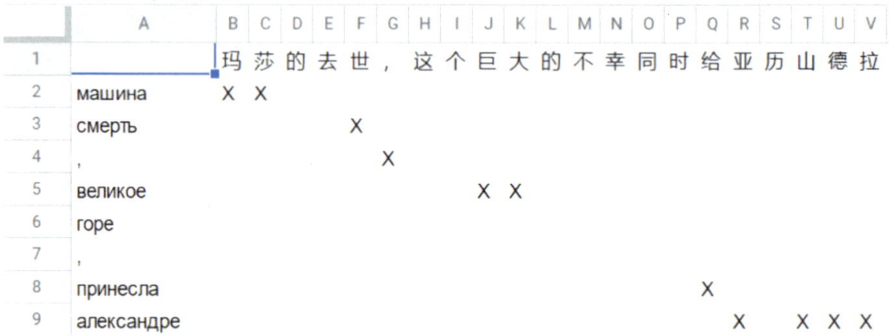

	A	B	C	D	E	F	G	H	I	J	K	L	M	N	O	P	Q	R	S	T	U	V
1		玛	莎	的	去	世	，	这	个	巨	大	的	不	幸	同	时	给	亚	历	山	德	拉
2	машина	X	X																			
3	смерть					X																
4	,						X															
5	великое									X	X											
6	горе																					
7	,																					
8	принесла																X					
9	александре																	X		X	X	X

Figure 1. Working page from Google Sheets with the Chinese sentence in column headers and the Russian sentence in row headers; the "X" in the matching area is the result of word-to-word alignment produced by an unsupervised learning model

2.1.3 *The alignment process*

At the start of the project, we aligned 125 pairs of Chinese sentences translated into Russian in a full manual mode (without using the aforementioned unsupervised learning model) and then applied the described process to another 327 pairs, bringing the total size of the gold dataset to 452 pairs.

Due to a limited number of annotators and time and resource constraints, we chose the iterative way (that is a first annotator manually aligns tokens by changing the automatic alignment, followed by the second annotator, who verifies the manual alignment and, in case of disagreement or doubts, puts the issue for the discussion) instead of having two annotators working parallelly on the same data. Consequently, based on the existing alignment guidelines, we developed our own alignment flow (see Figure 2); and four annotators got spreadsheets similar to the one shown in Figure 1.

In other words, our alignment process is structured in such a way as to make it transparent and objective, that is based on rules rather than on a personal opin-

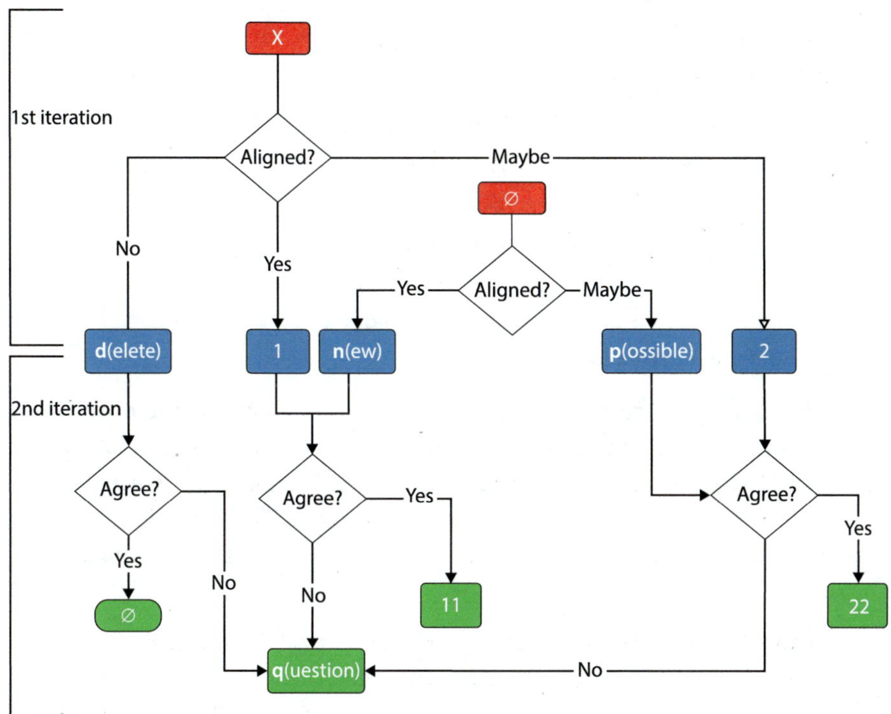

Figure 2. Align flow for peer review alignment

ion of a linguist-aligner. Disputed matches were discussed until an agreement on them was reached. Some cases became precedents for principles and exceptions, which provided a good base for the gold rules to be used by other linguists and bi-/multilingual datasets builders.

2.2 Alignment manifesto

To make the alignment as unambiguous as possible, we first developed the high-level principles, or alignment manifesto, and then implemented them in the form of more definite alignment rules.

Principle 1 stipulates that alignment should be based on word representation in the languages and not on the context. In other words, only tokens with clear semantic correspondences in both languages should be aligned, while those added or omitted due to context necessity, literal purposes, or to prevent tautology in a language should not. Example (1) shows that the Chinese expression 他们两人 does not have its counterpart in the Russian language but is embedded in the word forms of the Russian words making it clear that a speaker is talking about them, which is the reason for omitting them in a Russian context that does not tolerate tautology.

(1)

they	**two person**	indeed	"string of pearl and jade"[3]
tamen	**liangren**	zhenshi	zhulianbihe
他们	**两人**	真是	珠联璧合
		поистине	прекрасная пара
		poinstine	prekrasnaya para
		indeed	lovely/nice couple

'(They) are indeed a lovely couple'

Principle 2 is adopted from previous research and postulates that there are S(ure) and P(ossible) types of alignment. As it is shown in (2), Chinese 庆祝 that literally translates as "to celebrate" is expressed in Russian as "in honor of," which is a possible but not a direct translation of the Chinese token. Therefore, following the "paradigmatic, not syntagmatic" principle, 庆祝 is aligned as a P-alignment with the Russian "в честь."

(2)

10 month 1 day	FUT	run	**celebrate**	China	establish	70_years	milirary_parade
10 yue 1 ri	jiang	juban	**qingzhu**	zhongguo	chengli	70_zhounian	yuebingshi
10月1日	将	举办	**庆祝**	中国	成立	70周年	阅兵式

Китай	проведет	военный	парад	**в честь**	70-летия	КНР
Kitai	provedet	voennyi	parad	**v chest'**	70-letiya	KNR
China	organise-FUT	military	parade	**in honor**	70-year-PL	China

'(On 1st October) a military parade will be held to celebrate the 70th anniversary of the establishment of China.'

Figure 3 explains the difference between the so-called paradigmatic and syntagmatic alignments. The concepts of paradigmatic and syntagmatic relations come from Saussure's Basic Principles of Structural Linguistics, where he calls a relation between different grammatical roles of words in a sentence syntagmatic; and a relation between two interchangeable words paradigmatic. Therefore, in our project, words/expressions are aligned as S-alignments when they are the direct/evident correspondences of each other, as in the example in the center, where the Chinese and Russian words "beer" in bold represent the S-alignment. The left example on the diagram is an example of "paradigmatic" alignment, where a source word aligned to a rare synonym in the target language. Italics indicate that

3. idiom. perfect pair

this is a P-alignment, as in the Russian language, "beer" is translated euphemistically, with a possible but not a straightforward word/expression. An example of "syntagmatic" alignment is on the right. Chinese 一杯 corresponds to the ending of the Russian word "пива" that shows that it is only one glass of beer. It seems more complex and does not suit the purposes of building a gold standard of rules. The gold standard should be able to train the algorithm for finding sure/possible alignments for a language pair without any grammatical distinction – just with the ability to classify corresponding translations according to their commonness in respect to a searched word in a source language.

Figure 3. "Paradigmatic" vs. "Syntagmatic" alignments

2.3 Alignment rules

2.3.1 *Punctuation*

Punctuation is an essential part of the written form of every language. With proper punctuation marks, people differentiate ideas on paper when a speaker's voice is not heard. Thus, in a written context, punctuation marks are as crucial as words themselves.

Besides auxiliary verbs, question/exclamation words/expressions (like "What a nice ..." in English, "真 ... *(好看)*" in Chinese, or "Какой/какая ..." in Russian), and punctuation marks, which are the most expressive markers in the written discourse, Chinese abounds in modal particles that do not find proper word-correspondences in Russian. Particles express emotions, sometimes perform an exclamation or interrogative function, and could be divided into functional and non-functional particles. When a modal particle performs an interrogative/exclamation function, it is S-aligned with a punctuation mark in a Russian sentence, see (3). When a particle is non-functional and serves as an emotional decoder in written discourse, it is marked as a P-alignment to a punctuation mark in Russian. Sample (4) is an example of a non-functional particle alignment. Bold tokens stand for S-alignment and underscored tokens represent P-alignment, that is question marks in both languages, and a bold and underscored token is an S-alignment for a bold token in another language and a P-alignment for a respective underscored token, that is Chinese 呀 is a P-alignment to a question mark in the Russian sentence.

(3) You be this way think **Q** ?
Nin shi zhe yang renwei **ma** ?
您 是 这 样 认为 **吗** ?
Вы думаете ?
Vy dumaete ?
You think ?
'Do you think so?'

(4) Search who <u>EMPH</u> ?
Zhao shui <u>ya</u> ?
找 谁 <u>呀</u> ?
Кого надо <u>?</u>
Kogo nado <u>?</u>
Who.ACC need <u>?</u>
'Who are you looking for?'

Like in (3), the modal particle 吗 performs an interrogative function: even without seeing a sentence, an interlocutor can understand that it is a question because it is the "duty" of 吗 here to set a questioning tone; therefore, 吗 together with a question mark in Chinese is a sure alignment to a question mark "?" in Russian, as in the latter a question is expressed by means of intonation primarily.

2.3.2 *Pronouns and classifiers*

The Chinese language is well-known for its richness in classifiers. Russian, on the other hand, does not have that many classifiers; in rare cases, when it does, it often considers their use redundant or excessive. This results in a lack of correspondence with Chinese classifiers. In addition, the flexibility (that is the same sentence could be expressed/translated with or without pronouns without losing meaning) of the Russian language shown in (5) makes the alignment issue sharper. Following Principle 1, we set an additional rule for classifiers. It postulates that a Chinese classifier is left without alignment when a classifier or a similar word is omitted in Russian. In Russian, a demonstrative pronoun, a numeral or a so-called "classifier," that is the word denoting a container as in the case of (5),[4] is aligned with the Chinese classifier structure as an S-alignment. When a demonstrative and a "container"-classifier appear in Russian translation, every word is aligned as an S-alignment separately.

(5)

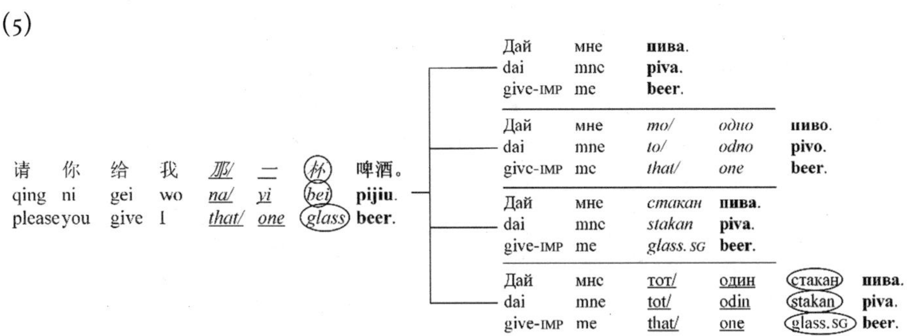

'Give me (that/ one/ glass/ one glass of) beer.'

2.3.3 *Chinese particles and verb complements*

Compared to inflected or fusional Russian, Chinese, as a representative of isolating languages, has many particles, some of which perform as members of nominal, verbal, and adverbial structures, and some represent the tense category. In the Russian language, these particles find their representation in inflectional changes, therefore, are attributed to "words on the left" in Chinese and aligned with the proper correspondences in Russian. For example, 的 is aligned together with the corresponding pronoun, noun, or adjective to a proper Russian token, 得 is aligned with a Russian verb together with the main verb in Chinese, and 地 is attributed to the corresponding adjective in Chinese. The same rule is applied to Chinese tense particles 了, 着, 过, etc.

Chinese directional compounds 去, 来, 下来, 下去, 上来, 上去 and resultative compounds 到, 见, 在一起, etc. are aligned together with the preceding Chinese main verbs (see (6) to (8)). However, when Chinese 去, 来, 到 are used not as compounds but as independent members of a sentence, that is as verbs or prepositions, they are aligned with their respective correspondences in Russian sentences, as in (9).[5]

4. Here, bold tokens stand for S-alignments, italicized represent P-alignments, underlined and circled show S-alignments and draw a clear line which tokens are aligned as S-alignments with each other.

5. Bold and underlined tokens both stand for S-alignments in the left example as 到 performs the function of a preposition and 去 of a verb; however, in the right example, Chinese 去 is aligned both with the verb and the preposition in Russian but as an S-alignment to the verb and as a P-alignment to the preposition.

(6) He call PST one CLF have-meat POSS cabbage_soup, immediately **sit**
ta jiao le yi fen dairou de baicaitang, jiu **zuo**
他 叫 了 一 份 带肉 的 白菜汤, 就 坐
down_DIR_COMP.
xialai.
下来.
Он спросил себе щей с мясом и **сел.**
on sprosil sebe shchei s myasom I **sel.**
he ask-PST himself shchi with meat and **sit-PST.**
'He asked for cabbage soup and sat down.'

(7) he look PROG Katerina, just **think RES_COMP** …
ta qiao zhe kajielinna, zhishi **xiang dao** …
他 瞧 着 卡捷琳娜, 只是 **想 到** ……
Глядя на неё, он только **подумал** …
glyadya na nee, on tol'ko **podumal** …
look_PTCP at she-POSS, he just **think-PST** …
'Looking at her (Katerina), he just thought …'

(8) she POSS pupil open V-AUX so big, almost and black POSS
ta de tongkong zheng de zheme da, jihu he heise de
她 的 瞳孔 睁 得 这么 大, 几乎 和黑色 的
iris_circle **join together PST.**
hongmojuan **he zaiyiqi**
虹膜圈 **合 在一起了.**
Зрачки её были расширены так, что почти **сошлись** с
zrachki ee bili rashireny tak, chto pochti **soshlis'** s
pipul.PL she-POSS be-PST dilated-PART so, that almost **get_together-PST** with
чёрными ободками радужки.
chernymi obodkami raduzhki.
black.PL rim.PL iris-GEN.
'Her pupils opened so wide that they were almost the size of the black circles of her iris.'

(9) he **go-PST** to Moscow.
on **poehal** v Moskvu.
он **поехал** в Москву.

她到 莫斯科 **去**了。 她**去**莫斯科 了。
ta dao mosike **qu le.** ta **qu** mosike **le.**
he to Moscow **go PST.** he **go** Moscow **PST.**

'He went to Moscow.'

2.3.4 *Prepositions*

In comparison to (5), Example (9) shows Chinese flexibility. The Chinese language allows, with a verb position change, for some prepositions to be omitted in certain sentences without any change in meaning. In contrast, in Russian, some verbs are not used without prepositions, such as the verb "to go (somewhere or to a certain destination)." Therefore, when Chinese does not have a verbal preposition, low right example in (9), and a Russian verb is used mainly with a preposition in a designated context, the Chinese verb is aligned with the Russian verb and its preposition, but, as it is shown in (9), as the S-alignment with the verb "поехал" and as the P-alignment with the preposition "в".

Some peculiar preposition usages are also found in Chinese. For instance, Chinese 在, when used as a preposition, often forms a frame structure, 在 ... 上 (on ... surface), whereas in Russian, it is expressed by one preposition only, see (10). Thus, to mitigate the grammatical differences between languages, the whole Chinese prepositional frame structure, 在 and 上, is aligned with the Russian preposition "на".

(10) Alexandra and Ana together sit **on** one CLF small sofa **surface**
yalishandela he ana yiqi zuo **zai** yi zhang xiao shafa **shang.**
亚历山德拉 和 安娜 一起 坐 **在** 一 张 小 沙发 上。
Александра и Анна сели вместе **на** маленьком диване.
Aleksandra i Anna seli vmeste **na** malen'kom divane.
Aleksandra and Anna sit-PST together **on** small sofa.
'Aleksandra and Anna sat together on a small sofa.'

Discrepant prepositional structures deserve special attention among all prepositional rules. Chinese and Russian not only differ in the lack or presence of prepositions but also have so-called "mismatched prepositional structures." At first sight, it looks that the Chinese structure 从这个案子脱身 (from this case free oneself) from (11) is easily aligned with the Russian "*сбросить с себя этот груз*" (throw off from oneself this burden). Moreover, all the components seem common between Chinese and Russian: 这个案子 (this case) corresponds to "*этот груз*" (this burden), 脱 (free) to "*сбросить*" (throw off), 身 (oneself) to "*себя*" (oneself), 从 (from) to "*c*" (from). However, a closer analysis shows that the Chinese 从 (from) refers to "(to get rid of) this case," whereas the Russian preposition "*c*" (from) is attributed to "(throw off from) oneself, from your body," if the Russian sentence is translated literally. Therefore, in the Chinese structure 从……脱身 (from … free oneself), 脱身 (free oneself) should be aligned as an S-alignment with the entire Russian expression "*сбросить с себя*" (throw off from oneself) and the Chinese preposition 从 (from) is to be left without a pair as in Russian "*этот груз*" (this burden) does not require any prepositions.

(11) Lao Xing have_to from this CLF case **free_oneself.**
lao Xing zhihao cong the ge anzi **tuoshen.**
老 邢 只好 从 这 个 案子 **脱身**。
Итак, ему ничего не оставалось, как **сбросить с себя** этот
Itak, emu nichego ne ostavalos', kak **sbrosit' s sebya** etot
So, he-DAT nothing no leave-PST, but **throw_off from oneself** this
груз.
gruz.
burden.
'(Lao Xing) he had nothing to do but to get rid of this burden.'

2.3.5 *Chinese verbs "to be" and "to have"*

The fact that Russian and Chinese belong to different language families causes more issues to be elaborated separately. Russian is considered to be a "to be"-language, and Chinese can be classified as a "to have"-language (see Freeze 1992). Russian flexibly uses the verbs "to be" and "to have," whereas Chinese, together with lingua franca English, has stricter rules and more regular usage. Therefore, following Principle 1, the verbs "to be" and "to have" are aligned when they have equivalents in Russian. For instance, (12) shows that in the present tense the verb "to be" is not translated/used in Russian, but in the past, as in (13), it appears and is aligned with the Chinese 是 (to be).

(12) I **be** student.
wo **shi** xuesheng.
我 **是** 学生。
Я студент.
ya student.
I student.
'I am a student.'

(13) You why with he break_up PST? he **be** CLF idiot.
ni weishenme gen ta fenshou le? ta **shi** ge bendan.
你 为什么 跟 他 分手 了？ 他 **是** 个 笨蛋。
Почему ты с ним рассталась? Он **был** дурак.
pochemu ty s nim rasstalas'? on **byl** durak.
Why you with he-ABL break_up-PST? he **be-PST** idiot.
'Why did you break up with him? He was an idiot.'

The verb "to have" does not depend on the tense (see (14)). Still, it sometimes could be omitted in the Russian language, as in (15), sometimes is embedded in negation or adverbs, as in (16), and even sometimes represented by synonyms (see (17)), which can only be P-alignments. Due to the word limits, we have presented different examples for adverb cohesion and synonym replacement. As for negation, it is usually presented as an S-alignment of Chinese 没有 to Russian "*нет*" in a present form.

(14) he **have/ FUT_have** house.
ta **you/ jiangyou** jia.
他 **有/ 将有** 家。
У него **есть/ будет** дом.
u nego **est'/ budet** dom.
At he-GEN **have/ have-FUT** house.
'He has/will have a house.'

(15) already **have** good many person EMPH.
yijing **you** hao duo ren la.
已经 **有** 好 多 人 啦。
Уже очень много.
uzhe ochen' mnogo.
already very many.
'There are already many people.'

(16) factory_building **in_total have** forty_eight CLF window.
changfang **yigong you** sishiba shan chuanghu.
厂房 **一共 有** 四十八 扇 窗户.
Вэтомпомещении **всего** сорок восемь окон.
v etom pomeshenii **vsego** sorok vosem' okon.
in this building **in_total** forty eight window.PL.
'There are forty-eight windows in this (factory) building in total.'

(17) small group nowadays just have organiser one person.
xiao zu muqian jin you zuzhizhe yi ren.
小 组 目前 仅 有 组织者 一 人。
Кружок пока что состоял только из одного организатора.
kruzhok poka_chto sostoyal tol'ko iz odnogo organizatora.
Club as_for_now consist-PST just of one-GEN organiser.
'The was only one person in the club; it was an organiser.'

2.3.6 *Alignment of speech figures*

The last rule we would like to present is the alignment of the so-called "translation peculiarities". What is evident in one language can be difficult to understand in another; thus, translators use communicative or adaptational translation methods to "rewrite" a source text so that it conforms to the rules of a target language and is smoothly acceptable by a target language. In (18), which is the translation of the Russian text into Chinese, a metonymy is included, that is "clothes" is used to denote a "person." However, this metonymy may interfere with the smooth understanding once translated into Chinese, so the metonymy was opened and translated into "the widow that wore a starched underskirt." Even though we are aware of this language phenomenon, following Principle 1, we aligned the Russian adjective "starched" to the Chinese noun "starch" and attributed to it possessive particle "de," leaving another part of metonymy, 衬裙上过 (put on the underskirt), unaligned. By doing so, we both follow our main Principle 1 and leave the ground for learners and researchers to study how speech figures are presented in the two respective languages.

(18) disappear-PRF-PTCP.SG, that[...] **starched** widow-DIM not have_time ...
ischez, chto[...] **krahmal'naya** vdovushka ne uspela ...
исчез, что[...] **крахмальная** вдовушка не успела ...
没 了 踪影, 衬裙 上过 **浆** **的** 寡妇 根本
mei le zongying, chenqun shangguo **jiang** **de** guafu genben
not PST trace, underskirt put_on **starch** **POSS** widow simply
来不及 ...
laibuji ...
do_not_have_time ...
'(he) disappeared (so fast) that the widow in a starched dress did not have time to ...'

Above are the main rules of our gold dataset. Due to space limitations and since the scope of the paper is to describe some general guidelines for building a Russian-Chinese gold dataset and test its role in algorithm training, some straightforward rules or those similar to ones already mentioned – like the alignment of Chinese auxiliary particles 被 and 把 that are similar in alignment principle with compounds (see Section 3.3.3) – have been omitted.

3. Evaluation

Among several existing machine learning models for word alignment (Dou & Neibig 2021; Nagata, Chousa & Nishino 2020; Li et al. 2019), Awesome Align by Dou and Neibig was chosen due to the availability of the code, ease in use, and, importantly, due to its sound performance on English-Chinese language pair (13.6% AER vs. 36.5% by Li et al. 2019). All the papers mentioned above use BERT as their base model; however, they perform worse or comparably to the chosen Awesome Align.

For a baseline, we used two statistical models: IBM Model 1, which is more straightforward, and fast-align, which considers the words outside of any context and is a reparametrization of IBM Model 2.

Due to significant language differences, we applied several tokenization options for statistical algorithms: BPE (byte-pair encoding) (Gage 1994) and MyStem (Segalovich 2003). MyStem is an algorithm that provides word lemmatization, that is bringing a word to its "normal" form (better – > good, walking – > walk, etc.). We used MyStem lemmatization and BPE for Russian sentences; and single character tokenization for Chinese. In pursuit of better results, we upgraded MyStem with lemmatization, which resulted in better model performance (see Table 1).

Table 1. Statistical models' results

Method	**Training**	**Ru-Zh AER**
IBM-model 1	No data preparation	75.2%
	Lemmatized data	67.8%
	BPE-tokenized data	79.5%
Fast Align	No data preparation	69.3%
	Lemmatized data	**61.1%**
	BPE-tokenized data	71.0%

All models were trained on 3.5 million (all available at that time) words from RuZhCorp and underwent training on three datasets: no preprocessing for either language; MyStem lemmatization for Russian, no preprocessing for Chinese; and BPE tokenization for both languages. Table 1 shows that fast-align with lemmatization had significantly better performance and thus was chosen as the primary baseline for our training model.

Awesome Align uses vectorized word representations of a pretrained multilanguage model. Each token (word, character, or punctuation sign) is represented with an ordered set of numbers, called a vector or embedding that also depends on the context. Such embeddings can be learned from multilingual but not aligned corpora, which allows for the use of big publicly available datasets. The model then calculates the distance between each pair of Russian and Chinese tokens; when that distance is lower than a predefined threshold, the pair is considered aligned.

Dou and Neibig (2021) proposed several ways to fine-tune the model. In a sentence-aligned parallel corpus, 15% of randomly chosen tokens in both languages are replaced with a unique [MASK] token, with a random token or left unchanged, with the probabilities of 80%, 10%, and 10%, respectively. Given a pair of masked sentences in two languages, the model learns to reconstruct an original token by itself.

Awesome Align, which can use different models as its core algorithm, also allows the model to be fine-tuned using a word-level pre-aligned bilingual parallel corpus. A combination of translation language modeling, self-training objective (a method similar to EM algorithm), and other methods described in the Awesome Align paper was the objective for such fine-tuning. Two algorithms were used for the experiments:

1. MultiBERT (also used by Dou and Neibig (2021)) was further trained on a multilingual corpus of Wikipedia articles. The model learned the embeddings using the masking approach described above and predicted whether a given sentence follows another sentence in a text.
2. LaBSE is trained by the same masking approach and by a translation model with parallel corpora. It learned to predict whether two sentences in two languages are aligned in a parallel corpus.

We have evaluated word alignments that can be extracted directly from publicly available versions of MultiBERT and LaBSE. Further, we additionally trained those models on RuZhCorp (~700,000 sentence pairs). As a final step, we fine-tuned those models on gold set of data (over 350 sentence pairs) manually annotated by humans. To compare the quality of the models, we use the AER metric introduced by Och and Ney (2000). All RuZhCorp texts (3.5 million words) were used for training. When training on annotated sentences from the novel dataset, AER is calculated on the rest of the dataset (test set of 102 sentence pairs).

In total, we conducted eight experiments, the results of which are shown in Table 2.

Table 2. AER of MultiBERT and LaBSE models after different trainings

Method	**Training**	**Ru-Zh AER**
Baseline (statistical model)	unsupervised on the parallel corpus	61.1%
AA – MultiBERT	Bare model (not explicitly trained for word alignment)	38.2%
	Pre-trained by Dou and Neibig	31.5%
	Fine-tuned on RuZhCorp (5 epochs)	28.7%
	Finer-tuned on the gold dataset	28.3%
AA – LaBSE	Bare model	31.8%
	Fine-tuned on RuZhCorp (1 epoch)	19.8%
	Finer-tuned on the gold dataset	**18.9%**

Table 2 shows that LaBSE achieves the best AER of 18.9% and MultiBERT follows with 28.3% only. That shows two facts: first, a gold dataset may improve the algorithms' performance (by 0.9 percentage points in the LaBSE case); second, in either fine-tuning scenario, LaBSE performance exceeds that of MultiBERT.

Summing up, in the absence of previous work on Russian-Chinese word alignment, we have compared our results with other resemblant pairs of non-similar languages that include one European and one East-Asian language: Li et al. (2019) list 36.57% as their best result for Chinese-English, Dou and Neibig (2021) show an AER of 37.4% for Japanese-English while providing a much lower 13.9% AER for Chinese-English. Therefore, our results are in line with or better than the previous research on similar language pairs and may become a valuable benchmark for future research on Russian-Chinese word alignment.

4. Conclusion

Word-alignment is a relatively novel and complicated task. In this paper, we described how we built a gold dataset of Russian-Chinese word-aligned sentences and the role of this dataset in algorithm training. We established the manual alignment guidelines for the Russian-Chinese language pair and showed that simple spreadsheets are helpful in the construction of a gold dataset as they allow for many-to-many alignments and peer-review. Having evaluated different models, we found that LaBSE with fine-tuning showed better results, and so we applied it to the RuZhCorp existing dataset. The alignment results are available online at < https://linghub.ru/rnc_parallel_chinese/search >

The good results after fine-tuning on the gold dataset are promising for further work, which we expect to undertake. First, we plan to increase the manually aligned dataset and train the model on a more extensive training set. Second, we hope to experiment with similar algorithms on other parallel corpora of the Russian National Corpus. Third, we want to try newer core models of the BERT family. Fourth, we plan to implement a translation relevance mechanism based on the word alignment, that is a mechanism that differentiates between more and less likely translations and arranges the sentences from sure correspondences to context or P-translations. We hope that our work, which is on par with current state-of-the-art models for similar language pairs, could facilitate the development of new word alignment methods and that the results of Russian-Chinese corpus alignment can benefit both students and professionals.

Funding

This work was supported by the "Development of online reference tools based on RuZhCorp to create an interactive educational environment" project funding from the Students' Academic Development Center of Higher School of Economics, Russia, and Jiangsu Province Excellent Postdoctoral Researcher Funding (江苏省卓越博士后计划), PRC.

Acknowledgements

We thank Kirill Semenov for his kind assistance during the project and for the allocated time for fruitful discussions. We also thank the reviewers for their valuable comments and everyone who helped us to proof the manuscript.

Abbreviations

ABL	ablative case
CLF	classifier
DAT	dative case
DIM	diminutive
DIR_COMP	directional compound
EMPH	emphatic marker
FUT	future
GEN	genitive case
IMP	imperative
PL	plural
POSS	possessive
PRF	perfect
PST	past
PTCP	participle
RES_COMP	resultative compound
SG	singular
V-AUX	auxiliary verb

References

Alkhouli, Tamer & Ney, Hermann. 2017. Biasing attention-based recurrent neural networks using external alignment information. In *Proceedings of the Second Conference on Machine Translation*, Ondřej Bojar, Christian Buck, Rajen Chatterjee, Christian Federmann et al. (eds), 108–117. Copenhagen: Association for Computational Linguistics.

Bahdanau, Dzmitry, Cho, Kyung Hyun & Bengio, Yoshua. 2015. Neural machine translation by jointly learning to align and translate. Third International Conference on Learning Representations (ICLR 2015). San Diego: oral presentation. <https://arxiv.org/abs/1409.0473> (30 July 2022).

Brown, Peter F., Cocke, John, Pietra, Stephen Della, Pietra, Vincent J. Della, Jelinek, Frederick, Lafferty, John D., Mercer, Robert L. & Roossin, Paul S. 1990. A statistical approach to machine translation. *Computational Linguistics* 16(2): 79–85.

Brown, Peter F., Pietra, Stephen A., Pietra, Vincent J. Della & Mercer, Robert L. 1993. The mathematics of statistical machine translation: Parameter estimation. *Computational Linguistics* 19(2): 263–311.

Chen, Jiang & Nie, Jian-Yun. 2000. Automatic construction of parallel English-Chinese corpus for cross-language information retrieval. In *Proceedings of the Sixth Conference on Applied Natural Language Processing*, 21–28. Seattle WA: Association for Computational Linguistics.

Chen, Wenhu, Matusov, Evgeny, Khadivi, Shahram & Peter, Jan-Thorsten. 2016. Guided alignment training for topic-aware neural machine translation. <https://arxiv.org/abs/1607.01628> (30 July 2022).

Cysouw, Michael & Wälchli, Bernhard. 2007. Parallel texts: Using translational equivalents in linguistic typology. *Language Typology and Universals* 60(2): 95–99.

Davis, Mark & Dunning Ted E. 1995. Query translation using evolutionary programming for multi-lingual information retrieval. In *Query Translation Using Evolutionary Programming for Multi-lingual Information Retrieval*, John R. McDonnell, Robert G. Reynolds & David B. Fogel (eds), 175–185. Cambridge MA: The MIT Press.

Dempster, Arthur P., Laird, Nan M. & Rubin, Donald B. 1977. Maximum likelihood from incomplete data via the EM algorithm. *Journal of the Royal Statistical Society* 39(1): 1–38.

Dou, Zi-Yi & Neubig, Graham. 2021. Word alignment by fine-tuning embeddings on parallel corpora. In *Proceedings of the 16th Conference of the European Chapter of the Association for Computational Linguistics*, Paola Merlo, Jorg Tiedemann, Reut Tsarfaty (eds), 2112–2128. Stroudsburg PA: Association for Computational Linguistics.

Freeze, Ray. 1992. Existentials and other locatives. *Language* 68: 553–595.

Gage, Philip. 1994. A new algorithm for data compression. *The C Users Journal archive* 12: 23–38.

Graça, João V., Pardal, Joana Paulo, Coheur, Luisa & Caseiro, Diamantino Antonio. 2008. Building a golden collection of parallel multi-language word alignment. In *Proceedings of the Sixth International Conference on Language Resources and Evaluation* (LREC'08), 986–993. Marrakech: LREC.

Han, Nway Nway & Thida, Aye. 2019. Annotated guidelines and building reference corpus for Myanmar-English word alignment. *International Journal on Natural Language Computing* 8(4): 25–38.

Kruijff-Korbayová, Ivana, Chvátalová, Klára & Postolache, Oana. 2006. Annotation guidelines for Czech-English word alignment. In *Proceedings of the Fifth International Conference on Language Resources and Evaluation*, Nicoletta Calzolari, Khalid Choukri, Aldo Gangemi, Bente Maegaard et al. (eds), 1256–1261. Genoa: ELRA.

Kuhn, Jonas. 2004. Experiments in parallel-text based grammar induction. *Proceedings of the 42th Annual Meeting of the Association for Computational Linguistics*, 470–477. Barcelona: Association for Computational Linguistics.

Lambert, Patrik, Gispert, Adria, Banchs, Rafael & Mariño, Jose B. 2005. Guidelines for word alignment evaluation and manual alignment. *Language Resources and Evaluation* 39(4): 267–285.

Li, Jinji, Kim, Dong-Il & Lee, Jong-Hyeok. 2008. Annotation guidelines for Chinese-Korean word alignment. In *Proceedings of the Sixth International Conference on Language Resources and Evaluation* (LREC'08), Nicoletta Calzolari, Khalid Choukri, Bente Maegaard, Joseph Mariani, Jan Odijk, Stelios Piperidis & Daniel Tapias (Eds), 518–524. Marrakech: ELRA.

Li, Xintong, Li, Guanlin, Liu, Lemao, Meng, Max & Shi, Shuming. 2019. On the word alignment from neural machine translation. In *Proceedings of the 57th Annual Meeting of the Association for Computational Linguistics*, Preslav Nakov & Alexis Palmer (eds), 1293–1303. Florence: Association for Computational Linguistics.

Macken, Lieve. 2010. An annotation scheme and Gold Standard for Dutch-English word alignment. *Proceedings of the 7th conference on International Language Resources and Evaluation* (LREC 10), Nicoletta Calzolari, Khalid Choukri, Bente Maegaard, Joseph Mariani et al. (eds), 3369–3374. Valletta: ELRA.

Mayer, Thomas & Cysouw, Michael. 2012. Language comparison through sparse multilingual word alignment. In *Proceedings of the EACL 2012 Joint Workshop of LINGVIS & UNCLH*, Miriam Butt, Sheelagh Carpendale, Gerald Penn, Jelena Prokić, Michael Cysouw (eds), 54–62). Avignon: Association for Computational Linguistics.

Nagata, Masaaki, Chousa, Katsuki & Nishino, Masaaki. 2020. A supervised word alignment method based on cross-language span prediction using multilingual BERT. In *Proceedings of the 2020 Conference on Empirical Methods in Natural Language Processing* [online], Bonnie Webber, Trevor Cohn, Yulan He & Yang Liu (eds), 555–565. Stroudsburg PA: Association for Computational Linguistics.

Nie, Jian-Yun, Simard, Michel, Isabelle, Pierre & Durand, Richard. 1999. Cross-language information retrieval based on parallel texts and automatic mining of parallel texts from the Web. In SIGIR '99: Proceedings of the 22nd Annual International ACM SIGIR Conference on Research and Development in Information Retrieval, 74–81. New York NY: Association for Computing Machinery.

Och, Franz Josef & Ney, Hermann. 2000. Improved statistical alignment models. In *Proceedings of the 38th Annual Meeting of the Association for Computational Linguistics*, 440–447. Hong Kong: Association for Computational Linguistics.

Och, Franz Josef & Ney, Hermann. 2003. A systematic comparison of various statistical alignment models. *Computational Linguistics* 29(1): 19–51.

Östling, Robert. 2016. Studying colexification through massively parallel corpora. In *The Lexical Typology of Semantic Shifts*, Päivi Juvonen & Maria Koptjevskaja-Tamm (eds), 157–176. Berlin: De Gruyter Mouton.

Sahlgren, Magnus & Karlgren, Jussi. 2005. Automatic bilingual lexicon acquisition using random indexing of parallel corpora. *Natural Language Engineering* 11(3): 327–341.

Segalovich, Ilya. 2003. A fast morphological algorithm with unknown word guessing induced by a dictionary for a web search engine. In *Proceedings of the International Conference on Machine Learning; Models, Technologies and Applications*, Hamid R. Arabnia & Elena B. Kozerenko (eds), 273–280. Las Vegas NV: CSREA Press.

Stahlberg, Felix, Saunders, Danielle & Byrne, Bill. 2018. An operation sequence model for explainable neural machine translation. In *Proceedings of the 2018 EMNLP Workshop BlackboxNLP: Analyzing and Interpreting Neural Networks for NLP*, Tal Linzen, Grzegorz Chrupała & Afra Alishahi (eds), 175–186. Brussels: Association for Computational Linguistics.

Stengel-Eskin, Elias, Su, Tzu-Ray, Post, Matt & Van Durme, Benjamin. 2019. A discriminative neural model for cross-lingual word alignment. *Proceedings of the 2019 Conference on Empirical Methods in Natural Language Processing and the 9th International Joint Conference on Natural Language Processing*, Sebastian Padó & Ruihong Huang (eds), 910–920. Hong Kong: Association for Computational Linguistics.

Wälchli, Bernhard & Cysouw, Michael. 2012. Lexical typology through similarity semantics: Toward a semantic map of motion verbs. *Linguistics* 50(3): 671–710.

Yadav, R.K. & Gupta, Deepa. 2010. Annotation guidelines for Hindi-English word alignment. *Proceedings of the International Conference on Asian Language Processing IEEE*, 293–296. Harbin: IALP.

CHAPTER 12

Building corpus-based writing aids from Spanish into English

The case of GEFEM

María Teresa Ortego Antón
CITTAC, University of Valladolid

The internationalization of the agri-food sector in Spain has led to an exponential increase in writing and translation services from Spanish to English. In this socio-economic context, the methodology used to develop GEFEM is described. GEFEM is a corpus-based tool that assists translators and technical writers in producing dried meat product cards in English. The output offered to users is based on quantitative and qualitative corpora analysis of dried meat product cards. This corpus-based writing aid includes the prototypical rhetorical structure with the most frequent moves and steps, the main model lines, the lexicogrammatical patterns, and a bilingual terminological database.

Keywords: translation, corpora, semi-automatic tool, English, Spanish

1. Translation and the agri-food sector

One of the pillars of the Spanish economy is the agri-food industry and, more specifically, the meat industry, which has become the most relevant one in terms of turnover and direct employment (MAPA 2022: 4–5). In addition to this, the main economic engines of rural regions located in Southern Sparsely Populated Areas (SSPA) are meat companies, which have a family structure, a small size, and a farming tradition. These small and medium-sized companies are mainly dedicated to the production of dried meats. In order to market their products abroad, they require writing and translation services from Spanish into English.

With this background, successful business expansion depends not only on the use of English as a *lingua franca*, but also on the following factors:

https://doi.org/10.1075/scl.113.12ort

> Successful communication will depend not only on the accurate transmission of relevant subject-specific information within the professional domain, but also on compliance with cultural conventions, both at the big and small cultural levels. To this end, acceptable usage language, plus an awareness of genre conventions, are paramount. (Pérez Blanco & Izquierdo 2021: 148)

Although one may think that neural machine translation systems could be the solution to meeting the requirements of dried meat companies, genres are characterized by different patterns depending on the target culture. Hence, the promotion of a given product needs to be sensitive to cross-cultural differences to guarantee that target texts satisfy the standards and expectations of the target community, "not only regarding the meaning but also register, style, geographical variant, etc." (Durán Muñoz & Corpas Pastor 2020: 164). One of the best tools to shed light on such similarities and differences are corpora, which have prominent roles in translation and contrastive studies.

Aware that agri-food translation is a field of knowledge still little explored in comparison with other domains, the ACTRES research group[1] is developing several corpus-based Spanish/English contrastive studies. This group analyzes pragmatic annotation in the agri-food corpus CLANES (Rabadán, Pizarro & Sanjurjo-González 2021a), the promotional texts on the food industry (Rabadán, Ramón & Sanjurjo-González 2021b), promotional texts on cheese (Labrador & Ramón 2020), texts on wine (Moreno Pérez & López Arroyo 2021), herbal teas (Pérez Blanco & Izquierdo 2020, 2021, 2022), or dried meat product cards (Ortego Antón 2019, 2020, 2021; Fernández Nistal 2020; Ortego Antón & Fernández Nistal 2020). Results enable the development and implementation of applications that can be integrated into linguistic tools based on natural language processing that will assist agri-food companies to overcome language barriers.

Thus, in this paper the methodology used to build GEFEM is described. GEFEM[2] is a corpus-based writing aid that assists translators and technical writers, among others, in transferring dried meat product cards from Spanish into English. It relies on the results of analyzing a unidirectional parallel (Spanish > English) virtual corpus[3] (P-GEFEM) and contrasting results with a comparable (Spanish-

1. ACTRES (Contrastive Analysis and Translation English-Spanish in its Spanish acronym) is an interdisciplinary research group led by Prof. Rosa Rabadán and Prof. Noelia Ramón (University of León, Spain): <https://actres.unileon.es/wp/> (30 November 2022).

2. GEFEM is the Spanish acronym for generator of dried meat product cards (*GEnerador de Fichas de EMbutidos).*

3. Aware of the lack of consensus among scholars to define 'virtual' corpus and the existence of multiple definitions, 'virtual' corpus is here understood as "a corpus in which there are not many texts but where the few texts included are suited to the field of knowledge, genre, and tex-

English) virtual corpus (C-GEFEM) in order to identify which patterns are typical from translated texts and which ones are common in texts originally written in English. Such patterns are included in GEFEM, so technical writers and translators can directly produce a proofread text with the terminology, the register, and the macrostructure that the target community expects.

2. Parallel and comparable corpora as a basis for developing a translation and writing aid

A methodology based on the design, compilation, and exploitation of virtual corpora is widely used in Translation Studies (Bowker 2002; Laviosa 2002; Beeby, Rodríguez Inés & Sánchez Gijón 2009; Corpas Pastor & Seghiri 2017; Sánchez Ramos 2019; Seghiri & Arce Romeral 2021; Ortego Antón 2022, among others). In fact, virtual corpora have multiple advantages in Translation Studies, such as their objectivity, reusability and multiple usage as a single resource. Besides, they are user-friendly and allow access and management to huge quantities of information in almost no time (Corpas Pastor & Seghiri 2009: 77).

Although an infinite number of taxonomies have emerged to classify corpora, in this paper comparable corpus is defined as "one which selects similar texts in more than one language or variety" (Sinclair 1996) and parallel corpora as "a text in one language that has been translated into one or more languages [...] since they, ideally, contain the same information in parallel with each other" (Danielsson & Ridings 1996: 1).

Following the protocol first used by Seghiri (2017) and applied in several studies (Ortego Antón 2019, 2020; Fernández Nistal 2020, Seghiri & Arce Romeral 2021, or Sánchez Carnicer 2022, among others), P-GEFEM (a virtual unidirectional Spanish-English parallel corpus) and C-GEFEM (a virtual English-Spanish comparable corpus) were compiled. The procedure for compiling P-GEFEM and C-GEFEM consists of four phases:

1. Searching for texts on the Internet to find dried meat product cards on the websites of renowned companies from different countries. Since the dried meat sector is very broad, I have selected dried meat product cards for three products (*chorizo, salchichón* and *lomo*) published on the web from 2016 to 2018. The collection of texts published on the Internet ensures authenticity

tual variety" (Corpas Pastor 2008: 91). It is "a corpus compiled from electronic sources exclusively in order to carry out a specific translation in any direction. Its principal objective is to construct a reliable resource quickly and at minimal cost, based on texts mined form the Internet, to satisfy the translator's documentation needs" (Corpas Pastor & Seghiri 2009: 78).

and, at the same time, has allowed us to select texts belonging to a wide variety of authors.
2. Downloading the texts manually in HTML or XML format.
3. Formatting texts to TXT UTF8 so that they could be processed by corpus management software.
4. Storing texts in a P-GEFEM or C-GEFEM folder, which was divided into two subfolders, BIBLIOTECA DIGITAL for XML files and a CORPUS folder for TXT files. Each subfolder was further classified by language into two subfolders: English (EN) and Spanish (ES) (see Figure 1).

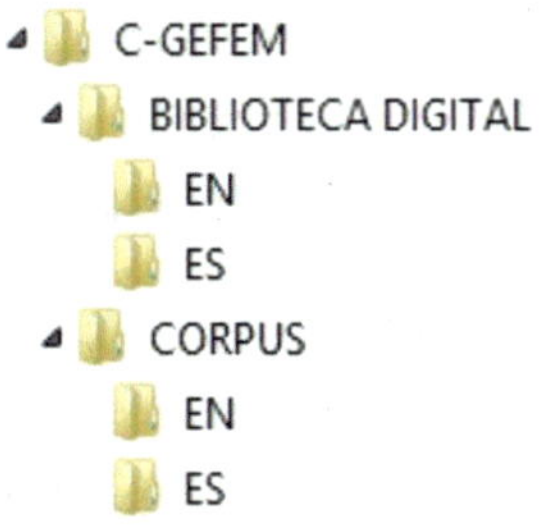

Figure 1. A sample of the structure of C-GEFEM

In addition, the files have been named using an ID (001DMwsMR160624FoodieEN.txt) composed of the number of the file (001, 002, etc.), the abbreviation for dried meats (DM), the indication that the texts have been extracted from the web (ws), the abbreviation of the company they come from (e.g. MR for Morrisons), the date they were downloaded (aammdd), the domain (Foodie), and the language (EN, ES, or TEN).

As a result, I have a virtual unidirectional (Spanish into English) parallel corpora (P-GEFEM) composed of dried meat product cards which include 100 texts in Spanish (18,449 tokens) and their translations into English (16,717 tokens) and C-GEFEM, a virtual (English-Spanish) comparable corpus composed of 100 dried meat product cards originally written in English (25,425 tokens) and 100 original texts written in Spanish (14,196 tokens). Both P-GEFEM and C-GEFEM are qualitatively representative because of the previously detailed procedure used to compile it. The difference in the number of words in each language in C-GEFEM is due to the fact that, in English, product features, packaging, and preparation and use are detailed, whereas in Spanish this information is much more synthetic.

To conclude the process, the quantitative representativeness has been checked with the ReCor software (Seghiri 2006; Corpas Pastor & Seghiri 2010), which calculates the minimum number of words that the corpus must include to be representative in terms of the basic terminology in this genre.[4] ReCor provides two charts: A and B. In chart A, the horizonal axis represents the number of documents whereas the vertical axis shows the quotient of types divided by the number of tokens. In addition, there are two functions, the red one for the files listed alphabetically and the blue one for the files listed randomly. When both functions are steady, the corpus achieves the quantitative representativeness. Simultaneously, a second chart (B) is generated, which shows the minimum number of tokens needed.

Regarding the Spanish subcorpus of P-GEFEM, quantitative representativeness is achieved with 70 documents and 15,000 tokens, as shown in Figure 2. Besides this, in the English subcorpus of P-GEFEM, fewer documents are needed to be lexically representative (50) and 11,000 tokens, as observed in Figure 3. Concerning C-GEFEM, the Spanish subcorpus is representative at 80 documents and 12,500 tokens (see Figure 4). The English C-GEFEM sub-corpus is representative at 90 documents and 25,000 tokens (see Figure 5).

Data gathered from P-GEFEM and C-GEFEM was examined in a multilevel analysis to develop GEFEM. Their analysis enabled us to establish the prototypical rhetorical structure, the model lines and the bilingual terminological database, in line of previous ACTRES-led research results (López Arroyo & Roberts 2015; Labrador & Ramón 2020; Ortego Anton 2019, 2020; Pérez Blanco & Izquierdo 2020, 2021, 2022, among others).

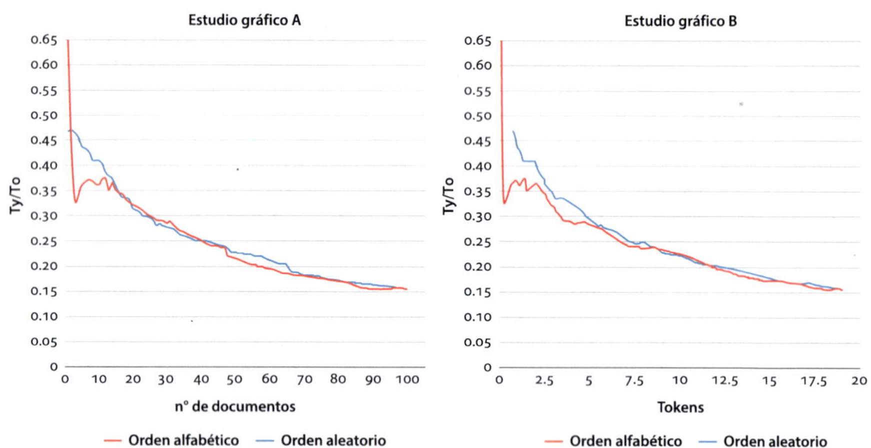

Figure 2. Quantitative representativeness of the Spanish subcorpus of P-GEFEM calculated with ReCor

4. More information about ReCor can be found at <https://rsoftuma.uma.es/es/software/recor/> (30 November 2022).

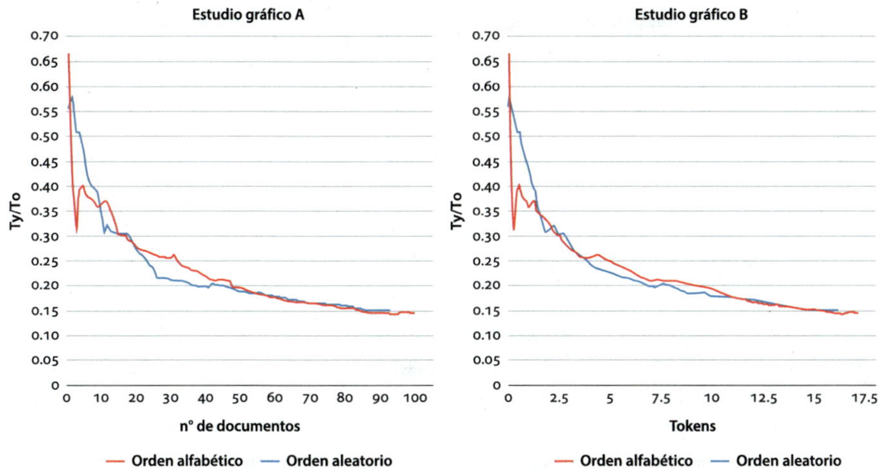

Figure 3. Quantitative representativeness of the English subcorpus of P-GEFEM calculated with ReCor

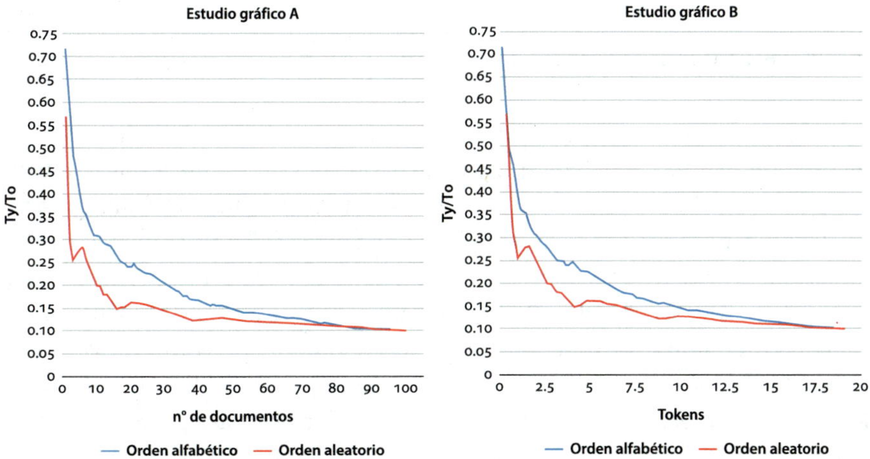

Figure 4. Quantitative representativeness of the Spanish sub-corpus of C-GEFEM calculated with ReCor

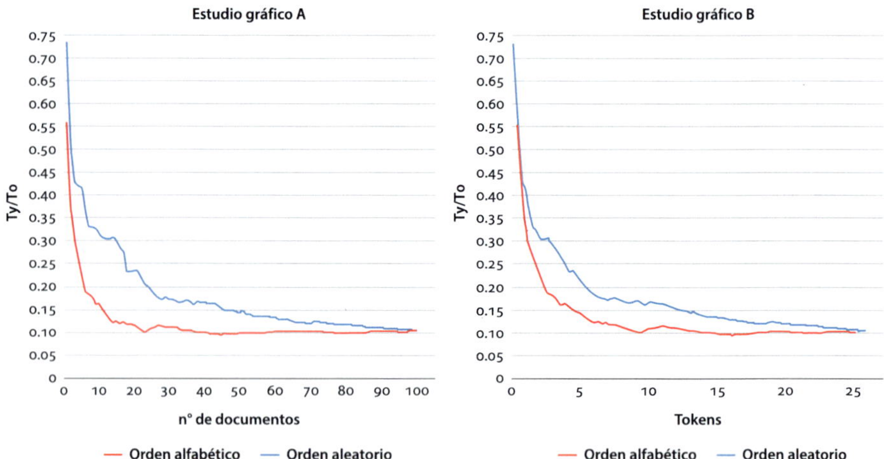

Figure 5. Quantitative representativeness of the C-GEFEM English subcorpus calculated with ReCor

3. The prototypical rhetorical structure

To establish the prototypical rhetorical structure – defined as "the hierarchical organization of a text [involving] the various sections and subsections of a text, moves and steps" (López Arroyo & Roberts 2015: 155) – the methodology proposed by Biber, Connor and Upton (2007) was followed. These authors consider that textual genres are characterized by a series of rhetorical components called 'moves'. A 'move' is defined as "a discoursal or rhetorical unit that performs a coherent communicative function" (Biber et al. 2007: 23). In turn, these moves can be divided into several steps, whose function is "to achieve the purpose of the move to which it belongs" (Biber et al. 2007: 24). The analysis proposed by these authors makes it possible to identify the linguistic characteristics of the moves; it provides a description of the typical structural and distributional characteristics of each move; it offers data on its relative position in relation to other moves; and it makes it possible to develop a certain textual genre.

First of all, 85% of the dried meat product cards share the same rhetorical structure in the parallel corpus (P-GEFEM), that is, the rhetorical structure in Spanish is reproduced in translated texts into English. In addition, 15% of them have slight variations such as the omission of tasting notes, the type of cut, the curing process or the ingredients. Thus, it can be stated that dried meat product cards translated into English share the same structure as the texts originally written in Spanish, as shown in Figures 6 and 7.

Figure 6. Dried meat product card in Spanish

Figure 7. Translated dried meat product card

Next, I checked whether the dried meat cards share the same rhetorical structure in Spanish as the texts originally written in English. The C-GEFEM texts were rhetorically tagged with a battery of tags associated with moves and steps with the aid of the Rhetorical Move Tagger®[5] developed by the ACTRES research group. Next, I compared the different moves and steps in Spanish and English with the Bilingual Comparable Corpus Viewer®.[6] This tool includes a menu that allows users to analyze and contrast the rhetorical information if browsed at the move or step level, as well as a concordance if a given word or token is searched for. I checked the percentage of moves and steps in each of the annotated sub-corpora, the occurrence of such moves and steps, the percentage of texts in which such moves and steps are included, as well as the total number of words in each move or step. The data resulting from this verification allowed us to develop the prototype rhetorical structure consisting of moves and steps in each of the working languages as shown in Table 1. The frequency of occurrence is represented with stars: from the compulsory nature shown by five stars (*****) to the little frequency labelled with one star (*).

Having established the prototypical rhetorical structure in Spanish and in English, the most frequently used lexicogrammatical patterns in each move and step were semi-automatically detected to solve problems in how to string words together, not only correctly and acceptably, but also idiomatically.

4. The model lines

Model lines can be defined as "typical sentences and parts of sentences found in a given text type where the content and format are fairly standard" (López Arroyo & Roberts 2015: 157). They are found in both writing templates and translation-based writing applications.

In C-GEFEM, when establishing the prototypical structure, I agree with Pérez Blanco and Izquierdo (2021: 157) that phraseological and lexicogrammatical patterns, even though formally diverging, were functionally equivalent. On the basis of this similarity, with the Bilingual Comparable Corpus Viewer® I examined all instances of each move and step in the English subcorpus of C-GEFEM, analyzed the occurrences and identified the most frequent model lines for the moves and steps. This examination was manually handled, paying attention to the phraseology whose content matched the communicative function of the chunk where I found it. Results show three different patterns: (a) compulsory patterns, which

5. Rhetorical Movement Tagger®: <http://contraste2.unileon.es/web/en/tagger.html> (7 March 2022).

6. Bilingual Comparable Corpus Viewer®: <http://contraste2.unileon.es/web/en/browser.html> (7 March 2022).

Table 1. Prototypical rhetorical structure in Spanish and English

Prototype of rhetorical structure in Spanish	Freq.	Prototype of rhetorical structure in English	Freq.
1. Denominación del producto (*****)	100%	*1. Product name (*****)*	98%
2. Imagen embutido (*****)	96%	*2. Weight (***)*	47%
3. Marca (***)	41%	*3. Product image (*****)*	87%
3.1. Nombre (***)	29%	*4. Product code (**)*	27%
3.2. Logo (*)	2%	*5. Conceptual information (***)*	53%
3.3. Descripción (***)	41%	*6. Description (*****)*	81%
4. Información conceptual (**)	29%	*7. Information*	
5. Código del producto (**)	21%	*7.1. Brand (**)*	27%
6. Descripción del producto (*****)	96%	*7.1.1. Brand description (**)*	27%
7. Información del producto		*7.2. Storage (***)*	59%
7.1. Peso (*****)	84%	*7.3. Origin (***)*	46%
7.2. Ingredientes (*****)	90%	*7.3.1. Packed country (*)*	10%
7.2.1. Aditivos (**)	16%	*7.4. Preparation and use (****)*	60%
7.3. Alérgenos (*****)	19%	*7.5. Packaging info (***)*	46%
7.4. Información nutricional (****)	66%	*7.6. Recycling (*)*	13%
7.5. Curado (**)	35%	*7.7. Other information (**)*	17%
7.6. Conservación (*****)	85%	*8. Ingredients (****)*	78%
7.7. Utilización (**)	40%	*8.1. Additives (*)*	10%
8. Origen (*)	7%	*8.2. Allergens (***)*	49%
9. Envasado (***)	46%	*8.3. Suitable for (**)*	12%
10. Fabricante (***)	52%	*9. Nutritional values (***)*	59%
10.1. Dirección (***)	51%	*10. Manufacturer (*)*	13%
		10.1. Manufacturer address (**)	36%
		11. Return to address (**)	24%
		12. Review (**)	26%
		12.1. Comments (**)	22%
		13. Follow on	9%

are represented with curly brackets, making it necessary to insert a word or group of words from a selection list; (b) optional patterns, which are emphasized with brackets to show that the information included in them is optional and can be omitted; (c) selection between two options delimited with braces and separated by a slash.

For instance, the step 'Allergens' has two different model lines which are shown accompanied by some examples to help translators and technical writers transfer the content into English:

1. MODEL LINE: [Dietary information]. {{Allergen / Allergy} information / Allergy advice}. For allergens, see {{highlighted / capitalised} ingredients /

ingredients in bold}. {{Contains / May contain} (ALLERGEN) / (ALLERGEN) free}.

   a. Example 1: Allergen Information: For allergens, see highlighted ingredients.
   b. Example 2: Allergy Advice: For allergens, see highlighted ingredients.
   c. Example 3: Dietary Information. Allergy Advice. For allergens, see ingredients in bold.

2. MODEL LINE: [Dietary information]. {{Contains / May [also] contain} (ALLERGEN) / (ALLERGEN) free / This product is (ALLERGEN) free}.
   a. Example 1: Dietary Information. May contain Milk. May Contain Soy. May contain traces of soya and milk.
   b. Example 2: Dietary Information. Contains Milk, May Contain Nuts, May Contain Soya / Soybeans.
   c. Example 3: This product is Wheat, Gluten and Dairy Free.

These model lines function as controlled language choices for the Spanish-speaking user to consider during their production of the English texts to ensure the idiomaticity, the grammatical accuracy and genre acceptability (Pérez Blanco & Izquierdo, 2021: 159–160). When a term has to be chosen, GEFEM also incorporates a terminological database.

5. The terminological database

GEFEM, the corpus-based writing aid, includes a terminological database with terms and equivalents. To select dried meat terms, first, term candidates were automatically extracted from the Spanish subcorpus of P-GEFEM using TermoStat Web 3.0. (Drouin 2003) and, then, terms were validated by applying the criteria proposed by L'Homme (2020: 72–75). Their equivalents were found aligning them with ParaConc, a multilingual concordance analyzer. Details of the analysis of P-GEFEM equivalents are fully explained by Ortego Antón (2019: 140–168; 2021b: 105), who concludes that there is a lack of standardization in Spanish terminology due to the usage of different terms to name the same concept, which gives multiple translation equivalents. She points out that the English language lacks lexicographic and terminological resources, so dried meat terminology is still not normalized.

Hence, using the same procedure to extract terms, as it has been explained previously with P-GEFEM, Spanish and English term candidates were extracted from C-GEFEM with TermoSTat Web 3.0. (Drouin 2003) and validated. In addition, equivalents were manually established taking into account the contexts of use. They were gathered in several Microsoft Excel spreadsheets organized by semantic field (additives, allergens, nutritional elements, packaging, ingredients, materials, origin and country) accompanied by the part of speech, the equivalents and an example of use (see Figure 8). This terminological database gave rise to e-DriMe (Ortego Antón, 2021a), an English-Spanish specialized e-dictionary about dried meats.

	A	B	C	D	E
1	ES	TIPO	EN	TIPO	EJEMPLO
2	aceite de ma	N	corn oil	N	Pork, Water, Salt, Nonfat Dry Milk, Dextrose, Paprika, Hot Paprika, Gar
3	aceite de oli	N	olive oil	N	Pork, Salt, Paprika, Olive Oil, Garlic, Antioxidant (Sodium Ascorbate), P
4	aceite veget	N	vegetable oil	N	Pork, Water, Salt, Nonfat Dry Milk, Dextrose, Paprika, Hot Paprika, Gar
5	ácido ascórb	N	ascorbic acid	N	Pork, Water, Salt, Nonfat Dry Milk, Dextrose, Paprika, Hot Paprika, Gar
6	ácido cítrico	N	citric acid	N	Pork, Water, Salt, Nonfat Dry Milk, Dextrose, Paprika, Hot Paprika, Gar
7	agua	N	water	N	Pork, Water, Salt, Nonfat Dry Milk, Dextrose, Paprika, Hot Paprika, Gar
8	ajo	N	garlic	N	Pork, Salt, Paprika, Olive Oil, Garlic, Antioxidant (Sodium Ascorbate), P
9	ajo molido	N	garlic purée	N	pork (89%), water*, sweet paprika, red wine, sea salt*, starter culture*
10	antioxidante	N	antioxidant	N	Pork, Salt, Paprika, Olive Oil, Garlic, Antioxidant (Sodium Ascorbate), P

Figure 8. Screenshot of terms belonging to the semantic field of ingredients

Next, a cross-linguistic comparison of results in parallel and comparable corpora allowed us to identify morphological and syntactic phraseological patterns of dried meat terminology in both languages. For example, 'Iberian' o '*ibérico*' is not used in the English language, which prefers the term 'Spanish', a generalization to show the origin of the product or the pig breed the meat comes from. In addition, the term 'acorn' is always omitted in English texts to the extent that we any occurrence of this term in the English subcorpus of C-GEFEM was found, while it appears 140 times in the English subcorpus of P-GEFEM, so translators usually transfer '*bellota*' into English ('acorn') using the technique of 'literal translation'. The shape of dried-meat products is another aspect that tends to be omitted in English discourse while it is widely used in texts translated into English (Ortego Antón 2021b: 104–105). On the other hand, features to show degrees of spiciness are always explained in English texts while omitted in translations into English. Hence, translated dried meat product cards do not ensure the idiomaticity, the grammatical accuracy or genre acceptability of English discourse, so researchers and language professionals should not faithfully rely on the exploitation of parallel corpora because they do not respect macrostructure conventions in the target culture and terms are translated using literal translations that do not suit in the target language.

6. GEFEM: The dried meat product card writing assistant

GEFEM 2.0.© is a dynamic web-based software with a user-friendly interface that guides translators and technical writers through the writing and translation of dried meat product cards. It is free of charge.[7] First of all, the software allows the user to create a blank document or to upload a document on which the user has already worked, as shown in Figure 9. When selecting the first option, '*Crear documento*', the application shows us a menu on the left that allows us to navigate between the different moves and steps (see Figure 10).

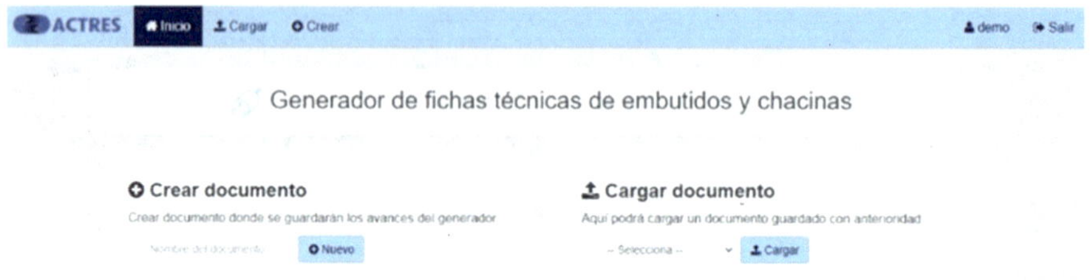

Figure 9. GEFEM start-up interface

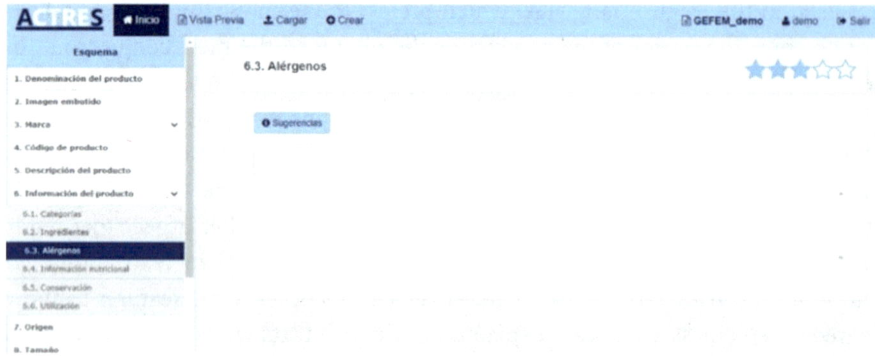

Figure 10. Menu with the structure of the dried meat product card

For example, the step 'Allergens' is selected, the 'Suggestions' button is pressed, and a pop-up window appears where the two model lines are shown so that the user must choose one of them by clicking on 'Add' (see Figure 11).

The tool offers different elements that guide the user with different colored buttons, that is, green indicates that a word or group of words must be inserted, purple shows two or more options from which the user must choose one, and orange corresponds to an optional text fragment. Therefore, the user completes

7. GEFEM 2.0.©: <https://actres.unileon.es/demos/generadores/applications.html#generatorsSection> (7 March 2022).

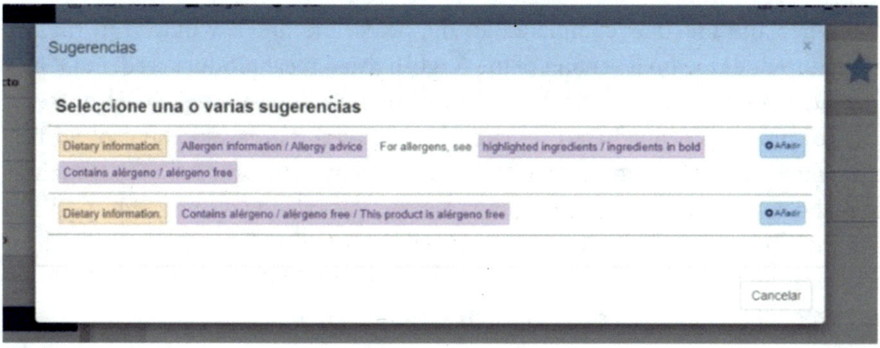

Figure 11. Model lines of the 'Allergens' step

the content of the dried meat product card following the instructions provided by the different windows. When users have to choose a lexical unit from the terminology database, it appears in green, as shown in Figure 12.

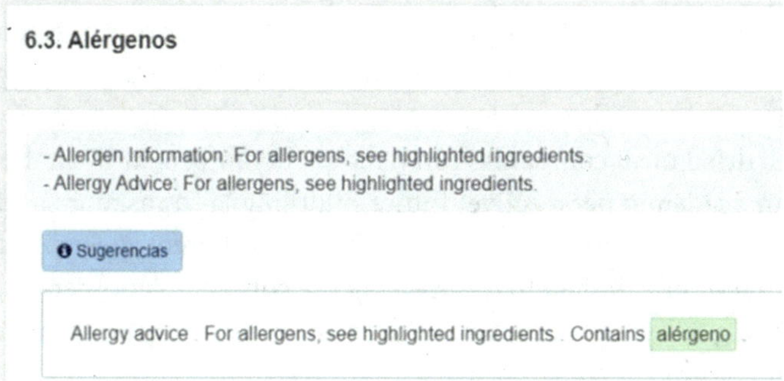

Figure 12. Example of a lexical unit from the terminology database

Clicking on '*alérgeno*' displays a window in which the user enters the first characters of the term in Spanish, and the English equivalents are offered (see Figure 13).

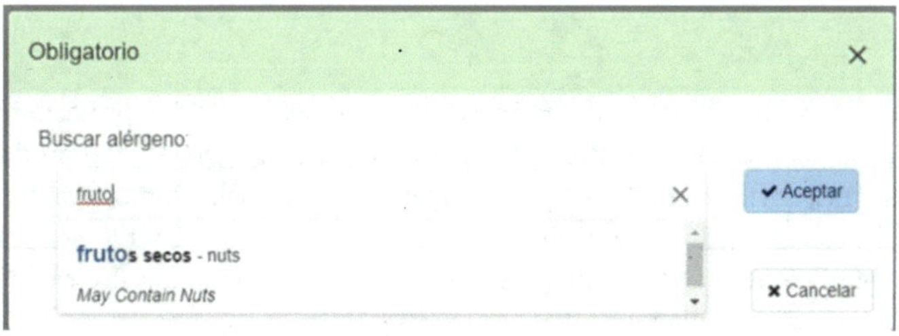

Figure 13. Example of a drop-down menu for choosing a lexical unit

When the user has completed all the fields, the preview button in the top menu provides the final version of the English dried meat product card, in DOCX format, adapted to the linguistic and cultural conventions of English discourse.

To sum up, corpus-based research has enabled the development of writing aids which are useful and efficient because they rely on the extraction and analysis of real data from comparable corpora. Among the existing writing aids, GEFEM is a tool that can help increasing the productivity of agri-food companies, as it shortens the translation process, since translators and language professionals are not generally trained nor specialized in agri-food genres.

7. Conclusions

Throughout this paper, the methodology applied to build GEFEM was described, that is, a corpus-based writing aid that assists users when translating and writing dried meat product cards from Spanish to English. The development of linguistic applications such as GEFEM makes it possible to transfer research results to the productive framework so that small- and medium-sized companies may reach the international market, and translators and technical writers can increase productivity. All in all, dried meat companies can offer quality information on the Internet.

From an academic perspective, future multilingual translators and technical writers must be trained in the particularities of the different specialized genres so that they are not only limited to transferring the content to another language, but also to ensure quality and acceptable texts that suit the communicative situation of the target culture.

Finally, a neural machine translation module is currently being added to GEFEM in order to supplement data which have not been included in the terminological database. At the same time, I continue to develop multilingual writing aids for other areas of the agri-food sector.

Funding

This work has been carried out in the framework of the national R&D project entitled 'Controlled natural languages, collaborative communication, and bilingual textual production in 3.0 environments' (PID2020-114064RB-I00), coordinated by Dr. Noelia Ramón García (University of León), and partially within the project 'TorreznoTRAD' (PROYEMER-2021-028), coordinated by Dr. María Teresa Ortego Antón and funded by the Emerging Projects Grants (Call 2021) of the University of Valladolid.

References

Beeby, Allison, Rodríguez Inés, Patricia & Sánchez Gijón, Pilar. 2009. *Corpus Use and Translating. Corpus use for learning to translate and learning corpus use to translate* [Benjamins Translation Library 82], 75–107. Amsterdam: John Benjamins.

Biber, Douglas, Connor, Ulla & Upton, Thomas A. 2007. *Discourse on the Move. Using Corpus Analysis to Describe Discourse Structure* [Studies in Corpus Linguistics 28]. Amsterdam: John Benjamins.

Bowker, Lynne. 2002. *Computer-Aided Translation Technology: A Practical Introduction.* Ottawa: University of Ottawa Press.

Corpas Pastor, Gloria. 2008. *Investigar con corpus en traducción: Los retos de un nuevo paradigma.* Frankfurt: Peter Lang.

Corpas Pastor, Gloria & Seghiri, Míriam. 2009. Virtual corpora as documentation resources: Translating travel insurance documents (English-Spanish). In Beeby, Rodríguez Inés & Sánchez-Gijón (eds), 75–107.

Corpas Pastor, Gloria & Seghiri, Míriam. 2010. Size matters: A quantitative approach to corpus representativeness. In *Lengua, traducción, recepción: En honor de Julio César Santoyo*, Rosa Rabadán, Trinidad Guzmán & Marisa Fernández (eds), 111–145. León: Universidad de León, Área de Publicaciones.

Corpas Pastor, Gloria & Seghiri, Míriam. 2017. *Corpus-based Approaches to Translation and Interpreting. From Theory to Applications.* Bern: Peter Lang.

Danielsson, Pernilla & Ridings, Daniel. 1996. *PEDANT: Parallel Texts in Göteborg.* Göteborg: University of Göteborg.

Drouin, Patrick. 2003. Term extraction using non-technical corpora as a point of leverage. *Terminology* 9(1): 99–117.

Durán Muñoz, Isabel & Corpas Pastor, Gloria. 2020. Corpus-based multilingual lexicographic resources for translators: An overview. In *Studies on Multilingual Lexicography*, María José Domínguez Vázquez, Mónica Mirazo Balsa & Carlos Valcárcel Riveiro (eds), 159–178. Berlin: De Gruyter.

Fernández Nistal, Purificación. 2020. Los corpus como herramienta de traducción para los traductores del siglo XXI: El caso del chorizo ibérico de bellota. In *Perfiles estratégicos de traductores e intérpretes. La transmisión de la información experta multilingüe en la sociedad del conocimiento del siglo XXI*, Susana Álvarez Álvarez & María Teresa Ortego Antón (eds), 143–160. Granada: Comares.

Izquierdo, Marlén & Pérez Blanco, María. 2020. A multi-level contrastive analysis of promotional strategies in specialized discourse. *English for Specific Purposes* 58: 43–57.

Labrador, Belén & Ramón, Noelia. 2020. Building a second-language writing aid for specific purposes: Promotional cheese descriptions. *English for Specific Purposes* 60: 40–52.

Laviosa, Sara. 2002. *Corpus-based Translation Studies. Theory, Findings, Applications.* Amsterdam: Rodopi.

L'Homme, Marie-Claude. 2020. *Lexical Semantics for Terminology. An Introduction* [Terminology and Lexicography Research and Practice 20]. Amsterdam: John Benjamins.

López Arroyo, Belén & Roberts, Roda B. T. 2015. The use of a comparable corpus. How to develop writing applications. In *Corpus-based Translation and Interpreting Studies: From Description to Application*, María Teresa Sánchez Nieto (ed.), 147–166. Berlin: Frank und Timme.

MAPA. 2022. *Informe anual de la industria alimentaria española periodo 2021–2022.* <https://www.mapa.gob.es/es/alimentacion/temas/industria-agroalimentaria/20220728informeanualindustria2021-20222t220k_tcm30-87450.pdf> (28 November 2022)

Moreno Pérez, Leticia & López Arroyo, Belén. 2021. A typical corpus-based tools to the rescue: How a writing generator can help translators adapt to the demands of the market. *MonTI* 13: 251–279.

Ortego Antón, María Teresa. 2019. *La terminología del sector agroalimentario español-inglés en los estudios contrastivos y de traducción especializada basados en corpus: los embutidos.* Berlin: Peter Lang.

Ortego Antón, María Teresa. 2020. Las fichas descriptivas de embutidos en español y en inglés: Un análisis contrastivo de la estructura retórica basado en corpus. *Revista Signos* 53(102): 170–194.

Ortego Antón, María Teresa. 2021a. E- DriMe: A Spanish- English frame-based e- dictionary about dried meats. *Terminology* 27(2): 330–357.

Ortego Antón, María Teresa. 2021b. Los corpus como herramientas para la traducción español-inglés en el sector chacinero en el siglo XXI. In *Los corpus especializados en la lingüística aplicada: Traducción y enseñanza*, Elisa Sartor (ed.), 89–112. Mantova: Universitas Studiorum Editrice.

Ortego Antón, María Teresa. 2022. *La investigación en tecnologías de la traducción. Parámetros de la digitalización presente y la posible incidencia en el perfil de los futuros profesionales de la comunicación interlingüística.* Berlin: Peter Lang.

Ortego Antón, María Teresa & Fernández Nistal, Purificación. 2020. Estudio contrastivo de la terminología de embutidos en inglés y en español con ParaConc y tlCorpus a partir del corpus paralelo P-GEFEM y del comparable C-GEFEM. In *El uso de los corpus lingüísticos como herramienta pedagógica para la enseñanza-aprendizaje de lenguas, traducción e interpretación*, Míriam Seghiri (ed.), 23–48. Berna: Peter Lang.

Pérez Blanco, María & Izquierdo, Marlén. 2021. Developing a corpus-informed tool for Spanish professionals writing specialized texts in English. In *Corpora in Translation and Contrastive Research in the Digital Age* [Benjamins Translation Library 158], Julia Lavid-López, Carmen Maíz-Arévalo & Juan Rafael Zamorano-Mansilla (eds), 147–173. Amsterdam: John Benjamins.

Pérez Blanco, María & Izquierdo, Marlén. 2022. Engaging with customer's emotions: A case study in English-Spanish online food advertising. *Languages in Contrast* 22(1): 43–76.

Rabadán, Rosa, Pizarro, Isabel & Sanjurjo-González, Hugo. 2021a. Authoring support for Spanish language writers: A genre-restricted case study. *RESLA* 34(2): 677–717.

Rabadán, Rosa, Ramón, Noelia & Sanjurjo-González, Hugo. 2021b. Pragmatic annotation of a domain-restricted English-Spanish comparable corpus. *Bergen Language and Linguistics Studies* 11(1): 209–23.

Sánchez Carnicer, Jaime. 2022. *Traducción y discapacidad. Un estudio comparado de la terminología inglés-español en la prensa escrita.* Berlin: Peter Lang.

Sánchez Ramos, María del Mar. 2019. Corpus paralelos y traducción especializada: Ejemplificación de diseño, compilación y alineación de un corpus paralelo bilingüe (inglés-español) para la traducción jurídica. *Lebende Sprachen* 64(2): 269–285.

Seghiri, Míriam. 2006. Compilación de un corpus trilingüe de seguros turísticos (español-inglés-italiano): aspectos de evaluación, catalogación, diseño y representatividad. Tesis doctoral, Universidad de Málaga. <http://hdl.handle.net/10630/2715> (10 September 2012).

Seghiri, Míriam. 2017. Metodología de elaboración de un glosario bilingüe y bidireccional (inglés-español/español-inglés) basado en corpus para la traducción de manuales de instrucciones de televisores. *Babel* 63(1): 43–64.

Seghiri, Míriam & Arce Romeral, Lorena. 2021. *La traducción de contratos de compraventa inmobiliaria: Un estudio basado en corpus aplicado a España e Irlanda*. Berlin: Peter Lang.

Sinclair, John McH. 1996. Preliminary recommendations on corpus typology [EAGLES EAG-TCWG-CTYP/P Technical document]. <https://www.ilc.cnr.it/EAGLES96/corpustyp/corpustyp.html> (30 May 2023).

Index